CRAVING COMMUNITY:
THE NEW AMERICAN DREAM

Todd Mansfield
Ross Yockey
L. Beth Yockey

Published by

abecedary press

A subsidiary of
Yockey Communication, LLC
721 South Rose Street, Seattle, WA 98108

First printing 2007

Printed in the United States of America

ISBN 978-0-9764839-3-9

Library of Congress Control Number 2007929240

Jacket and Book Design by L. Beth Yockey

Proofreading by Alexandra Gouirand

TABLE OF CONTENTS

INTRODUCTION

America as we know it began as a small new world of villages. The earliest arrivals from Europe disembarked from cramped ships to find natives clustered in villages. While the French and Spanish built mainly forts, the English built villages. And that is the chief reason we speak English today, because those villages were permanent places, designed to foster community.

Today's big cities of Richmond, Philadelphia, Boston, Salem, New York all began as villages. In villages, neighbors knew neighbors, formed bonds, shared duties and came to trust one another. In villages, churches and schools were possible; governments could be set up. In villages, shopkeepers could live above their shops, friends could meet at a public house, a "pub," and there, along with food and drink, find conversation about the weather or a book or what they should do about the latest tax imposition. In villages, people of different means lived near enough to one another that wealth could not hide from poverty nor poverty from wealth. In America's villages, displeasure with alien rule grew into revolution, and a nation was born.

Then the American Dream came to mean owning a home of our own. Agencies of government and business combined to convince us that our only hope of achieving that dream lay on the ever-expanding outskirts of those former villages. Filling our tanks with regular and ethyl, we drove toward our dream and invented sprawl.

Today, a new sort of revolution quietly brews. After nearly a hundred years of urban diaspora into neighborhoods where only concrete and automobiles could connect us, we are craving the community we lost along the way and searching out different sorts of dwelling places.

From ocean to ocean, Americans are rejecting the isolation of the suburban century and rediscovering the pleasures of connectivity. Whether in the hearts of cities or on their far fringes, we are demanding the right to live together again. Remarkably, a significant number of real estate development and urban planning professionals are responding to that demand. They are creating neighborhoods much like those original American villages.

How did this lifestyle revolution come about? Is it really something we need? How will it impact the way we work and play? Will it be better for the environment or worse? Will it truly bring us together or simply segregate us in different ways?

The answers to those and other questions may be found in *Craving Community: The New American Dream.*

CHAPTER ONE
The Quest for Community

We're all born attached. Then it gets tough: the umbilical cord's cut, the struggle begins. We've got to learn how to do it all on our own, and at the very same time develop relationships with others.

Fail the first assignment and we turn out overly dependent, unable to stand on our own two feet. Indecisive. We fall into identity crises and mid-life crises, line our walls with self-help books and wish someone would read them to us.

Fail the second assignment – developing relationships – and the results can be even worse. At the extreme, we become sociopaths, shooting up schools, stalking women, abusing children, blowing up buildings. More commonly, we suffer from isolation and loneliness, we lack connection and sense of place, we wish we *belonged* somewhere. Call it community deprivation syndrome, CDS. It's reasonable to suggest that millions suffer from it and that perhaps most of us will suffer from CDS at some point in our lives.

It will be argued that this condition does not need a name, that words such as "loneliness," "isolation" and "solitude" are sufficient. But are they really?

"The same forces that are causing standards of living to rise and longevity to improve also promote loneliness," observes Gregg Easterbrook of *The New Republic*. "Steadily smaller households, made possible by prosperity, mean steadily less human interaction. Telecommuting, a personal convenience made possible by technology, means less human interaction." In 1957, only three percent of Americans considered themselves "lonely." In 1990, 36 percent of us did. But "loneliness" and its familiar synonyms are words that lock us in to a focus on the individual. Cures proposed for loneliness therefore tend to be private and self-centered rather than societal.

In fact, what we usually define as loneliness is not the root cause of any problem but the result. We lack contact with others, therefore we feel lonely or isolated or solitary. Those feelings may be relieved by meaningful contacts with others, by relationships, by *community*.

And so, for lack of a better phrase, we coin the term Community Deprivation Syndrome.

The most unlikely people may suffer from CDS. For cases in point, consider Ike and Alex, Joanna, John and Robbi. Consider Natasha, Mildred and Jim. Had you met any of the first six of these eight individuals in the mid-1990s you'd have thought they had it all. But in fact their lives lacked a critical ingredient. As for Mildred and Jim, we'll come back to them later.

Start with Ike Eissinmann (who actually spells his first name "Iake," but even his best friends think it's "Ike" and that's how it's spelled in all his movie credits). Ike burst onto the Hollywood scene as a telepathic, telekinetic teen from outer space in Walt Disney's 1975 *Escape from Witch Mountain*. Three years after that he did *Return to Witch Mountain*. Twenty years later, Ike was still in Hollywood, picking up occasional bit parts, doing voice-overs and sound effects, married to writer-producer-actress Alex Shayne. They had a comfortable house in the San Fernando Valley, but they were "just tired of it." Ike wanted to be "someplace where I could walk, where I could bike, where I could meet people on the street and have a conversation. I wanted more of a connection. I wanted to *belong*." Community Deprivation Syndrome.

Consider John and Robbi Henrickson. After twenty years of moving every eighteen months, John was looking at retirement from IBM, but retirement to where? John and Robbi were out of touch with their neighbors in Litchfield, Connecticut. John wanted to stay active, stay connected, but he looked at the future and saw himself slipping from the desk chair straight into the rocking chair. Robbi became a "corporate escapee." She took early retirement and started looking around the country for a place the couple could make their own, a "real" place, not some prefab golf or retirement camp. "We knew we wanted something," John recalls, "but we didn't know what it was."

Take Joanna Slaybaugh, who had a successful career going as an executive recruiter, living a fast-track life. But at her Bellevue, Washington, condo she had no one to care for, no one to visit. Working 60-hour weeks at something that "made no difference" was a draining experience. It left no time for connecting. Joanna realized that she "couldn't be anonymous anymore. I wanted to develop a lifestyle that made room for community."

Or consider Natasha Redwine-Carter: career woman with hard-working husband, two beautiful children. But in her Seattle suburban high-rise, nobody said hello to her. Natasha and her husband Dan Carter had been renting in and near the city since they got married, but felt like they knew no one in their neighborhood. "I didn't get a chance to meet my neighbors," Natasha says. "If I had a problem or needed something, I would not feel comfortable knocking on my neighbor's door. If I bumped into someone on the elevator, it was an awkward situation, because we would never speak. Neighbors there did not speak to each other."

Four very different situations, yet all six lives missing the same essential ingredient. You would not have called any one of them "lonely" or "isolated," yet they all had this unspecified feeling that something was wrong, this angst, this Community Deprivation Syndrome.

For too long we've been pretending that the lives of people such as Ike and Alex, John and Robbi, Joanna and Natasha represented fulfillment of our collective American Dream. With a nice place to live, a well-paying job and things to spend our money on, we must have it made. Yet, at least since the 1940s, many of us have been living in denial of a basic human need: meaningful interaction with other human beings. We require connection to feel complete.

BABY BOOM ANGST.

Between the end of World War II and the start of the 21st century, three generations of Americans came of age, and those three generations are represented in the authors of this book. Beth Yockey, born in 1978, has moved to six different states, zigzagging around the country for years until finally achieving a sense of place in Seattle. Todd Mansfield, born in 1957, discovered the secret of community while he was planning places for other people to live. The third co-author tells a story that spans the half-century-plus.

Born in 1943, Ross Yockey, Beth's father, found himself among the baby-boomers thronging to New York City in the early 70s, where he experienced a shock. It wasn't the grandness and the spectacle, for he'd seen those concrete canyons in a hundred movies, and his journalist's spine was predisposed to the tingling of such media events as garbage strikes, gay rights marches, bra burnings in Central Park, Vietnam vets capturing the Statue of Liberty, the Mets winning the pennant:

those things might happen in a city of such magnitude, and he'd come prepared for the bigness of the place.

What surprised Ross was the *smallness* of the place. New York had neighborhoods where everybody knew everybody else and seemed glad to see a stranger. The San Gennaro Festival in Little Italy where everybody was a *paesan'*. Locals hand-waving directions to favorite restaurants down steep Chinatown stairs. A flour-dusted mom-and-pop team in Brooklyn's Middle East, tossing phyllo dough over a surface three ping-pong tables wide. A neighborhood pub with Christmas music all year long and drafts drawn by jolly bearded barkeeps in Santa suits.

What amazed him was the casual spillage of life onto the sidewalks, where a chance encounter might put a whole new spin on your day or on your future. What astounded him was the sudden immersion in a pool of humanity, actual people you could speak to or not, jostle or slide past or even introduce yourself to. Whether you moved to the Big City to start a career or to find a mate or to escape the small town or just for the sheer romance of it, there was an inescapable *sense of place* in New York City in the 1970s, a sense of somewhere you could belong if you just let yourself. You could walk or hop a bus to work or shop, to dine out or catch a movie. There was a thing too many baby-boomers had never known back home in their protected postwar suburbs, a thing called *community*.

The neighborhoods of baby-boom youth were sterile and homogenous in the main, one house much like another, this street the same as that one, few chance encounters, rarely a surprise. Dogs walked themselves. Kids could walk too, but to where? Your mom drove you to dance lessons or ballgames, a bus picked you up for school. Dad drove or took the bus to work.

And later on, when those baby-boomers ended their big-city sojourn and went home to raise their own kids, they moved into neighborhoods much like the ones they'd grown up in, only now they were farther from the centers of dying downtowns and somehow more isolated. But sure as paper covers rock and rock breaks scissors, fenced-in suburban yards beat barred city windows, two-car garages beat the city bus. A nice home in the suburbs – wasn't that the American Dream? Or was it about to become the American Nightmare? As Lewis Mumford wrote in *The City in History*, "the ultimate effect of the suburban escape in our own time is, ironically, a low-grade uniform environment from which escape is impossible." Most of America would take another twenty years to awaken to the truth Mumford discovered in 1961: we had designed ourselves a box in which happiness would always be somewhere beyond the next beltway.

Baby-boomers had left something behind in the big city, but most of them spent little time thinking about it. Work to be done, wages to be won. So you had long commutes, so the kids had nearly-as-long bus rides, so there weren't a whole lot of playmates within walking distance: didn't their backyard have a gym set? Weekends found you with half-acre lawns to mow and cars to wash and charcoal to light. Walter Cronkite assured you every evening, "that's the way it is," because there was nothing you or anyone else could do about it. The only choice for living seemed to be suburbia, a place like no place. And so the baby boomers, not realizing they might have been victimized by community deprivation, deepened and expanded the deprivation for the next generations.

As our population grew, so did our suburbs. Woods and wetlands between cities disappeared. Children ran less, couched more and fattened alarmingly. The landscape went from farmland to needle-track arteries punctured with strip malls and Dairy Queens and office parks. Suburbia jes' growed, until there was something beyond it, called exurbia, the same only farther away. Our gray air thickened, our tension mounted, our hearts strained. We drove miles for milk and margarine.

Many of those whose jobs supplied the necessary down payments bought larger and larger houses ever more distant from their jobs. We now spend more time at those jobs – and more time commuting to and from those jobs – than does any other nation, and those time commitments continue to grow. Ever higher percentages of our time must be given over to driving. We've made DVD players standard equipment in our SUVs, so our kids don't fuss on their long rides to school. We have clustered our shops and our service providers in "shopping malls" and "office parks" whose acres of auto lots seem larger than the neighborhoods we call home.

No place like home, right?

Back in the big cities, doors were plated in steel and framed in locks; guards and gates sprang up everywhere; eye contact became taboo. And as the suburbs sprawled, so did our social anomie, the general malaise and distrust of others. We surrounded our climate-controlled, self-sufficient home-castles with security-system moats because, really, who would keep an eye out for us?

"No longer forced outside by the heat and humidity, no longer attracted by the corner drugstore, and no longer within walking distance of relatives, suburbanites often choose to remain in the family room," wrote Kenneth Jackson in 1985's *Crabgrass Frontier*. "When they do venture out, it is often through a garage into an air-conditioned automobile. Streets are no longer places to promenade and to meet, but passageways for high-powered machines."[2] We had taken refuge, Jackson warned, in a "cult of domestic privatism."

Now, two decades later, we've got our satellite dishes beaming in news, sports and soaps from space, our movies ordered online and delivered to our mailbox, though we rarely communicate with the folks down the block. To ward off mental illness, we have resorted to drugs. Ten percent of us take prescription drugs for medication and millions more self-medicate as we retreat ever inward from meaningful interaction. We have learned to watch our own backs, because we have come to abide, many of us, in neighborhoods of the neighborless. We are living in denial of our need for community, a need that is well documented.

THE SCIENCE OF COMMUNITY: HARD-WIRED TO CONNECT.

Interestingly, it was during the 1950s, just as we were hunkering down and privatizing our lives in suburbia, that science began exploring our dependence on one another. One of the era's most famous studies was of the little slate quarry town of <u>Roseto</u>, Pennsylvania. In Italian-American Roseto, people drank and smoked as heavily as anyone else, worked as hard as people in nearby towns and cities, yet Rosetans seemed nearly immune to cardiac problems. Both the crime rate and applications for public assistance in Roseto were zero.

Stewart Wolf, a physician, and John Bruhn, a sociologist, concluded that Rosetans lived longer, happier lives because they built their houses so close together that the front porches almost touched, because they got together at social clubs and on evening walks. Despite a heavy intake of artery-challenging Italian food and wine, their gatherings "radiated a kind of joyous team spirit." Dr. Wolf concluded that a high level of community is a better predictor of healthy hearts than are low levels of cholesterol or tobacco use. "People are nourished by other people," he wrote.[3] Caring friends and neighbors reduce stress and the diseases brought on by stress.

Back in the 50s it seemed that every branch of science was waving the community flag. Sociologist Robert Ezra Parks insisted that our sense of self "depended almost entirely on our status within a community."[4] Psychoanalyst Erik Erikson warned we all were in danger of having an "identity crisis" if we didn't connect with our community. According to behaviorist Abraham Maslow's "hierarchy of needs," we needed community to realize anything approaching our true potential. In fact, for the past half-century, scientists – dare we say, the scientific *community* – have agreed that together we form a whole greater than the sum of our individual parts.

Scientists pressed on with their research, blithely disregarded by city planners and real estate developers everywhere. In the 70s, British psychologist John Bowlby concluded that social ties are "the hub around which a person's life revolves."[5] About twenty years later a team of San Francisco psychologists concluded that in many ways, "people cannot be stable on their own."[6] If science is to be believed, the case for community is overwhelming.

Despite all this evidence to the contrary, our culture – the things we do, the ways we behave, the expectations we have for ourselves and our children – holds up a vision of "self-sufficiency" as the ideal. The impossible ideal. As a result, we fall ever more frequently into anxiety, depression, narcissism and superficiality. And all of those tendencies promote violence and self-destructive behaviors, conditions to which we ironically refer as "anti-social."

So: relate or disintegrate.

Medical science tells us that when women are stressed their brain releases a cocktail of chemicals, including oxytocin, which promotes, among other emotions, nurturing behavior. As a result, they seek the company of other women. Once they have connected socially, the brain releases more oxytocin, helping them to relax further.[7]

So: connect and compose.

A 2003 report from the Commission on Children at Risk concludes that what our nation needs most is "authoritative communities," to combat a "crisis of American childhood" caused by a "lack of connectedness." There is a deficit between what America supplies in the way of community and what we all need. The study concludes that humans are 'biologically primed" for finding meaning through attachments to others. The need for community arises naturally from our basic biology and how our brains develop.

So: humans are hard-wired for community.[8]

And the research continues to bear out this most critical point. In 2005-2006, at Germany's Max Planck Institute of Evolutionary Anthropology, scientists learned that humans begin helping one another from a very early age, a characteristic that may be unique among animals. Working with toddlers as young as eighteen months, researcher Felix Warneken performed over and over such mundane tasks as hanging towels with clothespins and stacking books. When Warneken "accidentally" dropped a clothespin or let a book fall to the floor, each of the toddlers rushed to help. The babies looked at Warneken's face, decided he needed help, then wobbled over to pick up the clothespin or book, pull themselves up and hand it to the seemingly struggling adult. Warneken refrained from thanking the children, so as not to reward their actions in any way. Still, the children offered their help over and over again. The research concludes that "human children as young as 18 months of age (prelinguistic or just-linguistic) quite readily help others to achieve their goals in a variety of different situations. This requires both an understanding of others' goals and an altruistic motivation to help." Warneken suggests we are born with "pro-social motivation," a desire to be part of our community.[9] There it is again.

Antoine de Saint-Exupéry put it more poetically in *The Little Prince*: "Man is a knot, a web, a mesh into which relationships are tied."

How did we escape this natural web of community? Social commentator Robert Putnam, author of *Bowling Alone* and *Better Together,* says we have simply lost our sense of place over the past fifty years, becoming increasingly disconnected, unplugged from friends and family and society. (We will return to Putnam's work, which has been extraordinarily influential, although we find some of his conclusions flawed.) As for the causes of this disconnection, Putnam cites television, changed women's roles, evolving family structure, workplace transformation. But to the list of usual suspects he pointedly adds: America's sprawling suburbs. The places we live, Harvard sociology professor Putnam observes, actually have served to isolate us from one another. Our very homes have been designed to stifle community.

In this Putnam is correct. At least since the middle of the 20ᵀᴴ century, community has fallen victim to a set of circumstances, neither intended nor foreseen, by which the design – more accurately, in many cases, the *lack* of design – of our neighborhoods makes it more and more difficult for us to relate to one another. More often than not, we have created "communities" devoid of community.

One need not study, as Putnam did, the declining membership of bowling leagues to see the truth. The warning signs of Community Deprivation Syndrome are all around us. One finds them in the opinion pages of newspapers from one end of the country to the other. Here, on the Op-Ed page of *The New York Times:*

"Sometimes living in a home in the suburbs of Central Jersey can feel as lonely as floating on an island in the South Pacific." Loneliness set in the first week college teacher and mother Shirley Russak Wachtel moved into that Central Jersey neighborhood. "I would wheel my youngest around the block in the stroller and then go for miles before I would see anyone except a solitary jogger or a stray crow swooping down to peck an errant garbage bag." And after sixteen years in the neighborhood, Wachtel writes, "things are pretty much the same. We continue to commute to work, park in our garages, and venture out only to retrieve the mail or a newspaper. We have gardeners for the planting and hire kids to shovel our snow. When a house alarm goes off, no one bothers to check it out or call the police... But do we have to accept it?"[10]

We do not. Psychologist Kathleen A. Brehony, in *Living a Connected Life,* suggests we simply slow down and smell our neighbors' roses. "With the wild, swirling pace of today's world," she writes, "it can be easy to ignore our deep and innate needs for relationship and community. We sometimes forget that belongingness – the sense of being accepted and embraced by others – is not a luxury in life. It's our lifeblood. It's like air. We need it to live."[11] And when we don't have it, sometimes the worst can happen.

The worst happened to Mildred Stojkovic and Jim Sulkers, the final two of the eight individuals introduced at the beginning of this chapter.

Seventy-year-old Mildred lived in the rundown Chicago neighborhood of North Lawndale. Like most of her neighbors, Mildred only went out when she had to, because was afraid of what might happen to her on the street. The streets were lined with single-room-occupancy buildings like hers; there were few businesses, lots of barred windows and padlocked storefronts. Nobody talked to anybody else. North Lawndale looked as though it had been bombed out, with more empty lots than shops or markets, more violent crime than street life. Stojkovic is a fairly common Yugoslavian name, so Mildred may well have had relatives in the area, but if she did, they never came by to see her.

On July 13, 1995, the day the temperature hit 106 degrees in Chicago, Mildred probably stayed in her room. She had no air conditioning, no ice, no one to call. And in her room, all alone, she died.

But Mildred and many of the other 590 people who died in that Chicago heat wave did not die from the heat at all. Had they been on familiar terms with neighborhood storekeepers, they might have been welcomed into air conditioned space. Fearing victimization, they neither left their apartments nor trusted those few strangers who came to check on them. These people were victims, not of the heat, but, as the late social commentator Jane Jacobs observed, they died from "no functioning community."[12]

"Loneliness and a failure of belongingness are most chilling when they are complete," says psychologist Kathleen Brehony. "When there is no one to care or comfort, no one to embrace or include us. In spite of what other advantages we may have in life – a warm house, food to eat, money to spend – when we are disconnected, without attachments of the heart, we are psychologically and spiritually destitute."[13]

Even more chilling than the Chicago heat wave deaths is the story of Jim Sulkers of Winnipeg, Manitoba. Sulkers was reclusive, a 53-year-old who avoided his family and his neighbors at the condominium. One November evening in 2002 Jim went to bed and never woke up.

So little connection did Sulkers have with the outside world that nobody missed him until August 25, 2004. That's when police finally climbed into his tidy one-bedroom apartment and found him still in bed, his body mummified. He'd been dead just three months shy of two years, and no one had even noticed. Sulkers had done his banking and paid all his bills on the internet. The internet kept on automatically depositing his monthly pension, kept on subtracting his condo dues, his mortgage, his utility bills. The internet kept him virtually alive for 21 months.

"How can that happen, for God's sake? Two years!" Jim's nominal neighbor Sam Shuster asked the Canadian Press wire service. "I used to ask the president of the [condo] board, 'Where in the hell is he?' She said all she knew was the bank gets the monthly money, so we don't worry about it." No doubt Sulkers would have been found earlier had he not had an unusual medical condition that prevents decomposition after death. Otherwise, even though nobody really missed Jim, they'd have smelled him.

Jim Sulker's death at least taught some of his neighbors a lesson about community. Two doors down the hall, Gladys Lowry also lived by herself. "I know this could never really happen to me," she told reporters, "but my neighbor and I have decided to phone each other every other day…just in case."

STARBUCKS AND OTHER SIGNS OF REVOLUTION.

There are those who say the breakdown of community is irreversible. In *Better Together*, the 2003 sequel to his *Bowling Alone*, Robert Putnam sounds a troubling note of pessimism. In the United States today, he insists, we are "no longer building the dense webs of encounter and participation so vital to the health of ourselves, our families, and our polities."[14] If Putnam is right, the vast majority of us are in danger of dying the way Mildred Stojkovic in North Lawndale and Jim Sulkers in Winnipeg died, from a lack of community.

But this is where we part company with Putnam. He and other doomsayers have failed to identify a movement back to community; Americans are beginning to reverse the trend. Perhaps we are not joining bowling leagues and Elks Clubs, as Putnam laments, but we are finding remarkable new ways to live together. America is on a quest for community. We are discovering ways to make our existing neighborhoods more neighborly. We are using new technology to cure our Community Deprivation Syndrome. Most remarkably, the people who plan and design the places we live are at last beginning to heed the cry for community. The tide is turning. We are witnessing a revolution of reconnection, a determination to re-village ourselves.

Could be the tipping point came with the terrorist attacks of September 11, 2001, when, for the first time in generations, Americans seemed for a time united in the face of a common threat. Or it may simply be that our own mobility has stretched a society beyond endurance: we move more frequently than any non-nomadic culture in all of human history. Or perhaps it's just that community-deprived baby boomers are at last waking up to what they've missed most of their lives.

Whatever the reasons, it's happening. We are finding new places to live and we are making the old places better, simply for the sake of community. At least some of us are done with going it alone. Americans – and citizens of other countries as well – are not spiraling ever downward into depressing solitude; we are recognizing our hunger for community, finding new and imaginative ways to satisfy that hunger.

This quest for community is a movement formed of all strata of society – recently arrived immigrants, multi-millionaires, twenty-somethings and retirees, individualists and corporate citizens – all coming to grips with their chronic lack of community. Young adults congregate in city centers, forming "urban tribes." Creative types from all over build an annual temporary city in the desert. Fundamentalists break up their mega-churches, so that congregations can stop watching preachers on video screens and get to know each other, even as other churches expand by forming interest-communities – singles groups, couples-with-children groups, couples-without-children groups, divorced-women groups. Millions satisfy their connection craze by journaling in the blogosphere. Banks, suddenly placing a dollar-value on human contact, invite customers to eschew ATMs and meet their tellers face-to-face. In Chicago and San Francisco, dining clubs form on the internet and relationships congeal over lunch. In New York, apartment dwellers break the ice with e-mail and open their doors to strangers-become-friends. The movement spreads across the ocean, and National Cup of Sugar Week offers Britons a new excuse to meet the neighbors.

At least one American company is consciously brewing community around the globe. Taking its clue from Ray Oldenburg's 1989 *The Great Good Place*, which told us we all need a "third place" distinct from home and office to gather, the Seattle coffee-grinder Starbucks is out to become the third place for city dwellers and suburbanites the world over. Starbucks aims to give each new shop a sense of belonging to its particular neighborhood, a "sense of place." Unlike Burger King and McDonald's stores, every Starbucks looks and feels ever-so-slightly different from every other one. They want people to feel at home, to congregate together in their caffeine cafés.

"This seems to fly in the face of common business sense," observed Lawrence Cheek in the Seattle *Post-Intelligencer*. "Why spend so much money creating an environment that invites people to hang around for hours, writing essays on their laptops while nursing a $3.25 mocha?" The answer Cheek got from Starbucks Senior Vice President for Store Development Launi Skinner is that Starbucks is "less about the transaction, and more about the experience," more about nurturing long-term relationships than providing short-term refreshment.[15] Starbucks of Seattle has built its globally dominant enterprise on a combination of our thirst for coffee and our hunger for community.

At a Starbucks in Boston, software developer Moe Shephard has formed relationships with both baristas and latte lovers. "I've gotten to know everybody who's ever worked there," Shephard told the *Boston Globe*. "Everyone talks to you. There's a group of buddies I meet every morning to talk about the affairs of the world…I go for the coffee, the croissant, and my pals. And no one hassles you. You can stay as long as you want. It is a place that encourages community building of some sort. I've met people in there that I'm friends with now whom I never would have met otherwise."[16]

Much of this third-place activity is happening in cities, but perhaps most remarkable of all, the community-craving movement is re-inventing suburbia, where today well over half of all Americans make their homes.

In suburban pockets around the nation and around the world, homeseekers are speaking with their wallets, buying up houses and condos, renting apartments, opening shops and offices in what are best thought of as "New Villages." In later chapters we'll look more closely at New Villages, including some located in suburbs, others within central cities. Each one has its own identity, creates its own sense of place. For now, let's define the New Village simply as a more-or-less self-contained neighborhood that intentionally – that is, by design – offers residents opportunities for community interaction, on walking and biking paths, in shops and restaurants, in parks and other public spaces, and at places of business.

Of the six people we met at the start of this chapter, excluding the late Mildred Stojkovic and Jim Sulkers, five have relocated to suburban New Villages, and there they have found community. John Henrickson, the sixtyish white baby-boomer who traveled the world for IBM, has relocated with wife Robbi to DC Ranch, a New Village outside Scottsdale, Arizona. Natasha Redwine-Carter, an African American Gen-Xer who grew up in a crowded city, moved to the Seattle-area New Village of Issaquah Highlands. Former child actor Ike Eissinmann and his wife Alex traveled all the way from a Los Angeles suburb to put down roots in one of the prototypical New Villages, Celebration, Florida, created by a Walt Disney team working under Todd Mansfield. All of these people have become acolytes of community.

John Henrickson sips on a latte at the Market Street Coffee Company – there being no Starbucks in DC Ranch – huddled close to Robbi so as to be heard over the noise of conversation and the milk steamer. The Henricksons' golden retriever is parked outside the coffee shop, welcoming pats from passers-by. "We knew we wanted something," John nods, "but we really didn't know what it was. We're still discovering what 'community' means, because we have never had it before."

Robbi met John back in college in Minnesota and they've been looking for home ever since. "We lived in Hong Kong, we lived in Tokyo," Robbi says. "We've moved nineteen times in 36 years of marriage. This was the first time we moved for our own reasons." She was the one who found DC Ranch, picking it over dozens of nearby desert-landscaped subdivisions filled exclusively with single-family homes. "I had never felt so grounded, such good feng shui out here. This place just gave me a sense of community." John nods agreement. "So many times you hope for something, and you're disappointed. We're not disappointed now."

At DC Ranch, John has become involved in stewardship of the McDowell Sonoran Land Trust, giving lessons to hikers and campers on using Global Positioning System in the desert mountains. Most days, though, he and Robbi only have to take a few steps from their front door to find community. "On Saturday, we go to the market, and we see our favorite dog friends. We don't walk together, we just meet them on the paths."

In Celebration, southwest of Orlando, new friends are introducing themselves to Ike and Alex Eissinmann's polite yellow Lab whose leash is looped around a tree branch. Ike shouts introductions from an outdoor café table. "His name is Taggert." Alex squeezes her tea bag with determination. "After fifteen years of living in your typical 50s

Ike and Alex Eissinmann left an impersonal L.A. suburb for New Village-community. With dog Taggert and their neighborhood electric vehicle (NEV), they can go everywhere and meet everyone in Celebration, Florida.

Photo by the authors

suburbs, I was just *tired* of it," she says. "I wanted to come someplace where people wanted to meet their neighbors." Alex's spiked red hair is a beacon. She cannot sit long at the outdoor tables of Celebration's town center without being approached by a friend-slash-neighbor. "I didn't know what to expect from people here," she smiles, "but I knew that, regardless, it would be more of a connection. I wanted to belong."

Ike takes up the theme. "You start to develop friendships through just using the town. We love it. We're engaged, we're involved." Ike has designed the Celebration Food-Fest commemorative T-shirt. Together he and Alex operate the electric train that tours families and children around Celebration, which they consider the perfect master-planned development. "It's no big mystery that people came here looking for something," he says. "Peace of mind, safety, community, activity – we all came here looking for something. Those of us who are happiest have found it in some way."

In the far corner of the country from Celebration, Natasha Redwine-Carter is serving ice cream to her two kids and three of their friends. She is one of the stars of her New Village's marketing video. "On my first day here in Issaquah Highlands, one of my neighbors at the bus stop invited me to a Tupperware party of all things. And I thought that was so great. She didn't know me, she wanted to make me feel welcome to the neighborhood, and I appreciated that. I did attend the party and met a lot of moms in my area. And within 24 hours I was pretty much friends with all of my neighbors nearby. I had a great chance to meet other people with children and everyone was very warm and friendly.

"Now, when I meet someone who is brand-new on the block, the first thing I do is invite them over for tea or a margarita or whatever I think they'd like, just to make them feel welcome to the neighborhood. Just as other people made me feel welcome."

Joanna Slaybaugh had moved from Chicago to the city of Bellevue, right up the road from Natasha's Issaquah home. Working long hours with no time to connect, and neighbors who were less than neighborly: "When you are exhausted from working such long hours, the last thing you want to deal with is a neighbor knocking on your door for a cup of sugar." She knew she was lacking connection; she had gone to workshops on creating community. Finally she gave up on city living altogether and moved back to the small town she grew up in, Pomeroy, Washington, "so small that everybody refers to their phone numbers only by the last four digits."[17] Joanna was able to move back after 22 years and instantly rejoin her community. She has at last found success, happiness and a sense of belonging.

In 2002 the web magazine Salon.com lamented the "loneliness to American life today." The majority of us live in cities or suburbs where "most public spaces are indistinct, impeccably designed by corporate creatives telegraphing class – the towering pillars of the Banana

Republic at the outdoor mall, the endless escalators and tiled walls of the multiplex. Jobs come and go, people move away at the drop of a hat, relationships begin and end and begin again. It's understandable that so many of us long for some feeling of permanent connection, some certainty of a relationship that could withstand the constant flux we experience, year after year."[18]

The time has come to embrace the concept of community as a cure for a lot of what ails us. As Judge Richard Posner wrote shortly after the terrorist attacks of 9/11, "The category 'American' suddenly seems spacious and lofty, transcending the petty divisions that so preoccupied the politically active and the ideologically obsessed." Nothing like a common enemy for making friends, Posner wrote in *The Atlantic Monthly*. "We are learning that social diversity and social homogeneity, extreme individualism and national community, are compatible."[19]

In "The Desire for Hermitage," composer Samuel Barber used the text of a tenth-century Irish monk to account for rejection of community. "Alone I came into this world," sings the monk. "Alone I shall go from it."[20]

Yet none of us comes into this world truly alone; we enter umbilically connected…and we are destined to connect again. We are not hermits. Forming community – a group of people with whom we can share our stories, our achievements and our disappointments, our talents and our needs – is in our blood, in our very DNA. It is up to each of us to nurture that connectivity even as we nurture our individualities.

CHAPTER TWO
Defining Community and Satisfying Our Hunger for It

A band played and a big crowd cheered as the launch from S.S. *Nevada* eased up to the dock. Everywhere red white and blue bunting, news cameras flashing. "It's all on account of Annie's birthday," eleven-year-old Anthony Moore sniggled at his little brother Phillip.

Annie Moore searched the crowd for her mother and father. She hadn't seen them in two years now. She wondered what her life would be like in this new land so far from the Ireland where she'd spent all of her fifteen years. The crowd pushed her into the back of the man in front of her. He turned and snapped something at her, in a language she thought might be German. Just ahead of the German an officer was lifting the gangplank railing. The band was playing a song she'd never heard, steamer whistles were blowing and bells were ringing their frightening, beautiful music.

"Ladies first," said another voice from behind Annie, an Irish voice. A burly arm pulled the German aside and nudged Annie Moore forward. Annie stepped onto the gangplank and down to the dock, becoming the first immigrant to pass through the United States' new processing facility, the Great Hall at Ellis Island in New York Harbor.

She had only a basket of clothes and two brothers clinging to her skirts, but here came Annie, living the "American Dream." A Mister So-and-So from the U.S. Treasury Department shook her hand and asked her where she was from. "Cobh, County Cork," Annie stammered. Another dignified gentleman pressed a ten-dollar gold piece into her hand and told her congratulations. It was by far the most money Annie Moore had ever held. The American Dream was coming true.

That was on January 1, 1892. In the 62 years that followed, more than twelve million immigrants would follow Annie Moore into the Great Hall, until in 1954 the government shut down the Ellis Island port of entry. Today nearly 100 million Americans, about 40 percent of us, can trace our ancestry to men, women and children who followed

Annie's footsteps. As for Annie Moore herself, she eventually married a fellow immigrant, Patrick O'Connell, and with him she raised a family of five children in Waco, Texas. One of her descendants, Edward T. O'Donnell, is a nationally recognized historian who wrote about Annie in his "Hibernian Chronicle" column in the national Irish-American newspaper *The Irish Echo*.[21]

In Waco, where she lived until her death in 1923, Annie had a home of her own – a roof over her head and possessions beyond what she could carry on her back – in a community of families who looked out for one another, who shared her values, whose children grew up with her children. She lived the American Dream.

Yet in a way the success of Annie Moore and the millions of immigrants who followed her have contributed to a kind of national amnesia about that dream and what it was really all about. As city populations grew too fast for services to keep up, as wave after wave of new immigrants crowded into tenements uncared for by absentee landlords, our vision narrowed. The American Dream shrank to supplying basic needs: food and shelter. If we could just manage a paying job and a roof over our heads, that would be dream enough.

We forgot that we also need other people in our lives, that we need *community*. Alone, Annie might not have succeeded.

DEFINING COMMUNITY.

So what exactly do we mean by "community?" We need to have a clear idea of that before we proceed much further. Our English language employs the word to cover a multitude of concepts, from distinct components of society (the gay community) to a group of cohabitants (the Park Slope community) to an ecological habitat (the grasslands community). Our word is derived from Latin, *communis*, which means "common," but in turn *communis* has its own roots. The first part of the word is easy: *co, com, cum* – we use them all in English to suggest togetherness. The second part would seem equally obvious: *unus* means "one." So a community must be a group of people come together as one or for a single purpose. Hence dictionaries provide us with a list of choices. From the *American Heritage Dictionary*:

> ' A group of people living in the same locality and under the same government.
>
> ' The district or locality in which such a group lives.

- A group of people having common interests: *the scientific community; the international business community.*

- A group viewed as forming a distinct segment of society: *the gay community; the community of color.*

- Similarity or identity: *a community of interests.*

- Sharing, participation, and fellowship.

- Society as a whole; the public.

Multiple people, something shared: that's community. But there is another possibility, a fascinating option proposed by the online encyclopedia *Wikipedia*, which, itself, satisfies many of the former criteria. While agreeing with the *American Heritage* in the several uses of "community," the writer of the *Wikipedia* entry maintains that the second part of the word comes not from *unus* (one) or *unitas* (unity), but from *munus*, which is Latin for "gift," as in "munificent." Thus the article concludes, "Community literally means to give among each other. Community could be defined as a group of people who share gifts which they provide to all." A fascinating concept.

In spite of its multiple definitions and extraordinary weight-bearing load, "community" is the only word we can find to talk about the sort of connection Americans are looking for in the early years of the 21st century. So, while not denying the validity of those other definitions, we will establish our own definition, and we will avoid using it in any of its other senses (although those other senses may turn up in a direct quotation or two.) In this book, the word "community" means:

> **A place to live not in isolation but in the company of other people who share some values and interests and who interact for mutual benefit.**

That's what we mean by community, and we believe that's what most people mean when they speak of a "sense of community" or when they say, "our community is a special place." That's the "community" that Annie Moore found, first in New York City and then in Waco. And that's what new generations of immigrants are finding in the United States of America.

Between 1990 and 2000, the U.S. population grew by nearly 33 million, and almost half of that gain was attributed to immigration. During the decade of the 90s, thirteen states saw their foreign-born population more than double. As our native-born growth decelerates and our foreign-born population rises, the real estate and home-building industries have naturally begun to pay closer attention to what immigrants and their offspring are really looking for. According to the Harvard University Joint Center for Housing Studies, from 1998 to 2001 nearly eight percent of new home sales and eleven percent of existing home sales were to foreign-born households. Immigrants constituted twelve percent of those buying their first homes in 2001, and on average they bought more expensive first homes than their U.S.-born counterparts. Do we know anything of their version of the American Dream?

For some of those immigrant buyers, meeting basic needs is enough. Mislanys Rodriguez, in Spring Hill, Florida wanted "security for my daughter, the security of owning the roof over your head." On the other hand, there are those whose dream extends beyond the basics. Somalia-born Asha Abokor worked several years and studied her options carefully before buying a house in Phoenix. "I wanted it as an investment," she says, "to belong to a community with established roots. All those things were really important."[22]

Barry Checkoway, a professor of social work at the University of Michigan and a founding director of the Edward Ginsberg Center for Community Service and Learning, believes that immigrants and their offspring are making a big commitment to building community. Most new immigrant groups, he says, are more active within their neighborhoods than are people who've been here for generations. Latinos, according to Checkoway's research, are voting in higher numbers than ever. Similarly, young people are becoming more involved than their parents ever were. Checkoway's study, "Lifting New Voices" depicts the efforts of young people in economically troubled areas all over the country to improve their neighborhoods through civic involvement.[23] For newcomers as well as for generations brought up in suburban isolation, the American Dream is returning to its roots. More than simply a roof over our heads – even if it's an expensive roof of an impressive house – new Americans are dreaming of a place they can feel a part of.

We are also becoming more directly involved in the design and creation of our places. When the Urban Land Institute (ULI) studied immigration and population diversity in 2003, its report concluded that those factors were "changing the face" of many parts of the country and "creating demand for more development that fosters inclusivity rather than exclusivity." At the ULI's annual fall meeting in San Francisco, Arizona developer and Celebration alumnus Brent E. Herrington sounded the theme. "We've had to rethink how we brand communities and reconsider our messaging." he said. So Herrington's Scottsdale-headquartered DMB Associates has shifted its business strategy toward master-planned suburban developments that take into account the demographic changes resulting from immigration.

"Suburban communities that are named, gated or built around a single amenity such as a golf course," says Herrington, "are more apt to imply exclusivity rather than inclusivity to immigrants. That does not work well when you are reaching out to a diverse market." As a result, DMB is "reinforcing the message of inclusivity," through amenities such as multi-use, flexible spaces that foster socializing and interaction between people of different cultures. In other words, they are building more than homes; they are building community.

Another panelist at that ULI meeting suggested that especially among families from Central and South America, community begins with extended family. "It is inherent in the lifestyles of Latinos to have all family members under one roof, and to put down roots in the community," says Katherine Perez, executive director of the Southern California Transportation and Land Use Coalition. Perez reports that extended families have become such a driving demographic force in Southern California that builders are now offering "accordion" housing blueprints to immigrant suburban home purchasers. These show the possibilities for adding bedrooms or other living space as families grow through the birth of children or the arrival of relatives from across the border. "These accordion plans let families make additions so they won't have to move out of the community. It keeps the communities strong," she maintains.[24]

It is notable that the new master-planned developments of Arizona and the expandable housing designs of California are happening mostly in the suburbs, which over the last half-century have come to symbolize America's careless lack of planning and design. Yet as the population continues to grow, the reality is that we will continue to depend on extra-urban spaces to accommodate that growth. Is it possible that we are witnessing a conversion from suburban sprawl to suburban community? Can the revolution of reconnection redefine suburbia? To properly answer those questions, we need to step back for a moment and understand that where most of us live today is mostly a result of someone else deciding where we *ought* to live. Suburbia was thrust upon us.

BIRTH OF THE SUBURB BLUES.

World War II and the baby boom provide the usual, much oversimplified explanation for today's housing patterns in the United States. In fact, the official roadmap to suburbia was drawn up even earlier than that. The railroads – owned principally by real estate developers, called tycoons back then – started moving people from cities to the countryside in the mid-19ᵀᴴ century. People from the dank, overbuilt, crowded cities got their first breath of fresh rural air and naturally began wondering what it would be like to live there. Before the 20ᵀᴴ century dawned, trolley lines – owned by those same real estate tycoons – were replacing many of the interurban railroad lines. This enabled manufacturers to build new and bigger factories on less expensive "suburban" land, which, by today's stretched perspective would seem but a short distance from the city center. Trolley lines made it possible for city-dweller laborers to "commute" to work, where formerly most of them had simply trudged to the mill. Auto makers and road construction sped up the process, even as immigration and other factors continued to crowd cities and make them less desirable places to live. When the stock market crashed in 1929, America fell into the Great Depression and the federal government fell into the business of telling Americans where to live.

Our government-sponsored relocation program started in 1933, with a now forgotten agency called the Homeowners' Loan Corporation, or HOLC. A product of Herbert Hoover's administration, the HOLC sent an army of land appraisers and housing inspectors around the country to determine which places were suitable for new home building and which were not. When Franklin Roosevelt became President, he morphed the HOLC into the Federal Housing Authority, and that organization drew up the master plan for the new American Dream: a house in suburbia. FDR's New Deal proclaimed that new home construction, rather than renovation of existing housing in crumbling inner cities, would be the most effective means of stimulating the economy. A vast number of unemployed could be put to work building houses.

Because housing was considered an appreciable asset, lending institutions saw houses as collateral. With America's surviving banks barely making ends meet, the Depression-bound government was willing to guarantee home loans, but only on condition that the houses be built in "desirable" neighborhoods, where people were likely to pay their notes on time. Therefore an FHA-loan home could not be built next to a factory or a dump or in any "bad" part of town. Using

Morningside, begun in 1938, was one of the first real estate developments on the outer fringe of Charlotte, NC, in an area officially sanctioned by the Hoover-era Standard Acts.

Used by permission of Crosland, LLC

the earlier work of HOLC inspectors, the FHA institutionalized neighborhood desirability. The FHA *Underwriting Handbook* actually "red-lined" neighborhoods deemed unsuitable for loans. Inevitably, the red-lined parts of town were those occupied primarily by low-income households, often exclusively black or immigrant families, while the "suitable" parts were nearly always on the outskirts, insulated by trolley and automobile rides from the deteriorating inner cities. Across the land in the 1930s, home-building companies popped into existence literally overnight. The owners of the trolley systems – land speculators nearly to a man – began extending their lines away from the red-lined inner cities. Despite the Depression, car sales began to climb.

It seems likely that FDR's plan would have lifted the economy as intended, had not the Second World War intervened and made it a moot point. The home-builders shifted to government contracts, building military barracks and housing for shipyard workers, as North Carolina's Crosland Company did, shifting from home-building in Charlotte to shipyard workers' housing in Wilmington. When the GIs returned home in 1945, it was like a cork popping from a bottle of economic champagne that had been shaking and fizzing for nearly half a decade. Those GIs were ready for starting families, or for moving the families they'd already started into homes of their own. John Crosland moved his company back to Charlotte and started building those GI houses, as smart developers everywhere did.[25] The Veterans Administration joined the FHA as guarantors of low-down-payment, low-interest, long-term loans. The mothers and fathers of baby-boomers bought houses at the hitherto undreamed of rate of a million new homes a year, almost all of those in the suburbs. Besides, the best schools were being built out in the suburbs, and all those new mommies and daddies wanted their kids to get the best education American suburbia could offer. The race to suburbia was on and people needed wheels to get there. Small wonder that in the four years following World War II Americans bought 21.4 million cars, more than five times the number of new houses built during that period.

As for the great cities, largely unimproved over the previous two decades of depression and war, they had become places where the government and the banks did not want to make loans and where families who could afford something better no longer wanted to live. This stimulated the infamous "white flight" that would run riot through the 60s and 70s. Few government agencies or local real estate tycoons stopped to consider that in their rush to grow and grow rich they were setting in motion the inevitability of inner-city decay, separate-and-unequal treatment for those who stayed behind and, of course, suburban sprawl.

Inevitable, too, was the emergence of a new business model. What had worked downtown would not necessarily succeed in the suburbs. Department stores, the former flagships of downtown business, fled for their lives to the suburbs. Dining establishments were not far behind. In the 1960s a fast talker named Ray Kroc became the Johnny Appleseed of the fast food industry by betting on suburbia. As Harvey Levenstein writes in *Paradox of Plenty,* Kroc's "real genius" had nothing to do with hamburgers and golden arches. It was that "he knew how to exploit the new demographics." [26] While earlier fast food successes like White Castle remained stuck and shrinking in the decaying inner cities, Kroc put all his chips on the new commercial strips of suburbia, tying McDonald's and its horde of emulators to the automobile.

Not coincidentally, Kroc and his contemporaries were the first generation influenced by television. In the 1950s that new medium bombarded America with assurances that the suburbs were the only good place to live. Sure Ralph and Alice Cramden (Jackie Gleason and Audrey Meadows) survived in the city, but Ralph was a lowly bus driver and his buddy Norton worked in the sewers. Like the Cramdens, New Yorkers George "Kingfish" and Sapphire Stevens (Tim Moore and Ernestine Wade) lived in a run-down, dreary little apartment. That was simply the best the Kingfish could manage as a department store delivery man.

Neither *The Honeymooners* nor *Amos 'n Andy* provided ideal role models, merely laughs. Television did its best to let us know the cities were teeming with nasty criminals and vicious gangs. *Dragnet, Boston Blackie, Mr. District Attorney, Perry Mason, Peter Gunn* – there were a million stories in the naked cities, all of them unpleasant. And if the bad guys tried to get out of town, *Highway Patrol* would hunt them down; villains were not permitted in the suburbs of the 1950s.

No, the only problems in suburbia had to do with what time dad would be getting home, what mom would cook for dinner and how junior would ever explain that baseball hit through the neighbors' front window. The Andersons of *Father Knows Best* never spotted an unsavory character near their home at 607 South Maple Street in generic Springfield. *The Adventures of Ozzie and Harriet* – and of their sons David and Ricky – never included garbage strikes, sirens in the night or break-ins at 822 Sycamore Road. As for the Cleavers – Ward and June, Wally and Theodore – of *Leave it to Beaver*, moving up in the world meant moving to a more exclusive suburb. They put their house at 211 Pine Street up for sale: "Charming three bedrooms w/ den on beautifully landscaped grounds, modern dream kitchen, patio, spacious, airy. The ultimate in suburban living. Near schools and transportation." Their new house, at 485 Maple was even better. (Notice the street names: Maple, Sycamore, Pine – Kansas City *Star* syndicated columnist Bill Vaughan is credited with the line: "Suburbia is where the developer bulldozes out the trees, then names the streets after them.") In what was perhaps the most celebrated television relocation, Lucy and Ricky Ricardo, played by Lucille Ball and immigrant-made-good Desi Arnaz, in 1957 escaped a 99-year lease in Manhattan. They and their friends the Mertzes moved from 623 East 68th Street to the suburban nirvana of Westport, Connecticut, perhaps not far from Darrin and Samantha Stephens of *Bewitched*.

But it wasn't just television first pushing and then lamenting the suburban lifestyle; the 50s and 60s were awash in hit tunes about suburbia. Consider Jerry Wallace's "Primrose Lane," where life was always a holiday. At the climax of "Silhouettes" in 1957, the lead singer of the Rays nearly caused a suburban sensation when he saw the woman he took to be his girlfriend kissing another guy, then discovering, to his shock, he was on the wrong block. That was because in low-end suburbs such as Long Island's Levittown, all the houses looked pretty much alike. That phenomenon was satirized somewhat heavy-handedly in San Francisco protest singer Malvina Reynolds's "Little Boxes," in which the houses on the hillside were "all made of ticky-tacky and all look just the same."

The entertainment industry's most worrisome concern about those darned suburbs surfaced in the 1963 film *Wives and Lovers*. By this time the suburbs were being built so far out from the cities that house-bound wives simply could not keep track of their commuting husbands' whereabouts. Office hanky-panky loomed large in their imaginations. The warning in the film's theme song, by Hal David and Burt Bacharach, pretty much stands as a testimony to the times:

> *Day after day, there are girls at the office,*
> *And men will always be men.*
> *Don't send him off with your hair still in curlers –*

You may not see him again.
For wives should always be lovers too.
Run to his arms the moment he comes home to you...
I'm warning you.

If we wanted a house in the suburbs – and nearly everyone did in those days – we had to take the bad with the good. That suburbanization of sitcoms reversed itself, to some extent, in the 80s and 90s with shows like *The Cosby Show, Friends, Sex and the City, Seinfeld* and *Frazier,* showing viewers the idealized urban communities to be had in the Big Apple... or even in Seattle.

A "TRAGIC LANDSCAPE" OF McMANSIONS.

In 2006, television has come full circle with *Desperate Housewives,* in which suburban women are the decision-makers dealing with the angst and learning disabilities and drug problems of the children. It is the suburban women with those uncontrollable urges. Wives, they agree, should always be lovers too. Their desperate families live on Wisteria Lane (certainly not the lane of that name in Celebration), where life is anything but a holiday. "A staggering number of programs, just like the people who watch them, now live in the land of the two-car garage," reports *The New York Times. The Simpsons* live in Springfield, where once Father Knew Best. If we want more of the 'burbs, we can set our TiVos to record *Weeds, Big Love, The Sopranos, Laguna Beach* or *The O.C.* to find neighborhoods "crowded to overflow with pot-dealing PTA moms; hardware-store owners in multiple marriages; and tattooed, Wiccan home-swappers."[27]

But long before we could admit that we had not left all our personal problems and social dysfunction behind in the crumbling cities, we declared a suburban address first acceptable then preferable. By the 1980s in most parts of the United States a suburban zip code was very nearly essential. As proof of a family's rising socio-economic status, nothing else had the impact of an oversized, multi-car-garaged, palatial home in a stylish new suburb. If the lot could be three-quarters of an acre or larger, preferably fronting on a golf course, one's success was indisputable. To give home-buyers what they seemed to want, developers bought up tracts of farmland and forest ever farther from the central cities, where lots could be larger and homes could be called "estates." The notion that a man's home was his castle took on an almost literal meaning along long and curving blocks lined with look-alike castles. As the Suburban Century neared its climax, builders were tacking on so many amenities to houses in these exurban, isolated and often gated estate farms that within the industry they became known as McMansions.

During the 80s, architect Tom Low was involved in super-sizing the city and suburbs of Charlotte, which was (and at this writing, still is) one of the nation's fastest growing regions of the day. "I really didn't like the place that I was designing," he says today. The subdivisions, office parks, apartment complexes and shopping centers he designed "never added up to community. I really didn't like the way Charlotte was heading."

What bothered Low most of all was that so many of the city's financially successful people were isolating and insulating themselves from everything and everyone else around them. "The Millennium McMansion may be a great thing in its own right, but it is never attached to anything that really adds up to something. That is why people who buy these big mansions have to create an entire village inside their homes. The kitchen is called the 'café,' the TV room is now

Gated developments such as this one outside Dallas may be the antithesis of the community found in New Villages.

Photo by Dean Terry from the film Subdivided (www.subdivided.net)

the 'home theater,' the master bedroom is now called the 'master resort,' with its own juice bar and its own Jacuzzi. And every house has its huge recreation room with its own sports center. You need three or four living rooms to entertain because there is nowhere to go from where you live. You know, really it makes sense to have five thousand square feet, because the physical environment surrounding you is so miserable you basically have to create your own cocoon with all the amenities built in."[28] Low might be overstating the case, but we certainly have seen amenity-laden cocoons such as those he describes.

It took just a little while for many of us in America to realize we had become a nation of suburban dislocation. It was in 1993 that journalist and novelist Howard Kunstler published a wake-up call in *The Geography of Nowhere: The Rise and Decline of America's Man-Made Landscape.* If you picked up a copy at the chain bookstore in your local ten-acre shopping mall, you might have given a clench-lipped nod to the dust jacket copy:

> "Eighty percent of everything ever built in America has been built since the end of World War II. This tragic landscape of highway strips, parking lots, housing tracts, mega-malls, junked cities, and ravaged countryside is not simply an expression of our economic predicament, but in large part a cause. It is the everyday environment where most Americans live and work, and it represents a gathering calamity whose effects we have hardly begun to measure."

We aren't sure exactly what "economic predicament" we were in in 1993, and tragedy and calamity may seem harshly hyperbolic descriptions of the places most Americans live, but Kunstler had his point. There was generally nothing welcoming about the vast majority of suburban neighborhoods in a social sense. No matter how cozily and comfortably designed its individual "dwelling units," as the planners say, the neighborhoods themselves, auto-dependent and contact-discouraging, somehow turned us in on ourselves. People who moved into these neighborhoods often tried to do something to generate a spirit of community. They formed associations and clubs and welcoming committees which may have worked in some neighborhoods but which, with the passage of time, became primarily poorly managed power bases for the few and methods for denying access to the unwanted. Many of these "neighborhood associations" and "community associations" exist today primarily as grinding wheels for individual axes, promulgating regulations about what is not allowed within the neighborhood and keeping out any activities that might endanger home resale values.

When Beth Yockey and her parents moved to the 1960-vintage Charlotte suburb of Lansdowne in 1989, no member of the neighborhood association showed up to welcome them. They found in their curbside mailbox an annual solicitation for association membership dues, an occasional newsletter and announcement of the yearly come-one-come-all barbecue. In thirteen years of living in Lansdowne, they were never visited by anyone from the neighborhood association and were telephoned only once, with an urgent request that they attend a Zoning Board meeting to stop a group home for AIDS patients from moving in. That invitation was declined.

"Community associations in the US have a bad reputation," acknowledges Pat Wasson. She should know. As national president of the Community Associations Institute from 1996 to 1997, Wasson traveled around the country, "trying to put the community back into these communities. All these 'community associations' have no community in them. Whatever happened to the Welcome Wagon?"

Actually, Welcome Wagon still exists, though it has little to do with community as we have defined it. Founded by Memphis entrepreneur Thomas Briggs in 1928, Welcome Wagon was always a commercial venture, with paid "hostesses" greeting new homeowners and handing out promotional gifts and coupons for businesses in the area. Eventually Welcome Wagon spread from Tennessee to suburbs across the USA. In the 1980s a similar operation, Getting to Know You, sprang up on Long Island, New York. Sponsored by a local beverage company, GTKY was basically a neighborhood merchant directory sent through the mail to new residents. When these two organizations merged in 1998, they kept the Welcome Wagon name, but abandoned its former personal touch. As explained on the company's web site, "The home visits stopped in 1998 as an increase in two-income families meant fewer people were home to accept visits. Welcome Wagon began greeting new homebuyers through the mail with a gift of an attractive, customized address book...Although the day of door-to-door neighborly visits are [sic] a thing of the past, Welcome Wagon is still committed to connecting with new homebuyers through their mailboxes and the internet." [29]

Translation: personal contact stopped being profitable.

But, we and others maintain, that lack of personal contact can be damaging to us personally and to society at large. In the extreme, there are the *hikikomori* of Japan, young people who shut themselves up alone for weeks, months, even years, gradually losing the most basic of skills required to interact with others. Eventually *hikikomori* may lapse into a kind of waking coma, simply staring into space for hours on end, or committing heinous crimes when someone attempts to help them get on with life. Varying estimates put the number suffering from this strange condition at anywhere between 50,000 and 1 million. Nobody really knows, because families of *hikikomori* are embarrassed and reluctant to talk about it.

Hopefully, this extreme variety of Community Deprivation Syndrome will not spread like bird flu to other nations. Japan's principal *hikikomori* psychiatrist, Dr. Tamaki Saito, points out that his country's is a culture that for centuries lived in isolation from the rest of the world, and much of its poetry and music celebrates the "nobility of solitude."[30] On the other hand, Japan's influence on the rest of the world in the 21ˢᵗ century can hardly be called insignificant. Nor can that of China, whose rulers' superiority complex successfully isolated that vast country from the Western world right up until the 21ˢᵗ century.

"Cultural xenophobia is a frequent sequel to a society's decline from cultural vigor," writes the esteemed social critic Jane Jacobs. Her book *Dark Age Ahead* warns us that we are in danger of slipping into a "fortress mentality," in which we look backward and inward rather than forward and outward. "A fortress mentality not only shuts itself off from dynamic influences originating outside but also, as a side effect, ceases influencing the outside world."[31]

While certain politicians may preach the virtues of isolation, there is plenty of evidence that this is precisely what Americans do not want. Notwithstanding the demise of Welcome Wagon, people seem more bound and determined than ever to meet the neighbors. Americans and others around the world are rediscovering the importance, perhaps the urgency, of community. Whatever we call our neighborhood, neighbors are necessary. Despite the tooth-gnashing fears generated by *Bowling Alone*, a 2002 University of Connecticut survey found that nearly half of us Americans, 47 percent, spend a social evening with close neighbors at least once a month. An earlier poll by the University of Chicago put that number even higher, at 56 percent.

HIGH-RISE VILLAGERS, URBAN FARMERS, DESERT COMMUNES.

One of the chief distinctions between most big city dwellers and most suburbanites is the degree of proximity between them and their closest neighbors. In suburbia, next-door can mean a half-acre or more away; in the city, neighbors often live literally on top of one another. A little-noted byproduct of the sanctification of suburbia is that city-dwellers too have come to view distance as an asset, even when the only distance available is psychic. Over-friendly neighbors may be viewed as pariahs. Privacy is paramount. As a consequence, community can be as hard to find in the crowded city as it is in the sprawl of suburbia. However, as *The New York Times* has noted, that is changing. The revolution is afoot in Manhattan and Brooklyn, just as in Westport. Rather than simply creating their own little aeries in tall buildings, people are looking for ways to turn tall buildings into communities. "To one degree or another," declared the *Times* in a 2003 survey of developers, owners, managers and tenants, "many nests are becoming villages."[32]

From East 58th Street comes the assertion: "Our attitude is that we are a family unit rather than isolated units." Guy I. Smiley, president of the board of a 352-apartment co-op says, "After 9/11, I think everyone was looking for a connection... and where you live is a great place to have that."

At North Shore Towers and Country Club, a three-building, 1,800-unit co-op in Queens, owners are promised "a lifestyle, not just an apartment." This vertical village includes a full-service restaurant, a catering hall, an outdoor hot-dog stand, a clubhouse that serves breakfast and lunch, swimming pools, health clubs, lectures on art, seminars on medical problems, dancing classes and a 460-seat movie theater. North Shore's back yard is an eighteen-hole golf course. "This is small-town living," smiles resident Phyllis Goldstein, "and when you interact in the club, the movie theater, the coffee shop, over the years, you get to know everybody."

At Greystone, a less-pricey co-op apartment complex up the Hudson in Yonkers, residents have formed a social action committee to make their building more child-friendly, "more like a community." Ten years ago the Greystone was a cold place with lots of prohibitive rules: no scooter riding, no ball playing. Now kids frolic together by the pool and parents feel secure. There's always a neighbor ready to keep an eye out, says Lisa Sherman, ready to help with her three-year-old. "'I have to be down there, but I don't have to stay on top of him." And this is one of the most common refrains of parents in New Villages across the land: parents trusting neighbors with the welfare of their children.

Complexes like the ones in Queens and Yonkers are manifestations of a growing phenomenon labeled "microneighborhoods." Barrett Lee, a sociology professor at Pennsylvania State University, says he sees people in many parts of the country using simple geographical connectivity as the basis of community, forming neighborhood networks of support. "For certain kinds of support, like emergency help and borrowing the proverbial cup of sugar," Lee says, "proximity is most important."[33]

Microneighborhoods, declared *The New York Times* in 2002, were "blooming" across Westchester County, "in densely packed suburban neighborhoods with small homes, in more spacious neighborhoods with larger homes and even in urban apartment complexes." Joanne Fahey, who lives at Tappan Landing, told the newspaper that in her micro-neighborhood "everybody is very generous, caring and giving."

Also blooming in midtown Manhattan are community gardens, gardens planted on the interior of city blocks and cooperatively managed by the owners of the apartments and condominiums which surround them. The MacDougal-Sullivan garden, one of the oldest in the city, has 21 townhomes abutting it. Residents retain small private plots but share common space with a playground and pathways – a bit of "central European charm" in the middle of the city.[34] Residents plan egg hunts, picnics and cocktail parties together in their private garden.

Though it has become an amenity, raising the prices of the townhomes it serves into the millions, the McDougal-Sullivan Garden blossomed out of hard-times necessity. Alden Cohen recalled in 1974 that in the 1920s, "no one had very much money." As residents worked together to plan which vegetables to plant and formulate the rules for their new shared space, the garden "taught us many lessons in cooperation." The cooperation that comes from working together to grow veggies teaches skills that young people in inner-cities and suburbia alike are often lacking.

In Olympia, Washington, Blue Peetz saw a lot of kids who had "hunger as an issue in their lives." He founded an organization called Garden Raised Bounty (GRuB), and began working with them on planting vegetable gardens. He quickly learned that not only was their hard work solving the immediate need of putting food on their tables, but was also teaching them social skills, teaching them how to tackle problems, to manage a business and to relate to the community at large.[35] That experience has been shared innumerable times around the country at urban p-patches. The American Community Garden Association now has over nine hundred member organizations.[36]

While others are planting vegetables, college deans across the country are sowing the seeds of community as a way to involve more of their students in the learning process. As in microneighborhoods, universities are creating physical spaces in which students and teachers can begin to relate to one another as neighbors. "You create pockets all around campus that strengthen social bonds between students, which keeps them in school," says George D. Kuh, director of the National Survey of Student Engagement (NSSE) at Indiana University, Bloomington. "The creation of living-learning communities is not just about enriching the life of the mind," he says. "It is also about ensuring the livelihood of the college."[37] Nationally, schools are focusing their incoming freshmen into community-based learning groups, which are engineered to provide a stable structure for students adjusting to a new way of living. One such institution, The Evergreen State College in Olympia, has been ranked near the top in its level of academic challenge and student success. According to both NSSE and the school, Evergreen's emphasis on getting students involved in the community, and on attracting community-service minded students, is the key to that success.[38]

Another lesson in community building comes not from the campus but from the desert. One of the more unusual efforts at bringing people together, Burning Man began in 1986 with a group of twenty San Francisco friends building a bonfire on the beach in celebration of the summer solstice – or burning possessions associated with a certain ex-girlfriend, depending on which version of the story you believe. By 2006 the Burning Man festival had grown to nearly 40,000 people, culminating Labor Day weekend in the Nevada Desert. Actually, Burning Man is a year-round state of mind, with regional participant groups staying in touch all around the country. They work together on projects of "radical self-expression" and communicate extensively over the internet, with nearly 400 Burning Man groups on Yahoo alone.

The Burning Man Festival evolved out of "a heartfelt desire for connection and community" into a year-round community state of mind, culminating in the creation of a temporary town Labor Day weekend in the Nevada desert.

Photo by Todd Gardiner, 2005

For Beth Yockey, Burning Man is all about creating community, about forming bonds which have nothing to do with commercialism. For their week-long desertfest, participants are expected to arrive with whatever they need to be self-sustaining. Groups and individuals may give things away, but exchange of money – indeed exchange of any sort – is strictly prohibited. Infants to septuagenarians, people from every imaginary background create a city that provides such services as a daily newspaper, a radio station, air-lift emergency transportation, a fully-functioning community police department (called "rangers"), a department of public works and waste recycling.

Burning Man, writes Ethan Watters, is not an expression of antisocial behavior, but rather "of a heartfelt desire for connection and community in the cool *guise* of rebellion - the best of both worlds." In his book, *Urban Tribes: a generation redefines friendship, family and commitment*, Watters likens the festival to the social dynamics that eventually toppled the Berlin Wall. In Berlin there was no organized public movement, simply communication within networks of friends. "Personal networks were the most important contexts for mobilizing citizens."[39] The "burners," the citizens who participate in Burning Man, are likewise mobilized through personal networks. People meet, fall in love and get married at Burning Man. People discover geographical neighbors they never knew.

Beth's camp, which calls itself EPT, communicates daily through its Yahoo group. The tribe's eighty members host dinner parties and art events. They fundraise, support each other in times of need and feed each others' cats and dogs when necessary. Other Seattle-area burners have started non-profits, media collectives, shoe-making companies and cooperative housing. There are five "public" email listservs, as well as hundreds of private groups, like EPT's. Beth's tribe is a community, and it's also a part of the larger Seattle-burner community, which in turn is a part of the even larger international Burning Man community.

TECHNOLOGICALLY ENABLED COMMUNITY AND OTHER VARIATIONS ON THE THEME.

The community-seekers of Burning Man are hardly alone in their adaptation of technology to create community. While we'll deal with this subject at greater length later, let us note here two of the recently-emerged techniques for bringing people together, Friendster and Dodgeball.

Friendster is more or less an application of the "six degrees of separation" theory – I know somebody who knows somebody who knows…etc. At Friendster.com you fill out a basic profile, submit a photo of yourself and you're on your way to establishing your "personal network." Click on another Friendster name and see how you're connected to that person. As Matthew Continetti wrote in the *Weekly Standard,* "Chances are I have more friends than you do… I know for a fact that I have 112,842 friends." That was back in 2003; Continetti probably has made a lot more Friendster connections since then.[40] "Friendster is more like a dinner party" than an online dating service, says the *New Statesman.* "You meet new people through the introductions of existing friends."[41] Though the dinner party metaphor is questionable, as of the fall of 2006 it claimed to have more than 33 million "profiles" of men and women with whom users could connect, all of whom knew that first someone in real life before logging on.

While Friendster started out on the British desktop, Dodgeball is an American child of the internet-cellphone marriage. As Ben Gilbert reported on National Public Radio's *All Things Considered,* "Dodgeball allows a user to send a text message from a mobile phone to the Dodgeball server, a single e-mail address. From there, the Dodgeball server shoots the message out to a kind of virtual mailing list of friends that the user has previously designated on the Dodgeball web site. You tell the service where you are, and it tells your friends."

Available in more than twenty cities as of 2006, Dodgeball is a sort of personal global positioning device. The system looks for other users in a ten-block radius who share one degree of separation from your Dodgeball friends. "It tells you where your friends' friends are," says Gilbert, "and Dodgeball then tells those same people where you are." Sort of an "on-the-fly happy hour."

More traditional avenues of community-through-technology are I-Neighbors.org – which helps you set up a web page for your neighborhood, featuring information about local governments, who's available for babysitting and the like – and MeetTheNeighbors.org, which is sort of an electronic block party. "You just might turn a neighbor into a friend," says *Time* of the new icebreaker options.[42]

Sometimes we don't need technology to find community, sometimes we just need to get out of the house. Joel Clement, an environmentalist with Forest Dynamics, did that when he moved from the Seattle neighborhood of Fremont to the less-gentrified neighborhood called South Park. (Coincidentally, the neighborhood Beth Yockey calls home, too.) Clement calls South Park "a nutty multilingual mix of social activists, craftsmen, blue collars from Boeing, white collars from downtown, motorcycle enthusiasts, and apparently most of Seattle's musicians."[43] After having a drink at a neighboring-neighborhood's local bar, Joel decided that he needed to see what the South Park taverns had to offer. Overcoming an aversion to the County Line, where frequent drug deals happened and prostitutes openly solicited business on the front porch, Joel began a weekly happy hour event for South Park residents. By his encouraging residents to come together at the County Line, South Parkers have gained a neighborhood "third place" and fought crime at the same time.

"What I found in South Park is nothing short of the most welcoming, vibrant cluster of engaged neighbors I've experienced since my childhood in Maine." Writing in the *West Seattle Herald*, Clement says, "I knew right away things were different down here: neighbors walking their dogs stop and chat and fill me in on the latest South Park scuttlebutt; a mother and daughter sell steaming tamales door-to-door; neighbors loan each other tools, care for each other's pets, and generally look after one another; meetings, parties, and petty crimes are announced on a neighborhood e-mail listserv; and the monthly South Park meetings are actually packed and informative… In the meantime a new library is going up, a skate park is going in, Cesar Chavez Park is being completed, trees are being planted, the community center is providing a full menu of resources and activities for all ages, and the neighborhood association is tackling everything from the EPA's cleanup work on the Duwamish [River] to a hugely successful and well-attended Night Out Against Crime."[44]

On the other side of the country, in Todd Mansfield's adopted city of Charlotte, people are also finding opportunities to get out of their houses and join up with their neighbors. "People were actually created for community," declares James White, pastor of Charlotte's Mecklenburg Community Church, "so it's going to be a deep longing… We long to be part of a cause, a community, a team." White and his churchgoers create community by breaking up the 5,000-member congregation into "life groups" of people with similar interests and concerns, who meet regularly apart from the Sunday service. "Those things are important to people, whether they're aware of it or not."

In the northeast Charlotte neighborhood of Hartfield Downs, they've created something called "Meet in the Street." Twice a month, every other Friday in spring and summer, families in this neighborhood of about 60 homes carry their covered dishes and lawn chairs to somebody's front yard. Neighbors take turns hosting. "Everybody just parties in the street," says resident Diane Cato. "People aren't wound too tightly. They don't care if you run on their grass."[45] It is noteworthy that community is even able to trump a Southerner's reverence for his lawn. Turf fertilizers and crabgrass killers notwithstanding, people want to be part of something larger than themselves, to influence the world beyond their backyards.

Among the more interesting examples of community reclamation is the story of the little Nebraska Native American reservation of

Winnebago, near where Todd Mansfield's paternal grandmother grew up. Eighty miles north of Omaha, Winnebago's 28,000 acres had just 1,600 people, 70 percent of them unemployed. Most of the residents lived in trailers up on cinder blocks. Their only business was the B&H Bar. Their outlook, like the reservation itself, was bleak and uninviting. The best and the brightest were getting out.

Then a thirty-six-year-old Winnebago Tribe member, Lance Morgan, devised a plan to build a completely new village. It would take that, he figured, to bring his tribe together again. "Our original theory was, hey, let's fight the poverty in this community," Morgan told *The New York Times*. "If we fought poverty, then everything would take care of itself…We were going to have strip malls, and housing in the back. We thought that was cool."

At a development conference, Morgan got a different idea from Katherine Kraft of the Robert Wood Johnson Foundation. Kraft threw out terms like "walkability" and "density." Don't just build the economy, she advised, build community. As a result, Winnebago started planning apartments on top of shops, a commons, a mini-mall, and real houses, modular houses that are both relatively inexpensive and relatively luxurious.

The Winnebago tribe's general counsel, Danelle Smith, had moved off the reservation with her three young sons. "From a practical standpoint it was just easier for me to get a house in South Sioux City," she said. "It shouldn't be that way. You should be allowed to stay in the community to contribute back." [46] The place she may be able to do that is Ho-Chunk Village (Ho-Chunk is derived from Hochungra, the tribe's traditional name), where they're building a new kind of community.

"The Winnebago are thinking in big terms," says Andrew Lee, executive director of the Harvard Project on American Indian Economic Development, based at the Kennedy School of Government. In 2002 the Harvard Project gave Ho-Chunk Village a $100,000 award in recognition of its success in creating what could become a national model to help tribes lift themselves from poverty. "They're thinking about how to build a prosperous nation," adds Lee.

"People have hope," says tribal council chairman John Blackhawk, "and that has a snowball effect." [47]

By 2006, Ho-Chunk Village had twelve successful businesses generating $100 million in revenue. One of those is a housing manufacturer, which sells to the Winnebago and other tribes when it can, but not exclusively. The tribe has created more jobs than it has working-age people.[48]

But what if you don't have the resources at your disposal to build an economically-driven community center? What if you're not the type to pioneer a happy hour at a neighborhood dive? What can you do to build community where you live? The most important thing is the most obvious: get to know your neighbors. Start using your front door instead of your back door, or your front porch or lawn instead of the back (engineer what developers call "front-of-house living"). Wave at neighbors from your car, take walks after work. Don't wait until an emergency situation, ask your neighbors for their phone numbers, or email addresses. You'll find that you have something in common with them: you've all chosen to live in the same place, right?

Whether your neighborhood is in Winnebago or South Park or Evergreen College or Hartford or North Shore Towers, you can find community there, even if you have to make it happen. On the other hand, if you are planning to relocate, doesn't it make sense to look for a place that has a sense of place? Shouldn't "community" be just as important a factor in choosing a neighborhood – perhaps even more important – than, say, length of commute? If community is truly something we need and want, we need to know how to recognize it. We need to identify places in which we can live not in isolation but in the company of other people who share some values and interests and who interact for mutual benefit.

In *Building Suburbia: Green Fields and Urban Growth, 1820 to 2000*, author Dolores Hayden states that we can predict the level of community involvement by looking at how a neighborhood is designed. Hayden writes that people get to know you and you get to know them a whole lot better in neighborhoods where the homes sit on smaller lots, with front porches and sidewalks. "If you're thinking about moving into a new community, you might want to look at these things," advises Hayden. "If you're interested in living in a community where you will know your neighbors, it might be best to look for an older, established neighborhood with sidewalks, or maybe you should consider a new development that has been designed to support pedestrian life and provide a real feeling of living in a neighborhood."[49]

Among developers, planners, architects and builders – the professionals largely responsible for what sorts of neighborhoods get built and where they go — the cry for community is only just beginning to be heard. The Reason Public Policy Institute (RPPI), a national public think-tank based in Los Angeles, says that a new definition of community is emerging in the form of "master-planned communities." (To avoid confusion by overusing the C-word, we prefer to call these master-planned *developments*.)

Writing for the RPPI, Research Fellow Chris Fiscelli observes that such developments offer "the convenience of suburbia with the most cherished benefits of city life, like sense of place and belonging, and nearby services." These master-planned developments are actually self-contained living-working-playing spaces, most often laid out at the edges of cities, and, Fiscelli writes, the best thing about them is "that they are not some government version of utopia, but rather a private sector innovation. As planners, environmentalists, and smart growth advocates have been bemoaning suburban development for many years, developers have been doing something about it."[50]

What they have been creating is what will prove to be the most important breakthrough in housing since the postwar rush to the suburbs. This is the phenomenon we call the New Village.

CHAPTER THREE

Birth of the New Village

If you could design a perfect place to live, perhaps to raise a family or grow old gracefully, you might well find yourself thinking of an English village. Something endearing about that sort of place, something warm and comforting.

"A village," one English villager tells us, "is a place with a traditional center where people gather, a place where everyone knows everyone else. Corny as it might sound, it's a place where it's noticed instantly if Mrs. Jones hasn't been seen for a day, someone will go in and check if she's okay. Or a bowl of soup will be taken to elderly Mr. Smith, whose wife died a few months back." That definition is supplied not by some doddering spinster but by Katie Jarvis, a magazine editor and active mother of three. She lives and works in Minchinhampton, an English village that's looked much the same since the reign of Henry VIII.

THE COTSWOLD LIFE.

"A village is somewhere that tells you about the roots of the area," says Jarvis. "The small streets were made for horses, not cars. The old houses are built of materials that were dug out from within a mile radius." Indeed, the very pitch of Minchinhampton rooftops is determined by the strength of the yellow Cotswold stone from which its houses are built. "But it's more than an English rural film set," Ms. Jarvis points out – and this is crucial – "for ideally, it's somewhere people of all ages and 'classes' work, rest and play, as opposed to somewhere you just go to sleep at night."

Minchinhampton is one of dozens of villages in the Cotswolds, an area of gentle hills that stretch from near Bath to northern Oxfordshire in southwestern England, a distance of only 80 kilometers, or 50 miles. In days gone by the Cotswold Hills were famous for their long-haired sheep and cloth mills; today they are famous simply for their villages, *hundreds* of villages. Cotswold's villages have names such as Guiting Power, Upper and Lower Slaughter (named for nothing more sinister than the sloe tree), Shipton-under-Wychwood and Stow-on-the-Wold.

Rivers named Evenload, Coln and Windrush, dense with trout and ducks, run through them. Inns are called The Fox and Goose and breakfasts are served in thatched-roofed cottages that once held village smithies. Tour buses filled with Americans roll from one limestone gardened village to the next as the guides and tourists flip the pages of their memories searching for synonyms for "quaint" and "charming."

But for those who live there a village is simply "home." On a typical Minchinhampton morning Katie Jarvis walks her youngest son, nine-year-old Miles, to school, accompanied by a Springer spaniel called Josh. "We climb over the ages-old stone stile, which has a special opening for dogs to get through, and across the woodcutter's field – though it's too early for him to be here yet. Josh can wander at his own pace up the lane – which few cars visit – lead-less and free. But come the 'main road', he has to be harnessed for his own safety."

That main road is the only one in Minchinhampton that allows cars and trucks to careen by at breakneck speeds as high as 40 miles per hour. Along the road one sees unimproved grasslands where cattle have freely grazed for centuries. From the region's calcium-rich and nutrient-poor soil spring cowslips, wild thyme, orchids and grass in fields that stretch for more than 350 hectares (about 865 acres), fields where horses and cattle wander freely in the summer, without even fences to prevent their straying on to the roads. And those green fields, Katie Jarvis knows, are ripe for exploitation by subdivision builders. Minchinhampton is one of the most desirable villages in the area, and an ordinary three bedroom home here will set you back at least £373,000 (about half a million dollars US). There are lots of homes like that across the road, fronting on the village common and too many wealthy people crave the community of village life.

"Miles and I love walking the common together," Katie continues. "It feels like being on top of the world – a flat plateau of green, with the valleys of Stroud opening below us and rolling hills rising beyond. As we join the common, so we join a steady stream of walkers. Fellow schoolmates that Miles calls out to, dog walkers such as Rod and Maggie, who moved here many years ago from London, or locals, like Betty, whose fast-disappearing burr (accent) stirs up images of hay ricks and slow-eyed cud-chewing cows. Betty carries dog biscuits in her pockets: a dubious move for such an elderly lady. The local hounds flock to her like paperclips to a magnet, and refuse to leave, even when gratified. We walk about a mile to school, but it passes in a flash."

After dropping Miles off, Katie might stroll through "the piggeries" – former swine sties converted into retirement apartments – to pick up a morning newspaper. Then on to Taylor's Butchers, an historic family business that sells meat and homemade sausage from cattle grazed on the fields of the area. Wandering home to work can take a while. "People seem to have the time to talk in a way they don't in big cities. Minchinhampton of today has two antique shops, two charity shops (an ever-growing number as they're exempt from crippling business tax rates), a mornings-only bank branch, a post office, a butcher, newsagent, general stores, an estate agent, gift shop, two hairdressers, three restaurants/coffee shops, and a pub. Not bad for a population of about 5,000. But the useful shops are dwindling in favor of offices and tourist-type enterprises."

Quaint and charming as all this sounds, Katie Jarvis and her husband have chosen to live here not out of affection for the past but out of concern for their current and future family life. They moved to Minchinhampton not out of necessity or ignorance of anything "better" – in fact, Katie lived for two years in Paris – but out of choice. And what they love more than anything else about their village is its sense of community, a community to which they wholeheartedly belong.

"Church every Sunday is still a highlight; the flurry caused by the bishop's visit could hardly be surpassed if the Queen herself were to drop by for communion. There's Minchinhampton Country Fayre, where people dress up in medieval clothes to honor its origins. We have a Goodwill Evening at Christmas; the Cotswolds' traditional circus calls every summer; the drama society puts on regular plays. What more could you want? You might be able to go to the theatre every day of the week in London and see something different. But in the country, there's just as much excitement in seeing the local butcher play the dame in the village pantomime. Or in winning the Victoria sponge competition at the fête. The entertainment might be much more home-grown, but it's valued, nonetheless."

Jarvis says that when she lived in Paris she got to know people, but only a few of them lived within walking distance. "I had to travel to see friends, whom I'd met on the whole through special interests, people I had something in common with rather than people who lived close by. But in my village, I know so many different personalities because I pass them every day. I don't need to have anything in common with them psychologically; the fact that we love Minchinhampton is enough to hold us together."

Remarkably, each Cotswold village is unique, with its own sense of place, and the tourist bureau wants you to sample them all: "Bledington lies on the Oxfordshire Way walk and taking this route you can walk westwards up on the wolds via Wyck Beacon and down to Bourton-on-the-Water, or south-eastwards down the valley to Bruern Abbey and onto Shipston-under-Wychwood."[51] Note that word "walk." Imagine walking from, say, Charleston to Savannah, from Cape Cod to Boston, from Louisville to Cincinnati. In England and Europe, you can tour villages without a tour bus. "And even in unfamiliar villages in the area," Katie Jarvis attests, "people will nod and say hello to you as you walk along their streets."

Small wonder that so many American tourists return from the Cotswolds wondering why the places they live can't be more like the villages they've just experienced. Villages like these allow us to be ourselves while at the same time being available to our neighbors and having them available to us. Villages are meant for walking and bicycling, for shopping at places where we are recognized and greeted, meant for easy travel between home and work. Villages are designed with public spaces where we can commune with nature, dotted with pubs and sidewalk cafes where we can relax among friends and strangers who might well become friends. And villages such as those of the Cotswolds remind us that the countryside – what we more often think of today as the "natural environment" – and civilization are not mutually exclusive habitats. Ultimately, the country mouse and the city mouse want many of the same things.

FROM ÇATALHÖYÜK TO BOSTON TO LETCHWORTH: THE GARDEN CITIES.

Katie Jarvis's village can trace its ancestry back to around 10,000 years BCE. That's just about when human beings invented the village. Villages brought individual tribes – our modern-day "extended families" – together, bonding them with a sense of place. There was stability in a village, and there was opportunity to contribute individual talents to the common good.

One of the earliest villages we know anything about is called Çatalhöyük (or Chatal Huyuk), settled around 7000 B.C.E. on the Carsamba River in what today is Turkey. Archaeologists discovered the site in the late 1950s and today it tells us a good deal about Neolithic life in the Middle East, when families built their homes in close proximity to one another even though there was no lack of available real estate.

When a family moved into Chatal Huyuk, it built a house of mud bricks, just a foot or so from the house next door – zero lot-line, as modern realty terminology would have it. They used that little space between houses to hold the garbage, much the same as their descendents would use alleys; when the trash piled up too high neighbors would get together and make a trip to the village dump. The only door to the house was a hole in the roof. The rooftop was the equivalent of the family's front yard, and the way they visited or moved around was to step from one roof to the next, unimpeded by privacy fences or hedges. Families did a fair amount of cooking up on the roof and from time to time invited their neighbors over to throw a hindquarter on the grill.

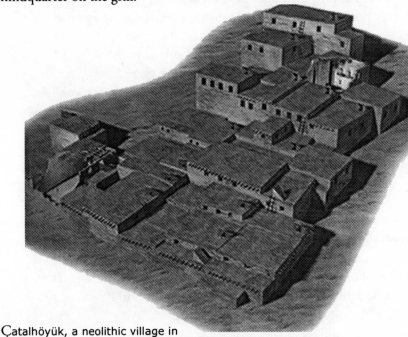

Çatalhöyük, a neolithic village in Turkey, shows that our earliest ancestors established village living as the preferred lifestyle.

Artist's rendition.

The Chatalites went on community hunting and fruit-gathering expeditions, bringing back red deer, boar, onagers, apples, hackberries and almonds, and they had a community garden where they raised wheat, barley and peas. A lot of their work was done in the home, keeping commute time to a minimum. As the epochs went by, Chatal Huyuk became a manufacturing and trading center whose craftsmen were renowned for their work in wood, copper, baked clay, stone and especially obsidian, which brought a premium when they turned it into daggers and arrowheads.[52]

All over the world villages became the norm. In Africa, in China, in India, villages were planned and laid out in neat arrangements, with private land separate from communal ground. Single-family and multi-family dwellings coexisted side-by-side. Villages provided places to shop and places to gather, places to learn and places to worship. The village functioned as the hub around which lives were built. Villagers held community functions and shared responsibilities. Indeed, in several early languages the words for "village" and "community" were the same.

Many of these early villages prospered and remained villages. Others expanded their boundaries and altered lifestyles so that different words had to be invented. The most commercially successful villages grew into towns and the most successful towns into cities, which began developing in several parts of the world at least by 3000 BCE.[53] Young people saw that while the village might have been a great place to grow up, a city offered more opportunities to earn a living. Sections of a city such as Damascus, thought to be the oldest city still in existence, were marked off for certain trades and occupations. Poor people clustered in one part of the city, with families crowded together, rich people gathered more comfortably in other parts. The indiscriminating livestock – horses, donkeys, cows, sheep, pigs – left their calling cards in every neighborhood. Garbage, along with its attendant stench, vermin and disease, became a fact of life in the city; nobody took the trash to the dump. One imagines grandmothers complaining, over the noise of city traffic, that life had been oh-so-much better back in the village. People began inventing excuses to get out of the city. Those with transportation discovered that while all roads led to Rome, on weekends and in the summertime they also led out.

Eventually, the rich people got smart and built villas – a word derived from the same root as "village" – out in the countryside, close enough to see the city but far enough away that they couldn't hear or smell it. This practice continued quite literally for ages. Old World nobility built their country homes and hunting lodges; and when cities in the New World became overcrowded, dirty, noisy and smelly, those who could afford country estates built them. Ultimately, people who saw themselves as upwardly mobile became outwardly mobile, emulating the lifestyles to which they aspired, and so the suburbs were born. Some of this growth happened by accident, but much of it was planned.

Combining the best elements of the city and the country has always been the goal of the loosely affiliated group known as city planners or, in today's more inclusive vernacular, regional planners. Urban design has been with us at least since Babylon. The so-called father of town planning, Hippodamus of Miletus in 408 BCE. supervised the building of the new city of Rhodes, using a grid design that is not so different from what we find in cities today. Renaissance man Leonardo da Vinci designed several model cities, but none got farther than Leonardo's drawing board. The history of modern planning begins – or almost begins – with the architect Christopher Wren, who saw his big chance after the Great Fire destroyed London in 1666. Within the first week of the fire, in fact, while the ashes were too hot for surveyors' feet, Wren had his new street plans drawn up, with plenty of mews and public parks, places to live and work. But Wren's ambitious plans, like Leonardo's, were never adopted. Not until the early 19TH century were any of London's sections laid out according to a scheme, about the same time that Baron Georges Eugène Haussmann, under the aegis of Napoleon III, was laying out the city of Paris.

In all these years, from Christopher Wren on up to the 20TH century, the number-one preoccupation of planners was getting rid of densely overcrowded, disease- and crime-infested slums. Out in the countryside and in the villages there may have been no operas or factories, but there also were no slums. For any city planner, the first question was, "What do we do with the slums?" Which, ultimately, became: "What do we do with the poor people?"

It was the same with cities everywhere, particularly in the United States, where continuing waves of immigration had stuffed the cities' low-income neighborhoods to overflowing. New York, New Orleans, Chicago, Philadelphia – they all had prodigious slums. In 1888 readers in London got a look at the mess that was Boston by way of a curious novel called *Looking Backward*. In this Rip Van Winkle-esque story, a well-off Bostonian named Julian West falls asleep under the spell of a "doctor of animal magnetism," and wakes up 113 years, three months and eleven days later, in September of the year 2000. Author Edward Bellamy imagines in our own present-day a "glorious new Boston with its domes and pinnacles, its gardens and fountains, and its universal reign of comfort…with its homes of simple comfort and its gorgeous public palaces… a city whose people fared all alike as children of one family and were one another's keepers in all things." More instructive is Bellamy's nonfictional description of the city he knew at the close of the 19ᵀᴴ century.

Boston of 1887 is "a shabby place," many of its people "meanly dressed and hungry." In the South End, manufacturers work against one another rather than for a common purpose. "These mills and shops were so many forts, each under its own flag, its guns trained on the mills and shops about it, and its sappers busy below, undermining them." Nearby hovels present "a scene of squalor and human degradation." Boston's streets and alleys reeked with "the effluvia of a slave ship's between-decks." Swarms of children, half-clad and brutalized, "fought and tumbled among the garbage that littered the court-yards."

Bellamy's descriptive passages crossed the Atlantic to disturb a Parliamentary stenographer named Ebenezer Howard. Born a shopkeeper's son, Howard had visited Chicago as a young man. Recently destroyed by fire as London had been 200 years earlier, the Windy City was in the painful throes of rebuilding. Howard returned to London and found work writing Parliamentary reports, which exposed him to the challenges of housing and labor in Britain. No idle dreamer, and not by any means a wild-eyed reformer, Ebenezer Howard found in the novel *Looking Back* a plan for making better places for people to live.

"The festering mass of human wretchedness about me offended not now my senses merely, but pierced my heart like a knife," Howard read in Bellamy's book. "Every stone of the reeking pavements, every brick of the pestilential rookeries, found a tongue and called after me as I fled: What hast thou done with thy brother Abel?" Like the novel's Julian West, Ebenezer Howard wanted to cry out, "I have been in Golgotha. I have seen Humanity hanging on a cross!" And like West, he knew that it did not have to be this way. "It was not the crime of man, nor of any class of men, that made the race so miserable, but a hideous, ghastly mistake, a colossal world-darkening blunder." The blunder was simply that cities had been allowed to grow out of control, unplanned and untended, like gardens gone to seed.

Howard ordered 100 copies of the novel and passed them out to his friends and to people he knew in the government. Then he sat down to write a book of his own, not a novel but a simple idea for correcting that "world-darkening blunder," the 19th century city. Howard envisioned a new kind of city, actually a network of towns of limited size, each planned out in advance, and surrounded by a permanent, undefilable belt of green agricultural land: a "garden city." His book was *To-morrow: A Peaceful Path to Real Reform*, and the money to print it in 1898 came out of Howard's own pocket. His aim was to show the world how to design a place that would promote "a healthy, natural, and economic combination of town and country life" through a balance of work and leisure, a place in which industry, home life and agriculture could peacefully coexist.

Much about the book was not new. Since 1852 Frederick Law Olmsted had been applying some of Howard's principles in America. But what Howard's approach lacked in originality it made up for in optimism and passion. Britain's reaction to the book was mixed, which is to say it created controversy. That translated into readership and eventual profitability. Soon Ebenezer Howard was touring England, preaching the merits of his proposed Garden Cities. By June 1899 he had formed a Garden City Association that attracted politicians, industrialists, lawyers, architects and builders. In 1903 the first Garden City, Letchworth, was begun. The movement to create true communities blending the advantages of town and country and populated, in Howard's words, "by a happy people," was on.

Impressed by a visit to Letchworth, Mary Muhlenburg Emery returned to the United States to establish Mariemont near Cincinnati. The widowed daughter-in-law of an English immigrant who made a fortune in lard, Emery donated $7 million to build a park, a school, a church, and, perhaps most importantly, places of employment. This enabled working-class families to earn enough money to afford living in the village. The village of Mariemont still thrives today and still pays tribute to Mrs. Emery's vision.

Sunnyside Gardens, in Queens, NY, opened in 1924 as the first Garden City to include rental apartments. In the "First Regional Plan for New York City," published in 1929, Garden Cities such as Sunnyside were proposed as ideal models for development. Developers caught the Garden City fever, especially after completion of the subway system in the 1920s drove the population of Queens over a million people. Soon New York had other planned developments – Jackson Heights (where Todd Mansfield's parents lived during World War II), Forest Hills Gardens and Flushing Meadows. Each of these village-like developments offered a mix of apartment buildings, private homes, shopping, parks and access to public transportation. Forest Hills was specifically designed to resemble an English village.

Across the Hudson in the borough of Fair Lawn, New Jersey, the City Housing Corporation accepted a proposal by a pair of architects who had visited Ebenezer Howard's developments in England, granting them in 1929 permission to construct the village of Radburn. Billed as "a Town for the Motor Age," one of Radburn's chief design concerns was providing safe places for children and others to walk without being threatened by automobile traffic. Radburn had – and still has – every sort of housing, along with commercial and industrial areas, so that the village would be self sufficient, each element depending on the others for success.

Such large-scale developments demand not only clarity of vision but depth of pocket as well. In the era after World War I, the United States economy was making a lot of people rich; land speculators thrived and utopian reforms could hope for financing. But just as New York, New Jersey and other parts of the country began to contemplate true regional planning, Wall Street collapsed and the world was plunged into the Great Depression. Those deep pockets were turned inside-out, demonstrably empty. It would take World War II to start filling them up again, and by that time most of the world would have forgotten Ebenezer Howard's dream of the garden city. But during the early years of the Depression, that dream seemed like just the right cure for much of what ailed the United States. To Rexford Guy Tugwell, one of President Franklin Roosevelt's "Brain Trust" members, the dream Howard and his adherents had planted in England would yield its most bountiful harvest in the United States. Roosevelt bought into Tugwell's plan for 3,000 "Green Belt Towns" to be built from sea to shining sea, rescuing in one grand swoop America's cities, its construction industries and its homeless.

Tugwell, then teaching economics at Columbia University, was named Under Secretary of Agriculture. In 1935 he helped author the

Emergency Appropriation Act, authorizing construction of the first 25 Greenbelt Towns. In these direct descendents of Ebenezer Howard's Letchworth, the U.S. government would own the land, the homes and apartments and would lease them to residents and small-plot farmers. With great fanfare and the enthusiastic support of Eleanor Roosevelt, construction began outside Washington, D.C. on Greenbelt, Maryland, outside Cincinnati on Greenhills, Ohio, and outside Milwaukee on Greendale, Wisconsin. Jersey Homesteads near Princeton was identified as a fourth "Tugwell Town," although it had been planned originally under an earlier New Deal program aimed at resettling agricultural and industrial workers.

One of the residents of Jersey Homesteads (renamed Roosevelt, New Jersey after the President's death), was the artist Ben Shahn, hired by Tugwell to paint an immense mural on the wall of the school building. "It was a good idea," Shahn told an interviewer in 1968, "because the people who didn't know each other should have some focal point, you know. It worked that way beautifully because when relatives and friends came to visit they would take them over to the school and explain the mural and so on."[54] After he finished the painting, Shahn moved to Roosevelt and lived there until his death a few months after that interview. Ben Shahn involved himself in village life, serving three years on the Roosevelt Town Council. His wife, artist Bernarda Bryson, served three years on the Board of Education. They considered themselves friends and neighbors to everyone in Roosevelt and at the annual community picnic Shahn would sketch portraits of his neighbors at 50 cents a head.

One of the gathering places in Greenhills, Ohio was the Community Church, available for both Protestant and Catholic services. Reverend Raymond Scott and his wife Barbara, close friends of Ross and Beth Yockey, spent most of the 1980s there and still remember Greenhills as the place they most enjoyed living. "We didn't call it the Presbyterian Church," Ray smiles. "It was the Community Church, Presbyterian. By that time the Catholics had built a church across the street. But for years the Catholics and Protestants had shared the Community Center and had the same choir. By the 80s we each had our own choir but still shared a music director."

The events and aftermath of World War II, including the rise of Communism, effectively ended America's interest in Ebenezer Howard's dream. It was too much big-government, too much like socialism. "The papers were violently against it," Ben Shahn recalled. The concept of mixing land uses and integrating spaces for living, playing and working – a notion first imagined by our Neanderthal ancestors – seemed no longer acceptable. And among city and regional planners, now organized as the American Planning Association, Howard's name is, if not mud, certainly sullied.

"After 100 years, Ebenezer's Howard's proposal for Garden Cities is as irrelevant as it was in 1898," the APA was told in 1998. The speech came, somewhat ironically, from New York City Planning Commissioner Alexander Garvin. "The notion that people should live and work in the same small community was unrealistic," Garvin said. "Most people don't want to be trapped in company towns. They want the ability to move from job to job. They want to choose their residence based on their personal assessment of schools for their children and available shopping and recreation opportunities. They want to be able to sell their home and move elsewhere whenever they desire." [55]

Although the Commissioner's argument might have reflected the current sentiment of many homebuyers, it lacked historical perspective. In the early years of the 20th century, when Garden Cities flourished, moving "from job to job" was hardly possible, let alone desired. Indeed, one of the primary objectives of Mariemont was to provide decent steady employment as well as decent housing for Southern Black families who had relocated to Cincinnati in the Great Migration. Then, post-World War II, urban America launched an even greater migration by automobile to the suburbs of the nation's cities. All but a handful of the United States' mushrooming tribe of real estate developers were content to take what they were given: small chunks of farmland at the cities' outer perimeters, which they could quickly turn into neighborhoods and profits. The notion of the suburban village, with its walkways and friendly shops, was buried under tons of concrete roadways and cinder-block shopping malls, inspired by Austrian immigrant Victor David Gruen's mid-50s Northland Center near Detroit and Southdale outside Minneapolis.

The postwar situation in England and Europe proved to be something else entirely. There cities and towns had been destroyed in conflagrations every bit as devastating as the fires of London and Chicago. Returning to the dream of its one-time clerk, Ebenezer Howard, Britain's Parliament first passed the Abercrombie Plan of 1944, intended to relocate 1.5 million Londoners to new and expanded towns throughout the country, and two years later passed the New Towns Act.

With Letchworth and its 1919 successor, Welwyn Garden City, as models, the postwar New Towns Act aimed at preventing further congestion of England's largest cities, into which job-seekers were pouring from all corners of the Empire. These New Towns were to be attractive, healthful and self-sustaining. That is, they would provide local employment for residents of varied income levels. The primary difference between Letchworth-Welwyn and their latter-day counterparts lay in their financing. Howard's Garden Cities had been established with private capital, but the postwar New Towns of England, Northern Ireland, Scotland and Wales would be financed in large part by the government. In addition to stemming the migratory tide, it was hoped that these new villages would stimulate economic growth and provide urgently needed housing for industrial areas.

Excepting the U.S., Ebenezer Howard's borrowed dream was sweeping much of the globe. France built nine *villes nouvelles,* five outside Paris. Brazil transported concrete by airplane to its vast, empty center to create Brasilia. Hong Kong built "satellite cities" such as Tsuen Wan and Kwun Tong. Japan borrowed the British idea and constructed thirty new towns, mostly near Tokyo and Kansai, but they intentionally ignored one of Ebenezer Howard's most important lessons: build places for people to work. Japanese commuters are still suffering from that decision. The Dutch built Hoofddorp and IJmuiden near Amsterdam and Hellevoetsluis near Rotterdam. In Poland, where most cities had been destroyed during the war, the new communist regime celebrated the nation's proletariat future in new towns like Nowa Huta. Singapore spent twenty years, starting on 1952, developing the new town of Queenstown, and later Tampines, which won a World Habitat Award from the United Nations in 1992.

In the United Kingdom, the first new town was Stevenage, Hertfordshire, founded in 1946. Wales built Cwmbran and Newtown. Scotland built Cumbernauld, East Kilbride, Glenrothes, Irvine and Livingston. All told, the British Isles boasted 28 new towns either finished or under construction by 1963, the year they finally made an impression on an important real estate figure from the United States. That was the year James Rouse decided to forgo his annual summer vacation in Canada and take the family on a tour of Europe.

HAIL, COLUMBIA AND JAMES ROUSE.

A Maryland lawyer and mortgage banker, Rouse had been hired two years earlier by Nelson and Mary "Tod" Rockefeller to explore the possibility of developing some property they owned in Westchester County, New York, a place called Pocantico Hills. Rouse had made money building shopping malls, and in the process he'd become deeply involved with urban renewal efforts in Baltimore and in Paterson, New Jersey. Rouse saw Pocantico Hills as an opportunity to build something more useful than another golf course surrounded by homes for the moderately wealthy. His goal, to which the Rockefellers at first subscribed, was to create *community.* To figure out exactly what he meant by that, Rouse gathered an impressive group of consultants, including the world-renowned anthropologist, Margaret Mead. In a letter to Mead, Rouse wrote, "Community planning in the United States has been unimaginative and uninspired."

Indeed, post-World War II development in the United States was epitomized by the work of Brooklyn real estate lawyer Abraham Levitt and his sons, who had built their three so-called "Levittowns" on Long Island, in Pennsylvania and in New Jersey. These were simply low-cost, cookie-cutter housing on a massive scale. Although the Levitts had their emulators – Rohnert Park in Sonoma County, California, "a country club for the middle class," is one notable example – and although their houses were highly sought-after in their day, their Levittowns did not provide the same sense of place one would find in an English village or a Scottish new town.

Quickly they became objects of satire more than of admiration and imitation. Around 1958 *Mad Magazine* had taken advantage of the identical scansion of "Levittown" and "Xanadu" to publish a takeoff on Samuel Taylor Coleridge's "The Ballad of Kubla Khan." It began: "In Levittown did Irving Cahn a lovely Cape Cod house decree…" And from the early- to mid-1960s, Levittowns and their attendant publicity were inspiring a disconnected, sporadic backlash, a renewed interest in developing American towns for the sake of community.

On South Carolina's Hilton Head Island, Charles E. Fraser turned cutover timberland into Sea Pines Plantation. Architect William Pereira began a master-planned development on the immense Irvine Ranch in Orange County, which was rapidly being swallowed by the suburbs of Los Angeles. New York real estate tycoon Robert E. Simon bought eleven square miles of northern Virginia in 1961 and began turning it into the master-planned development of Reston. All would have an impact, but none of those other developers would influence the future of place-making in the United States to the extent that Maryland's James Rouse would.

"We believe that the knowledge exists today," Rouse wrote Margaret Mead in 1961, "from which a plan could be evolved that would provide a decent environment for the growth of people, and we believe that the purpose of community planning should be first and foremost the growth of people."[56]

The Rockefellers at first bought into Rouse's idealistic plan, but the timing was all wrong. In November, Rocky and Tod's youngest son, Michael, was reported missing on an anthropological expedition in New Guinea. The following week, the Republican governor of New York and his wife announced their separation after 31 years of marriage.[57] Eventually the Pocantico Hills deal fell apart. However Libby Rouse insisted on Jim's following through with the community-building scheme, even if he had to do it without Rockefeller money. She thought her husband's ideas, not the Levitts', were the ideas America needed.

Libby was "deeply lonely" living in one of Baltimore's most fashionable suburbs. Echoing the laments heard in Chapter One, she complained, "I had to drive the children everywhere they went: to school, to doctors, to dancing class, to their friends' houses, to shop, to a movie, to everything. The children had no autonomy or independence, and I had no free time to do the creative things I wanted to do." An actively religious woman, Libby asked herself "What would Jesus do" about America's suburbs? "He would want families close to one another…in small communities, so they could be more loving, sharing warmth and friendships and support." Wouldn't it be better, she asked her husband, if "all these bits and pieces of life" could be woven together in one place?[58]

On their trip to Europe in 1963 Libby and Jim visited cities and new towns where the bits and pieces of life were indeed woven together. Rouse was particularly impressed by Vallingby, outside Stockholm, which "gave a wonderful lesson in a thoughtful but unselfconscious use of the land in sitting houses and apartments on it and relating them to one another." The chief difficulty in replicating Vallingby, or any of the European new towns, in the United States would be a lack of government financing. If Rouse wanted to build a new town he would have to find private financing for it.

He returned home in time to deliver a speech to a conference on "The Metropolitan Future" at the University of California, Berkeley. In the United States, Rouse told the conference, planners were not coming up with the right answers because they were not asking the right questions. "Planning deals with highways, land uses, public buildings, densities, open spaces, but it almost never deals with *people*." A crucial point, to which we will return. In many of the developments that have arisen since Rouse first promulgated his ideas, planners have focused myopically on architectural details such as front porches and back alleys, whereas what mattered in Rouse's mind was the connections among neighbors. "People grow best in small communities," Rouse insisted, "where the institutions which are the dominant forces in their lives are within the scale of their comprehension and within reach of their sense of responsibility and capacity to manage."

One month after giving that speech, on October 30, 1963, Jim Rouse held a press conference to announce that his vision was about to become a reality. In Howard County, Maryland, fifteen miles southwest of Baltimore and twenty miles north of the nation's capital, on tobacco farmlands lining the old Columbia Pike, Rouse was going to build a true new town, a master-planned development consisting of a cluster of villages. Its name would be Columbia.

The virtues and shortfalls of Columbia, Maryland, are chronicled in a number of other books and much is available about Columbia online. Its creation is lovingly and painstakingly limned in Joshua Olsen's biography of Rouse, *Better Places Better Lives*, published by the Urban Land Institute in 2003. The important thing here is that in Columbia James Rouse provided an American realization of the vision of a place built around the central idea of community. Columbia was not designed to maximize real estate profits or to satisfy any political agenda: it was all about community. Thus Columbia lies in a direct line from Chatal Hoyuk to the New Villages of the 21st century.

Six years after Rouse's news conference, in 1969, the Chabon family took out the first Veterans Administration loan on a house in Columbia, an event which made the front page of the local paper. Fiction author Michael Chabon would grow up in that house and later write about the experience in an essay for *Architectural Digest*. Chabon says his family and the other early residents of Columbia considered themselves pioneers. "They were colonists of a dream, immigrants to a new land that as yet existed mostly on paper. More than four-fifths of Columbia's projected houses, office buildings, parks, pools, bike paths, elementary schools, and shopping centers had yet to be built."

And as Chabon grew up, it all got built. Columbia was perhaps the first master-planned development in the U.S. to have it all: biking paths, parks, places to work, shop and be entertained, all in walking distance of single-family homes, apartments and condominiums, homes priced for everyone from low-income to high. It remains that way today. At its center is 27-acre man-made Lake Kittamaqundi, named for the first recorded Indian settlement in Howard County. Kittamaqundi actually means "meeting place" and it serves that purpose for the 96,000 residents of Columbia. At the lake's center, reachable only by boat, is the whimsically named Nomanizan Island. Even the names in Columbia are meant to foster community.

Michael Chabon considers Jim Rouse "a man with grand ideas about the pernicious nature of the suburb, and the enduring importance of cities in human life," a man who felt that "we were all branches of the same family; that we shared common roots and aspirations." As Rouse was building his dream of community in the 1960s, Chabon notes, other cities around America were in flames, torn by riots. "The City was a discredited idea in those days, burnt and poisoned and abandoned to rot, but James Rouse felt strongly that it could be reimagined, rebuilt, renewed."

From the vantage point of adulthood Chabon concludes: "The judgments of Columbia's critics may or may not be accurate, but it seems to me, looking back at the city of my and James Rouse's dreams from 30 years on, that just because you have stopped believing in something you once were promised does not mean that the promise itself was a lie."[59]

The noteworthy truth is that Rouse had the courage to make the promise in the first place, in a nation he considered largely unlivable. "There isn't a metropolitan area in the U.S. that has a comprehensive plan to accommodate its growth," Rouse told *Time* magazine in 1966. "The best prospect we have is that we will become a nation of Los Angeleses."[60]

Perhaps because Columbia lay just outside the Washington Beltway, it could not help but be noticed by a few politicians and bureaucrats. In 1970 the federal government made another tentative foray into the development of new towns with Title VII of the Housing and Urban Development Act. Passed during the Nixon administration, Title VII provided loan guarantees of up to $50 million to support development of new towns or villages that would set certain goals in affordable housing, affirmative social programs and environmental management. During the 1970s and 80s thirteen new towns were launched on the basis of Title VII. Of those, only The Woodlands near Houston did not default on its loan.

Like Columbia, The Woodlands began as the vision of one man. In this case the visionary was George Mitchell, a self-made oil and gas tycoon who turned to real estate development to diversify his business. Mitchell and his people spent considerable time with James Rouse trying to figure out how to make The Woodlands work and, after a few years on the brink of financial disaster, it finally did work. By 2006 The Woodlands would be home to more than 75,000 residents and 3,000 employers. "What makes it a real hometown," proclaims the jacket of a book on the development, "is not just that it is where people sleep at night, but that it is where and how they spend the rest of the day. The Woodlands community has won international acclaim for its successful mix of commercial, retail and residential components; its ability to attract and sustain jobs; and its protection of the natural environment."[61]

Perhaps because each successful development was the product of an impassioned individual – a Rouse or a Simon or a Mitchell – there was no sense of a "movement" to change the way we live and relate to one another in the United States. Each of the New Towns of the 1960s and 1970s was viewed as a sort of experiment, as though by scientists at scattered research facilities who failed to publish in the appropriate journals. But in the late 1980s and early 1990s, three streams of activity merged into one gushing torrent, with the potential for dramatically altering the status quo. These three streams were: the emergence of a new-old school of architecture; a welling desperation by state and local governments to channel growth; and a creeping, almost penitential angst among a small group of real estate developers.

THE NEW URBANIST COWBOYS.

To give them their due, America's architects were perhaps the first to see the light. One of their most distinguished leaders was and is Vincent Scully, who has been teaching architecture at Yale University since 1947. In lectures to architecture students at Yale and at other colleges around the country, Scully berated his profession for its participation in the nation's loss of community.

"The yearning to rebuild community, which is felt by most Americans today," Scully repeatedly told his college audiences, "now seems obvious to almost everybody – as it did once before, in the 1870s, when the Colonial Revival began – that community is what America has most conspicuously lost, and community is precisely what the canonical Modern architecture and planning of the middle years of this century were totally unable to provide."

In a lecture entitled "The Architecture of Community," Scully argued that since World War II American architects had been pursuing individuality at the expense of the common good. Their greatest achievements celebrated the individual, but separated the individual from the forces of history and time. One could not make a community out of those buildings, developments and subdivisions, Scully said, because "the individual human being seems wholly liberated from the entire human community."[62]

Out of this self-flagellatory concern arose a group of architects calling themselves the New Urbanists, whose aim was quite simply to create a new school of architecture along with a new approach to planning. New Urbanists were vitriolically vocal in their opposition to postmodernism, the anti-modernist movement that arrived with the 1950s, in which style and form existed for their own sakes – that is, to please the architect rather than to satisfy some requirement of those who would use or inhabit their designs. Led on the East Coast by the husband-wife team of Andrés Duany and Elizabeth Plater-Zyberk and on the West Coast by Peter Calthorpe – all graduates of Scully's Yale School of Architecture – the New Urbanism school insisted, as did their mentor, that the planning and design of living spaces must "assert the importance of public over private values." At the center of each neighborhood should be public space "activated by locally oriented civic and commercial facilities." The New Urbanists declared war against the strict zoning laws common to most cities, insisting that every neighborhood "accommodate a range of household types and land uses." Their ire was particularly aimed at the institution of the automobile, around which nearly every American neighborhood had been designed since the 1940s. And in a nod to Frank Lloyd Wright they proclaimed: "Architecture should respond to the surrounding fabric of building and spaces and to local traditions."[63]

Duany and Plater-Zyberk (with Jeff Speck) published in 2000 what may be considered the bible of New Urbanism, *Suburban Nation: The Rise of Sprawl and the Decline of the American Dream.* In *Suburban Nation,* Duany and Plater-Zyberk identified the five components of "sprawl" as shopping centers, office parks, civic institutions, roadways and housing subdivisions. And they continually drove home the theme that postwar suburban growth was bad for America: "The problem with suburbia is not that it is ugly. The problem with suburbia is that, in spite of all its regulatory controls, it is not functional: it simply does not efficiently serve society or preserve the environment."[64]

New Urbanism got its official start in 1981 when developer Robert Davis consulted with Miami architects Duany and Plater-Zyberk about doing something with an 80-acre tract of sand and scrub on Florida's northwest coast. The result was Seaside, a resort village of pastel-painted "cottages" surrounded by white picket fences, so idyllic, quaint and

Some New Villages, such as this one in Southern California, reject some New Urbanist design elements. There are no front porches here, but *mucho communidad* – a lot of community.

Photo used courtesy of The Corky McMillan Companies

charming that it was chosen by the producers of Jim Carrey's film, *The Truman Show*, as the perfect Panglossian neighborhood.

The developer and architects of Seaside wanted a cohesive neighborhood with a strong sense of place, the sort of neighborhood one might find in Charleston, Savannah, Nantucket or Cape May. Rather than putting multimillion-dollar homes on the oceanfront for the privileged few, as in Malibu and other coastal developments, Seaside left its beaches and its views accessible by the public. Seaside's streets were designed to accommodate cars and parking but to encourage walking. Residents could easily stroll or jog to the public beach or to Central Square – which started out as a tented vegetable and flea market but which evolved into a collection of legitimate shops and restaurants. Seaside was picturesque and nostalgic. However, because it was basically a vacation- and retirement-home locale, Seaside had no need for that critical element in Ebenezer Howard's vision, the workplace. Seaside turned heads but not the direction of neighborhood design. For that, New Urbanism would require a different laboratory.

SMART GROWTH: NEW LAWS, NEW LINGO.

As the decade of the 80s advanced, the nascent new planning approach found unexpected allies in a few state governments that were investigating ways to somehow bridle the sprawl of their cities. While city governments had long been concerned with controlling growth, the cities had sprawled way beyond their own political boundaries, and if government was going to control that sprawl it would have to be done at the state level. The spaces between those cities – not so long ago scenic woods and cherished farmland and vital waterways – were turning into deserts of concrete. With the federal government more inclined to build new highways rather than new villages, state governments began laying down the law against sprawl. The first statewide growth legislation was enacted in Hawaii in 1961. The 70s brought Vermont, Florida, Colorado and Oregon into the fold, and somewhere along the way the term "Smart Growth" entered the planners' lexicon.

Governments and chambers of commerce had nearly always operated under the assumption that "growth is good." Advocates of the new Smart Growth, such as the Audubon Society and the Sierra Club, argue that we identify areas of the land not by their numbers of factories or population densities but by the way they have evolved through time and the forces of nature. Population or tax-base growth should not be allowed to doom our scenery, our water and air quality. While factories and shopping malls may provide temporary or even long-term upswings in a state's economy, they may also do irreparable harm to streams or to wetlands or to an area's natural beauty. This sort of thinking caught on, and by the end of the 20th century, a number of state governments were ready to accept responsibility for establishing parameters of growth. Those states drew "growth rings" around their cities, demanding that anyone seeking to build a subdivision or a shopping mall outside that ring first receive the state's permission, a permission not casually granted.

The State of Maryland, home to James Rouse's Columbia, is generally recognized as an early leader of the Smart Growth movement. In 1997, Maryland Governor Parris Glendening, a native of Florida, put into effect a plan called "Priority Funding for Smart Growth Areas." In essence, this meant that the state would provide infrastructure funds – roadways, schools, water, sewers – in areas that were already developed to a large degree, but not in undeveloped areas. At first this seemed like a form of favoritism – only chosen parts of the state would receive state money – but the governor's plan was applauded by mayors across Maryland. Smart Growth, said Mayor Gary Allen of Bowie, would "strike a real balance in protecting local government authority while providing an appropriate state incentive for concentrating development in and around existing and planned communities."[65]

By 2005 all fifty states and most of Canada's provinces had launched their own Smart Growth movements. Naturally, every state also had its Smart Growth opponents, people who warned that urban aesthetes and leftist environmentalists were threatening to shut down highways and otherwise impede the American way of life. But, like that of New Urbanism, the Smart Growth Age had dawned.

Meanwhile, as legislators drafted laws and repentant architects wrote their books, another force was at work, one that would channel the intentions of both these groups into a unified movement for change. That third force was, purely and simply, American capitalism, but capitalism infused with vision. This was the same vision shared by Ebenezer Howard and James Rouse and a thousand others between them, that housing, labor and economic success for humans need not be fatal blows to Nature. A few farsighted land developers began to understand that they could make money today without wrecking tomorrow, that vibrant new places – "New Villages" – could be planned out and built for generations to come.

THE PROFITABILITY OF COMMUNITY.

In the late 80s and early 90s, at least four New Villages were under construction in the United States, the most master-planning activity in this country since Howard's Garden City concept crossed the ocean. The four were Laguna West near Sacramento, Rancho Santa Margarita in Orange County, Kentlands in Maryland and Celebration near Orlando, Florida. These in many ways anticipated New Urbanism and Smart Growth legislation. They worked, to some degree at least, because their developers saw an opportunity to make money by exercising far more civic responsibility than developers had in the past.

In Maryland – where else? – shopping mall developer Joseph Alfandre paid $43 million for a 352-acre farm eleven miles northwest of the Washington, D.C. Beltway. Undoubtedly influenced by the success of Columbia, Alfandre decided to create something more meaningful than a shopping mall. Among the army of consultants he brought in was the firm of Duany Plater-Zyberk (DPZ). With Seaside, Florida, under their belts, this was the Duany group's first opportunity to test their New Urbanism tenets on such a large, "real life" scale.

By this time DPZ had coined the unfortunate misnomer "Traditional Neighborhood Development" to describe the projects of New Urbanism. The TND handle was meant to recall pre-World War II inner-ring city development, but it is misleading and possibly off-putting because, for most homebuyers, "traditional" is the kind of neighborhood they grew up with: the typical suburban neighborhood of Sprawlville. For most of its residents, there would be nothing traditional about it, but Alfandre's Kentlands, Maryland has gone down in the New Urbanist books as "the first true TND." Kentlands has its picket fences and its front porches, like Seaside, but it also has a sense of permanence. More than four times the acreage of Seaside, Kentlands has six distinct neighborhoods built around a central shopping-and-working district called Market Square. It has single-family homes and apartments, town houses and condominiums. There are walkways and biking paths and parks and playgrounds. In short, Kentlands is very much like Katie Jarvis's village in England. While Kentlands ultimately succeeded, it almost went under due to Joseph Alfandre's vision exceeding his reach. One difficulty in creating a New Village is that it requires an enormous amount of front-end investment simply to create a sense of place before that place is occupied by the people who must, in the end, pay for it. Alfandre underestimated the amount of up-front capital required, providing an important lesson for others who would come behind him.

As the eastern contingent of the New Urbanist school was creating Seaside and Kentlands, their western counterpart, Peter Calthorpe of Berkeley, was working for Sacramento developer Phil Angelides, who wanted to create a neighborhood like the one where he had grown up. Together they designed Laguna West, an 800-acre New Village between Interstate 5 and the Union Pacific Railroad tracks. It would include 2,300 homes and 1,000 apartments, 65 acres of lakes and a town center with recreational facilities and shops and a nearby business park to supply jobs for the residents. Like those in Kentlands, Laguna West homes would have front porches and back garages that opened onto alleys. Neighbors would be encouraged to walk and ride bikes and gather in the public spaces.

Meanwhile, to the south of Calthorpe's development, the inheritors of a huge Spanish land grant were building Rancho Santa Margarita, "A Small City with the Soul of a Small Village." Concentrating on employment and affordable housing, the rural Orange County developers included a 450-acre business park and one million square feet of retail and entertainment in the town center, which itself included 1800 homes. They built in plenty of bike and walking trails, a man-made lake, parks and other public spaces.

When asked how Rancho Santa Margarita intended to reconcile its high density of residences with America's, and particularly California's, expectation of wide open spaces, RSM vice president for pre-development Richard Reese said he had found the answer – of course – in the villages of Europe. In villages such as Minchinhampton, he said, "high density and compactness are the norm." And, because people need other people far more than they need private putting greens and backyard badminton courts, "emphasis is placed on public rather than private open space."[66]

All three of those New Villages have proven successful, in financial and in sociological terms. But in terms of influencing public thought, none has captured the imagination as vividly as has the New Village of Celebration, Florida. And this would seem only natural, since the place was dreamed up by the "Imagineers" of The Walt Disney Company.

THE EISNER VERSION.

In the 1960s, when Walt Disney and his people were planning their second theme park, Disney World, Walt said he expected Disney World's showcase would be EPCOT – the Experimental Prototype Community of Tomorrow, an idea that may have been born when Walt took in the "World of Tomorrow" at the 1939 New York World's Fair. There, from revolving balconies that seemed suspended in space, he and other fairgoers looked out on "Pleasantvilles," home-filled suburbs, and inner-city "Millvilles," bustling with manufacture and trade. These miniature master-planned developments were linked by super-roads, carrying people in speedy automobiles from peripheral neighborhoods to their jobs at the center, through acres left green for recreation and agriculture.

As Robert Kohn, chairman of the fair's Board of Design, saw it in the late 30s, America's city of the future would no longer be "a planless jumble of slums and chimneys, built only for gain." Urban design would be put to work as "an effective instrument for human activities, to be used for the building of a better world of tomorrow."[67] That "better world," in fact became what would be almost universally decried as suburban sprawl. Disney, like Ebenezer Howard before him, knew in his heart that humans could do better.

Twenty-six years after Kohn's speech, on November 15, 1965, Walt held a news conference to announce the building of Walt Disney World in Orlando. His company had surreptitiously bought up 28,000 acres of central Florida's citrus farms, swamps and cattle ranches – 43 square miles, equal to the area of San Francisco and twice the size of Manhattan – forever altering the persona and economy of Florida. As in California's Disneyland, a new Magic Kingdom would be the "wienie [sic] to draw the kids in," but Disney believed EPCOT would be the substance:

"I would like to be part of building a model community, [said Walt to the assembled media] a City of Tomorrow, you might say, because I don't believe in going out to this extreme blue-sky stuff that some architects do. I believe that people still want to live like human beings. There's a lot of things that could be done. I'm not against the automobile, but I just feel that the automobile has moved into communities too much. I feel that you can design so that the automobile is there, but still put people back as pedestrians again, you see. I'd love to work on a project like that. Also, I mean, in the way of schools, facilities for the community, community entertainments and life. I'd love to be part of building up a school of tomorrow…This might become a pilot operation for the teaching age – to go out across the country and across the world."

Disney was a New Urbanist and Smart Growth-er before his time. But ultimately, EPCOT became merely a theme park, a showcase of "future technology" as envisioned from the past. Though it kept Walt's acronym, it never really became a "prototype" of anything. That distinction would have to wait for the end of the 80s, when Walt's eventual successor, Michael Eisner, and his team were trying to figure out what to do with a chunk of the original Florida real estate purchase, in Osceola County on the wrong side of State Highway 192 from Disney World.

These 4,000 acres were totally undeveloped, populated by alligators, and unneeded for any future expansion of the theme park. The Disney Company formed the Osceola Multi-Use Project team, headed by Peter Rummell, Todd Mansfield and Tom Lewis. Later, the team expanded to include Don Killoren, Charles Adams, Chris Corr, Joe Barnes and David Pace. As 1989 drew to a close, 25 years after Walt's vision, the Osceola team was still working on its own vision statement, but their ideas were starting to crystallize around creation of a New Village. In a December 6 memo to Michael Eisner, Peter Rummell described what that would entail.

"I have decided that much of its strength will come from its simplicity," Rummell wrote. "I want to develop the point of view that says we are building another theme park south of [US Highway] 192." But this so-called theme park would be "a dramatic departure from some of our basic principles that we have adhered to so far. Much of the magic from the Magic Kingdom comes from the suspension of reality when you walk in the door. Our new park will be exactly the opposite; it will not be controlled-access or even gated in the traditional sense. Quite to the contrary, it will be the ultimate in reality: a place where people actually live, work, shop and play on a 24-hour basis."

This New Village, Rummell added, would be "place making at its best." The aim of the Disney team, harking back to Walt's original hopes for EPCOT, was to build "a living laboratory for The American Town." Rummell went out on a limb: "I promise we will also develop some ideas that will be copied in many other places in years to come. And it will be developed carefully enough that it will become a model for new town development everywhere."

As we shall see, that prediction has proven 100 percent accurate.

THE COMMUNITY GAMBLE.

In the beginning, the New Village in Central Florida was to be called "DisneyTown," but the team decided it wanted no Mouse on this Main Street. They quickly changed the name to Celebration, Florida. They would use the Disney Company resources, but would disassociate themselves from Disney fantasy and magic. Appreciating the emergence of New Urbanism and Smart Growth, anticipating the revolution of reconnection, the Disney developers believed they had a historical opportunity: "The time and place is right for all of these forces to come together," Rummell wrote Eisner in Burbank. "The result can be one of our greatest collective accomplishments."

The word "collective" is important. Up until this point, New Towns and New Villages had been created mostly by individuals with the passion for creating community or simply for doing "something better." In Celebration the passion was a commitment from a team of corporate entrepreneurs. One of America's most successful, most highly scrutinized companies was committing itself to *community*. In his book on this breakthrough development, Andrew Ross notes:

> "The company had staked its brand name on the premise that residents would forge common bonds that exceeded the mere 'sense of community' featured in the advertising for the town. This was something of a gamble, since the outcome of overly zealous community building can easily threaten the property interests of residents and the developer. But the genius of the marketing concept would override any potential conflict. In Celebration, residents would be protecting their private interests precisely by building strong community bonds. The

more community-minded the town became, the more its property values would improve, since its homes were built to attract buyers who wanted to come and be community builders."[68]

Interestingly, one of the reasons Celebration was almost ten years in planning was resistance from the Disney executive corps. Far from embracing this vision, the top brass saw it as somehow unworthy of Disney. Yet in 2000, after Celebration's place in planning history was secure and its profits far in excess of anything the company had imagined, Eisner told Rummell that he considered it "my most significant achievement."

Success, as they say, has many fathers.

Although Celebration isn't perfect, and has inspired more than a few detractors, it also has spawned a host of imitators. It has become as Andrew Ross observes, "a stepping-stone on the career path for most who were involved with it." Nearly all of the people involved in creating Celebration agreed with Community Manager Brent Herrington that this would not be "a one-project deal." Worried that The Disney Company might cave in under pressure to halt what was at first only a huge drain on its resources, Todd Mansfield at one point asked Eisner to sell the Celebration Company to him and other members of the development team. He and the others "on the ground" in Florida believed so strongly in the concept that they were ready to replicate Celebration in other parts of the country.

But Disney stuck with the plan and finished Celebration. After it was completed, Mansfield, Herrington, Don Killoren, Charles Adams, Perry Reader, Amy Westwood and others involved with the project spread the gospel to the Carolinas, to California, to Arizona, to the Puget Sound. The New Village became the Smart Growth-New Urbanism vehicle for transforming not only America's cities but its much-maligned suburbs as well.

In subsequent chapters we will get to know many of the people who build and live and work in New Villages. We will see that, ultimately, the community-dreams of Ebenezer Howard and James Rouse and Walt Disney are coming true precisely because of the accuracy of Peter Rummell's prediction in 1989:

"We will be very profitable."

CHAPTER FOUR

Mixing Business with Pleasure...
and with Housing of All Types

On the far side of sixty and diabetic to boot, the man walks to stay alive.

Nearly every day sets him out from his condo in one of four directions in which he comes fast under the spell of roses, rosemary and lavender that fight for sidewalk space with big waxy clusters of rhododendron in all their dozen colors, with waves of azaleas and pink and white dogwoods and a hundred more flowers he's yet to learn the names of.

Depending on the direction of his travel, the man might pause for a gape at the Olympic Mountains' year-round snow cape across the Puget Sound or at the splashy city skyline across Elliott Bay, bracketed by the Space Needle on the north end and the praying mantis orange cargo cranes on the south. He might slow for a labored conversation with Bob, whose stroke has hobbled him into a slow and sweaty drag. Or he'll just walk on, pondering the butt of outsized modern mansions against bungalows and tiny "craftsman cottages," of chic townhouses against "classic brick" apartment buildings, of retirement homes against a bar and tattoo parlor.

The man might exchange a wave and a chat with the boys at the firehouse or the woman whose son surprised her by edging her lawn or the girl leaving the Jehovah's Witnesses Kingdom Hall. He might drop in on Allen at Hart's Gift Shop to see what new cards and novelties he's stocked or browse the upscale furniture store or get Al the locksmith to make him another mailbox key. Maybe he'll say hello to Mary Ellen at Megawatt, an organization whose mission is energizing community. He might pick up a half-gallon of one-percent milk at Safeway or a two-percent grande latte at Speranza Coffee House or pay about twenty percent more than the law should allow for a chunk of cave-aged gruyere at the Metropolitan Market. He'll likely stop at the old Carnegie Library for some jazz CDs and the novel they shipped him from the Capitol Hill branch. And on the way back he'll wave to Amanda in the frame shop and Jason in Zats Bagels and John and Frances, the jewelry crafters at their little shop called Click! next to Blockbuster. Later in the evening he might walk with his wife to one of a half-dozen restaurants or to the old Admiral Theater for an almost-first-run movie. The man and his wife live in the North Admiral district of West Seattle, the oldest and largest of Seattle's neighborhoods, and after just two months in this neighborhood, the couple can count perhaps a dozen individual and family neighbors as friends.

This same man spent the tail end of his forties and all of his fifties walking around an essentially different neighborhood in the suburbs of Charlotte, North Carolina. That walk started out the same, but its description ended about one sentence in, with "…azaleas, pink and white dogwoods." This other neighborhood was called Lansdowne and like the majority of neighborhoods in suburban America it contained only single-family homes. Even the flowers in that neighborhood were mostly distant, viewed across lawns big enough to hold outdoor concerts by the Charlotte Symphony.

The only Lansdowne neighbors the man saw with any regularity were a retired schoolteacher named Lemma, determined to make it to age 100 and around the block, and a Vietnamese man who ran behind an oversized stroller pushing his grown and mentally disabled son. With other neighbors his most frequent contacts involved waves to and from passing cars. As for neighbors who could be called friends, in thirteen years that number grew to seven, including the people who lived on either side of his house, the rabbi and his wife across the street, the retired fellow down the street who needed help eating his backyard tomatoes and the boy who kicked his soccer ball through the hedges into the man's back yard.

As for shops and restaurants, they were in strip malls some miles distant and required considerable negotiation with fast-moving cars and trucks. There was really no place to walk *to*, none of what the New Urbanist architects call "walkable destinations." The man eventually bought a treadmill and watched the birds and squirrels in his back yard. Then he and his wife left Lansdowne and moved 3,000 miles across the country to West Seattle.

THE BLESSINGS AND THE CURSE OF ZONING LAWS.

Lansdowne and West Seattle: two environments designed for human habitation. Two neighborhoods, but not two communities. They are roughly the same distance from their central cities, about 7 miles in Charlotte, 6 miles in Seattle. They both have nice homes, trees, flowers, birds, paved sidewalks, access to public transportation – but that pretty much ends the similarity count. Lansdowne residents depend almost exclusively on automobiles to get around. West Seattleites have cars, but they also transport themselves by bus, bicycle, roller skate, motorbike and foot. Lansdowne streets are busy only during morning and evening rush hours, shutting down almost totally after dark. West Seattle has both quiet and active streets, the latter alive well into the night. Lansdowne people, for the most part, drive each evening from climate-sealed Central City offices in climate-sealed cars to the garages of climate-sealed homes, rarely encountering one another. West Seattle people may work in the big city across the bay or they may work down the block or at the end of a bus ride.

The Castletown

$11,750

One of Crosland's most popular plans, designed for privacy and convenience.

	VA	FHA
Total Cash	$ .00	$400.00
Monthly Payment (Includes everything)	$83.50	$ 86.00

In 1950s suburbia, houses within a given neighborhood stayed within a narrow price range. In Charlotte's Edgebrook, the range was $11,750 to $14,500. At the low end, you had to park your car on the street.

Used by permission of Crosland, LLC

Yet the most important distinction between these essentially different neighborhoods is the interpretation of their local zoning codes. To be sure, Seattle has zoning laws just as Charlotte does, but the North Admiral district came into existence before the laws did; Lansdowne was built from scratch after World War II, during the period of zoning's most profound effects on life in America. In fact, Charlotte today is what Hollywood was to F. Scott Fitzgerald in 1940: "a perfectly zoned city."

In his unfinished novel *The Last Tycoon,* Fitzgerald quipped that one could drive through Hollywood and "know exactly what kind of people economically live in each section, from executives and directors, through technicians in their bungalows, right down to extras." Who you were depended on where you lived. In fact, where you lived all but set the limits to your possibilities.

Success in Charlotte these days is gauged not by minutes on the silver screen but by the height of one's office in one of the city's skyscrapers, nearly every one of which has gone up since 1990. Charlotte is second only to New York in the amount of money that passes through its ether, the number-two financial center in the U.S. The Queen City is home to Bank of America and Wachovia, and to a host of big-time investment players. One's financial success is visible in Charlotte only if one maintains a proper address. At the top of the address list are Eastover and Myers Park, old-school estate neighborhoods close in to the city. New Money centrifugates further from the center, out past moderate-income Lansdowne toward the city's southern rim, in neighborhoods such as Ballantyne Commons ("Nothing common about it," Henny Youngman might have observed.) Each of these Charlotte neighborhoods was once an unpretentious cotton field or dairy farm; today each is zoned R-1, meaning residential, single-family. Access to such neighborhoods is almost exclusively by automobile, though the city does supply transportation along its major roadways, thus permitting entry by maidservants. From the 1950s until quite recently, Charlotte, like Fitzgerald's Hollywood, could have been cited as one of America's perfectly zoned cities.

Louis XIV would have been amused by Hollywood and Charlotte, because Louis took zoning into his own hands. Toward the end of the 17th century Louis moved his entire court to the newly created and meticulously zoned Parisian "exurb" of Versailles. Created out of another hunting lodge, Versailles was intended to exist in harmony with nature. As historians Will and Ariel Durant have described it, Versailles was "a garden of the gods, built with the pennies of twenty million Frenchmen who would rarely see it, but who gloried in the glory of their King."[69] In Versailles's outdoor amphitheaters, the aristocracy gathered to attend the sublime music of Lully and the witty plays of Molière. The latter, in *Le Bourgeois Gentilhomme*, actually satirized the growing numbers of middle-class Frenchmen who wanted to up-zone but possessed none of the requisite aristocratic credentials.

It took thirty-six thousand men, six thousand horses and the equivalent of $500 million to create the immense apartments, galleries, dance halls, guard rooms, administrative office, servants' quarters, parks and gardens, but Versailles shows what one can accomplish with serious planning and very deep pockets. Since the nobles and their families and their mistresses resided in the palace, around the central *chambre du roi*, in a carefully determined pecking order, Versailles stands as an early example of zoning. Courtiers who rose in favor were invited to move nearer to His Majesty, although their servants were required to live off the grounds of the palace proper in neighborhoods of their own.

More than 200 years later, many of Charlotte's maids and lawn-tenders live in neighborhoods of their own, low-income neighborhoods such as Cherry and Grier Heights which abut but do not connect socially with the upper-class streets of Myers Park and Eastover subdivisions. As in Louis XIV's Versailles and Louis B. Mayer's Hollywood, this class distinction is by design; the neighborhoods are arranged to recognize and maintain status. That is what zoning means to most Americans: what kind of buildings can be constructed in which parts of town, where you go to work and where you go to be at home, who can live next to whom. Nearly every American city – Houston being the largest and most notable exception – has strict zoning laws that make it harder to create a New Village than it might be for a Hollywood gaffer to live next door to the Playboy mansion.

WHO ZONED YOU.

Zoning-as-law has not been with us since the beginning of time. It was officially invented in New York early in the 20th century by a lawyer named Edward M. Bassett, though his models were indeed

Versailles and its European spinoffs. Bassett became fascinated with the idea of separating the various functions of a city when he visited a city-planning display in Dusseldorf, Germany. There, in 1908, he saw models of cities with coherently-designed streets and sidewalks, parks and public spaces. "I was taken off my feet," Bassett later wrote, "by the impressions given me by these new fields of work."[70]

New fields indeed. In the first decade of the 20th century, the words "city" and "planning" were almost mutually exclusive in the United States; Edward M. Bassett had found his life's work. Back in New York, he became a member of the Public Service Commission and in 1913 he agreed to chair a commission to propose regulations that would govern the height of new buildings. Thanks to new steel-girder building techniques and improved elevators, skyscrapers were going up everywhere, blocking light and crowding out the tenement houses and brownstones. (The 42-story Equitable Building then rising on lower Broadway was a notorious case in point.) On lower Fifth Avenue ugly warehouses and factories were shoving aside once-fashionable retailers. Under Manhattan's already crowded street corners, subways were depositing their daily hordes from outlying boroughs. City government quaked in fear of total congestion.

Bassett's commission led to the city's adoption of a zoning plan in 1916, the first in the U.S., and Bassett was appointed counsel to the Zoning Committee of the City of New York, the agency created to implement the new plan. The New York Zoning Resolution was a relatively simple document, establishing height and set-back controls and establishing functional incompatibilities: factories and homes, shops and warehouses. From this point on, every building constructed in the city would have to be approved by the Zoning Committee. Skyscrapers would have to be built like wedding cakes, with smaller successive layers to let the light and air in. Noxious industry would not be permitted near dwelling places, making it unlikely that factory workers would be able to walk to and from their jobs.

Not satisfied with zoning New York, Bassett took his passion on the road, speaking in every state in the union over the succeeding ten years. Bassett's most influential convert was the man selected in 1921 as Secretary of Commerce by newly-elected President Warren G. Harding. His name, certainly more familiar than that of Edward M. Bassett, was Herbert Hoover. An internationally-acclaimed mining engineer who had directed America's European relief efforts after World War I,

Hoover had developed a passion for using government to leverage improved living conditions, especially housing, in America's cities.[71] Zoning seemed to Hoover the perfect answer. With careful zoning, you could keep all the attendant mess of industry and commerce, their dust and grime and ruckus, out of people's homes.

Moving from geological engineering to social engineering, Herbert Hoover recognized that not only poverty and disease but all manner of moral and social issues might be addressed through the proper laying-out of cities. "The lack of adequate open spaces, of playgrounds and parks, the congestion of streets, the misery of tenement life and its repercussions upon each new generation, are an untold charge against our American life," he wrote. Nearly all development and economic growth in those days was within cities, with their dense concentrations of people. While expansion of commerce and industry was essential to fuel the nation's economy, Hoover felt that only by regulating that expansion could the nation assure its future. "Our cities do not produce their full contribution to the sinews of American life and national character," he proclaimed.[72]

Hoover immediately appointed a commission of his own, with Bassett as a member, to draft "A Standard State Zoning Enabling Act" (SZEA) in 1921. Defying accusations of communism, Hoover's Commerce Department followed this in 1927 with A Standard City Planning Enabling Act (SCPEA). When they were finally done, Bassett and associates had firmly established zoning as an essential ingredient of a "comprehensive city plan."

By 1930 the Commerce Department would report that 35 states had adopted legislation based on the SZEA and fourteen cities in ten states had modeled zoning ordinances on the SCPEA. By this time Republican Herbert Hoover had been elected to the Presidency of the United States, not because of his groundbreaking efforts to establish zoning and city planning, but mostly thanks to his response to the Great Mississippi Flood. The Flood of '27 inundated 16.5 million acres of seven states, causing $400 million in damages and taking 246 lives. As he had done after the war in Europe, Commerce Secretary Hoover took responsibility for relocating the victims. Of the 700,000 people displaced by the flood, nearly half were African-American farm workers, most of whom were first sent to relief camps and later became part of the Great Migration to northern cities. In his acceptance speech as the Republican Party nominee, Hoover declared, "We in America today are nearer to the final triumph over poverty than ever before in the history of any land."

He was, of course, incorrect on that last point.

It is an irony of history that Mr. Hoover's name has become more recognized for his hands-off response to the 1929 Wall Street crash and the subsequent Great Depression – when homeless thousands camped in "Hoovervilles" on the edges of America's cities – than for his important contribution to city planning and zoning. Once America recovered from the Depression and World War II, city planners and zoning boards would alter the nation's landscape as few institutions before or since. We have Herbert Hoover and Edward M. Bassett to thank – or blame – for much of the alteration.

The Hoover-Bassett SCPEA neither required states to adopt zoning nor threatened them with sanctions for failure to enact planning legislation. In fact the suggested "comprehensive plan" could be interpreted just about any way a local government chose. But the Standard Acts, as they are still known in the planning and architectural trades, supply the underpinning philosophy under which state, regional and local governments determine the ways in which lands within their purview shall be used.

Zoning laws effectively state to a property owner that the government, not the individual, has the right to determine what may or may not be done with that property. The most basic question posed by that philosophical stance is that it seems to be at odds with this provision of the Fifth Amendment to the United States Constitution: "…nor shall private property be taken for public use, without just compensation." That guarantee is reinforced by the Fourteenth Amendment: "…nor shall any State deprive any person of life, liberty, or property, without due process of law."

THE LAWS ACCORDING TO EUCLID.

Those constitutional provisions might have stopped zoning in its tracks, had the U.S. Supreme Court ruled on December 22, 1926 in favor of a pair of Cleveland attorneys named Newton D. Baker and Robert M. Morgan. The two lawyers had argued on behalf of their property-owner client that zoning laws were unconstitutional at their core because by arbitrarily determining to what use someone's property

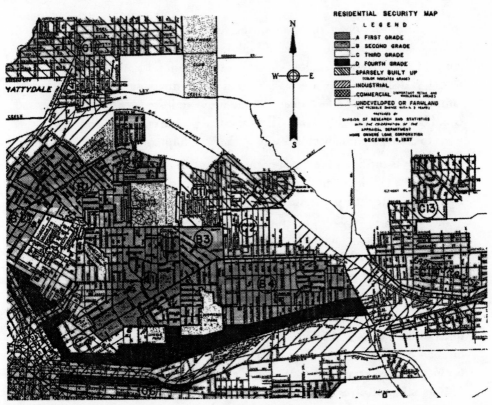

The Homeowners Loan Corporation (HOLC) began the tradition of zoning in America. In this 1937 "Residential Security Map" of Syracuse, NY, the darkest area was colored red, for "fourth grade" – hence the term "redlining."

could be put, a zoning board thereby determined how much that property was worth.

The client, Ambler Realty Company, had been holding on for several years to a 68-acre tract of land on the western edge of the Lake Erie village of Euclid, Ohio. There were railroad tracks on the edge of the property and, what with the rapid expansion of Euclid's big brother-city Cleveland, just twelve miles away, Ambler believed its land would soon be ripe for industrial development. Then on two sides of the Ambler property builders started putting up single-family houses, and in 1922, the Euclid Village Council adopted an ordinance establishing a comprehensive zoning plan for regulating and restricting the location of trades, industries, apartment houses, two-family houses, single-family houses and just about any other structure they could imagine.

Just as zoning ordinances in other cities had done, the Euclid ordinance determined how much lot-area each type of building required, how high it could be and how far back from the street it had to be set. It broke down the more-or-less rectangular map of Euclid into "zones" and said what types of buildings would be allowed in each zone. Much to Ambler Realty's chagrin, a significant portion of its 68 acres was declared "U-2," the classification permitting only one- or two-family dwellings and a few other uses: no heavy industry. No steel mills could be built on Ambler land. The real estate people cried foul and went to court, eventually all the way to the U.S. Supreme Court.

This was the first time the Supreme Court had been asked to consider the legality of any government denying business people the right to operate their businesses in residential areas. In its fascinating and landmark 1928 decision,[73] the court observed that while the Constitution is sacrosanct, the conditions under which it is interpreted must be viewed as fluid. Not so long ago, it reasoned, before the automobile age, traffic regulations "would have been condemned as fatally arbitrary and unreasonable."

The justices knew they were handling a hot potato. "The serious question in the case," they wrote, "arises over the provisions of the ordinance excluding from residential districts apartment houses, business houses, retail stores and shops, and other like establishments. This question involves the validity of what is really the crux of the more recent zoning legislation, namely, the creation and maintenance of residential districts, from which business and trade of every sort, including hotels and apartment houses, are excluded. Upon that question this court has not thus far spoken."

To find their voice, the justices considered what had been said on the issue by state and appellate courts. They quoted at length from the Supreme Court of Louisiana, in State v. City of New Orleans (97 So. 444). The Louisiana court had declared that any business operating within a residential zone "furnishes an excuse for any criminal to go into the neighborhood, where, otherwise, a stranger would be under the ban of suspicion. Besides, open shops invite loiterers and idlers to congregate; and the places of such congregations need police protection…Places of business are noisy; they are apt to be disturbing at night; some of them are malodorous; some are unsightly; some are apt to breed rats, mice, roaches, flies, ants, etc."

Almost equally unsavory to the New Orleans justices were multi-family dwellings. "With particular reference to apartment houses, it is pointed out that the development of detached house sections [i.e., one- and two-family homes] is greatly retarded by the coming of apartment houses, which has sometimes resulted in destroying the entire section for private house purposes; that in such sections very often the apartment house is a mere parasite, constructed in order to take advantage of the open spaces and attractive surroundings created by the residential character of the district. Moreover, the coming of one apartment house is followed by others, interfering by their height and bulk with the free circulation of air and monopolizing the rays of the sun which otherwise would fall upon the smaller homes, and bringing, as their necessary accompaniments, the disturbing noises incident to increased traffic and business, and the occupation, by means of moving and parked automobiles, of larger portions of the streets, thus detracting from their safety and depriving children of the privilege of quiet and open spaces for play, enjoyed by those in more favored localities – until, finally, the residential character of the neighborhood and its desirability as a place of detached residences are utterly destroyed."

The result of this ruling was that New Orleans' number-one upscale neighborhood, the Garden District, would remain to this day almost completely devoid of commercial establishments or apartment buildings. Because it is on some of the city's highest ground, the District escaped the floods of Hurricane Katrina in 2005. Many of the "malodorous" and "crime-infested" lower-income neighborhoods were not so fortunate.

The U.S. Supreme Court clearly was swayed by the Louisiana court's ruling, though its decision may also have been influenced by an *amicus curiae* brief filed by the chairman of Cincinnati's new planning commission, Alfred Bettman, a former member of Hoover's SZEA committee. Euclid's zoning ordinance was upheld and Ambler Realty had to find other ways to get rich.

For its part, the Village of Euclid soon afterward declared itself the City of Euclid, and a thoroughly-zoned city at that. Its name has become an integral piece of the jargon whereby architects and planners know one another. No longer do they speak of simply zoning; it is *Euclidian Zoning*. Although the Greek mathematician is considered the Father of Geometry, his formulas for the areas of polygons and circles have nothing to do with this distinction. It belongs to the former village named in Euclid's honor, which today crows on its web site: "Euclid's city planners assured orderly growth by segregating commercial and industrial land from residential neighborhoods, becoming pioneers of modern zoning concepts."[74]

So, thanks to Messrs. Bassett and Hoover, the town of Euclid and the Supreme Court, we live in a carefully zoned nation. Most of us do not live in the shade or shadow of monstrous buildings, most of us spend our days unbothered by industrial din and our nights undisturbed by heavy traffic. Most of us who own our homes have no fear of low-rent high-rises that might diminish the value of our property or even (thanks to our curved and dead-end streets) of desperate rush-hour drivers cutting through our neighborhoods in order to get to and from their own neighborhoods. In the 21st century, these are the benefits of Euclidian zoning.

What must also be pointed out is that zoning – dare we say, "draconian zoning" – has been and still is one of the great destroyers of community in America. Because those benefits – separation of commercial and residential interests, segregation of housing types and isolation of neighborhoods – have been established as the primary objectives of the nation's zoning boards, *community* has little if any place in their deliberations. Zoning has become all about what a piece of real estate is worth, not about how we live together as neighbors and laborers and professionals and business people and families. Perhaps the logical outcome of zoning regulation hit the American psyche in 2005 when the Supreme Court ruled that a city government has the right to bulldoze private homes and businesses if it thinks some other use – say a shopping center or an office complex – might generate more tax revenue. The court declared that residents of a working-class neighborhood in New London, Connecticut were obligated to sacrifice their homes in favor of a developer who wanted the space for a hotel, health club and offices.

This is not to say that zoning by its very nature does a disservice to neighborliness. On the contrary, such advocates of New Villages as Andrés Duany and David Sucher insist that some sort of determination of what goes where is essential. The zoning that makes great cities great is quite rigid, Sucher points out in *City Comforts*. "It is a short zoning code, and severe. But out of these limits grow hospitable, attractive neighborhoods. The builder must put his creativity into narrow confines: the detailing of windows, the color of the siding, the arrangement of the entry, etc. Like any other tight and limiting form

– the haiku, the sonnet – the creative and personalizing impulse must focus on only a limited set of variables."[75]

But just as there can be awful poetry, so can there be awful zoning. The intentions of zoning have ever been noble, but its application has tended to be overly simple, standardized, dogmatic and politically charged. American zoning almost always separates land-use into three main categories: industrial, commercial, housing. And housing is nearly always subdivided into multi-family (apartments) or single-family; the latter-day additions of condominiums and townhouses generally fall into a classification between the other two. For the most part, zoning is either/or, rarely inclusive. Cookie-cutter zoning has produced cookie-cutter residential neighborhoods, apartment complexes and shopping malls – and while this is itself an oversimplified statement, it makes the point.

Since most postwar suburban developments were zoned exclusively single-family, strip malls, such as this one in Buffalo, New York, sprang up along major arteries.

Photo used by permission of Charles Phoenix collection

MULTI-LAYERED LIVING: EXCEPTIONS TO THE ZONING RULE.

Across the ocean, Londoners have taken a different approach. After the Great Fire, architect Christopher Wren tried and failed to introduce what Mr. Hoover's commission would call "comprehensive planning." Instead the government there adopted a more pragmatic, case-by-case approach. If a church had stood on a certain corner before the fire, a church was built to replace it, likewise apothecaries, shops, banks, ale houses and row houses. Whatever had suited peoples' needs pre-conflagration would probably suit them post-. And that curious zoning habit has become entrenched over the intervening four centuries, making for a quite livable and interesting city.

One needn't travel to London or Paris to see what's possible without Euclidian zoning. Saratoga writer James Howard Kunstler visited Portland for his 1993 book *The Geography of Nowhere*. In Portland, Kunstler was awed to see that "office towers rise alongside apartment buildings. Museums, theaters, and commercial emporiums nestle in between. High-priced boutiques mix with grocery, hardware, and stationery stores…Portland is alive day and night. Because people live there at a high density, the city can support a variety of eating places, bars, cafes, clubs. The rich, up in their sky-high condos, live around the corner from the middle class, who live up the street from the not-doing-so-well. The important thing is that they all live together in proximity, not as though their worlds were separate, dirty secrets. The texture of life is mixed, complex, and dense, as a city ought to be, the way all cities used to be before the automobile and curse of Modernist planning."

Where "perfectly zoned" cities like Charlotte created "overstreet malls" – trans-tower walkways lined with convenience shops and kiosks for busybusy workers, Portland had passed a zoning code requiring buildings to put display windows at sidewalk level. They provided tax incentives to builders for buildings less than twenty stories high with reasonably priced apartments and shop-filled lobbies. And on the edges of the business district they changed the rules to allow multi-unit residences as well as single-family homes. Portland re-thought zoning and became a city built around community. As Kunstler says, "It is a living organism based on a web of interdependencies—which is to say, a local economy. It expresses itself physically as *connectedness,* as buildings actively relating to one another, and to whatever public space exists, be it the street, or the courthouse square, or the village green."[76]

It is remarkable how deeply we can miss this connection to the economy once we have experienced it. Andy Toomajian learned that the hard way when he agreed to spend a year as live-in caretaker of an "earthship" in New Mexico. For an environmentally sensitive, thoughtful thirty-year-old like Andy, it was energizing to be in a place that was one with nature – a beautiful house, climate controlled and powered by solar energy, in the sort of setting landscape artists and photographers drool over. He had his books, his music, a collection of films on DVDs and the woman he loved close at hand. Andy figured he had landed in heaven.

But as the year wore on the pleasure gave out. The electricity didn't work consistently; the DVDs and music were pleasures saved for special occasions. He longed for life back in the Mission District of San Francisco, for his horticultural job, for the people he met at clubs, in coffee shops or just on the street. Even his relationship became strained because "we only have each other to talk to." Andy says, "The desert, New Mexico, it's all very nice, pretty…but I miss the city. I miss walking to the store instead of driving 45 minutes to get a pizza. I miss having neighbors."

Living in the Mission District, Andy not only saw people, he "bumped into" them. He encountered the people who lived around him in the places he went to shop and eat, at the corner grocery and the corner bar. Strangers bumped into a second or third time are no longer strangers. After a few bumps strangers can become friends. In the language of sociology this is termed "multistranded connectedness." We have different layers to our lives, built around the places we live and work and shop and relax, and when we encounter someone in more than one of those places we develop a "multistranded relationship." Robert Putnam explored this phenomenon in his sequel to *Bowling Alone:*

> "Again and again, we find that one key to creating social capital is to build in redundancy of contact. A single pitch is not enough, whether you are pitching unionization or Christian salvation. Common spaces for commonplace encounters are prerequisites for common conversations and common debate. Furthermore, networks that intersect and circles that overlap reinforce a sense of reciprocal obligation and extend the boundaries of empathy."[77]

Not only is this multi-layering good for community, it's good for business. Bumping into people is one of the best ways to encourage and strengthen business connections. "The unplanned and serendipitous encounter [is that] upon which business grows," writes David Sucher. "The possibility of the accidental meeting is what makes the city a fertile place. From the chance conversation springs the new lead for a deal."[78]

Thus, in their desire to engineer a spirit of community, designers of New Villages, both urban and suburban, throw out the decades-old assumptions of Euclidian zoning. Places to live and places to work and places to shop must *not* be segregated from one another. This is a credo of both the New Urbanists and the Smart Growth-ers. For developers of community, it is simply common sense.

BUILD IT AND THEY WILL SHOP.

Early on in their research into successful place-making, the Walt Disney team knew they would need to include retail and office components in their proposed Central Florida subdivision. Todd Mansfield recalls walking onto the land when it seemed fit only for alligators and wild turkeys. It was difficult even for people who called themselves "Imagineers" to look at this spongey landscape and conjure up a vision of shops and restaurants and movie theaters and offices. If you built a downtown, who would shop there? If you built houses, where would the people who bought those houses go to buy groceries and sit down to chat over coffee? The Disney planners relocated the gators, ignored the turkeys, and started construction – and they started from the center.

Celebration's Town Center became literally that. It had to live up to its name. It came together at the edge of a man-made lake, created to filter stormwater, with a movie theater and four restaurants in four different price ranges. Town Center got its own bar, required by edict to stay open until the last movie let out, even if no one was drinking. The Disney people wanted everything just so – down to arguing with the chef at Columbia Restaurant that surely one could make a Caesar salad without raw eggs. Only indigenous flora would be planted on Main Street, none of those spindly palm trees native to the Middle East that everyone associates with Miami Beach and Las Vegas. But, then, indigenous shade trees such as Florida water oaks turned out to be impractical along the commercial street: their mossy-draped and evergreen branches hid the storefronts. Who knew where the stores were? The planners threw up their hands and went back to the palm trees. However, the Columbia's chef did not have to resign over the uncooked egg yolk question.

Unsure exactly how all this would work, the Disney team decided to hedge their bets on the exact nature of future demand for space in downtown Celebration. Thus they built apartments that would pass inspection up to the stricter retail code rather than just the less demanding multi-family code.

Among the many ideas swirling in the heads of the Celebration team were those that would soon become the tenets of New Urbanism. Any residential development worth designing would require a grocery store where locals could pick up the essentials and, of course, bump into one other. A corner store, in the embryonic New Urbanist view, would do "more than a social club to build the bonds of a community." But in order to accomplish such a goal, the corner grocery and other shops would have to be built even before there were people to shop in them; the retail component of Celebration had to be subsidized by the developer, Disney. "Since it can be effective in marketing real-estate – if properly staffed with a gregarious busybody – the corner store is a fairly easy concept for enlightened developers to understand," Celebration's architects would write later.[79] In fact, running a store where nobody shops is not generally considered good business, but in this case it worked.

One of the first stores to open was Village Mercantile, selling clothing, gifts and personal items. Vicki Puntonet moved to Celebration from Coral Gables and went to work for the store's owners. Before too long, she says, most of Celebration's stores were making lots of money, selling not only to residents but to tourists who had to see for themselves what Disney had wrought in remote Osceola County. "In the beginning we knew everyone who came into the store," Vicki said in 2004. "Now, not so much, since Celebration has about nine thousand residents." Vicki has a village home on Campus Street, a half mile from the store that she now owns. She wouldn't live or work anywhere else.

"One of our biggest challenges was getting the commercial area open before the residential area," says former Disney team member Tom Lewis. "The hope was that showing people the town center would make it easier for other developers to get money this sort of development in the future. It was a vision of what a great idea this was, and we wanted other people to do it. And for us, it did drive value."

Tom Lewis's job was to negotiate with people in government who generally see things only the way they're written down in the rule books. One of his proudest achievements was to convince the U.S. Postal Service to build an actual post office in Celebration Town Center, a place where residents would have to go each day to pick up their mail rather than have it delivered to their houses. "There is a belief that you cannot create a town unless you have the center first," Lewis says. You can build these places to different scales, big villages or small ones, but you still need the center. It's important for the residents to have a place to go, and that's why it's important for the developer to have deep pockets."

The success of Celebration's New Village design, mixing business with pleasure and with housing of every type, has been copied from one end of the country to the other, and with each iteration the area's

Euclidian zoning denies Americans the opportunity to shop and enjoy life's social pleasures within walking distance of their homes. New Village residents can walk to shops, offices, schools, restaurants and entertainment venues close by their single-family homes, condos and apartments, some of which are built right above the shops in the background.

Photo used courtesy of Celebration Associates

zoning laws have to be rewritten to accommodate community. In each case, also, the developer has to figure out how to get the retail stores up and running before the shopping and dining population arrives. It is, says Chesterton, Indiana developer Kevin Warren, the old chicken-and-egg puzzle turned inside out.

Warren's Lake Erie Land Company began planning the New Village of Coffee Creek, about fifty miles southeast of downtown Chicago, in the late 1990s. In 2002 Coffee Creek's success looked like such a sure thing that Kevin delivered a speech to the American Planning Association on "Zoning Out of the Box." But by the end of 2003 locals were still waiting for the appearance of a town center.

"The commercial projects which have come to fruition at Coffee Creek Center – or those which are still working their way through the pipeline – have had, strictly speaking, little of the quaint or retro about them," groused a writer for the Chesterton Tribune. At that point Coffee Creek had a family health care center, an orthopedic institute and a Hilton Garden Inn. Under construction just off the nearby Indiana Toll Road, Highway 49, was a 370,000-square foot shopping center and a big gas station. "Each of these projects has its own virtues," the report continued, "yet none of them, to be fair, really speaks to the New Urbanist vision."[80]

Exactly one year later, the vision was at least visible with the grand opening of Pavilion Center. For the moment it was only two shops, a women's boutique and a spa, both with addresses on Sidewalk Road, but it was a start. "We're still in the early stages," said Kevin Warren. "Right now we have about a hundred and fifty apartment renters – the apartments are already very successful – and ten single-family homes occupied. But even now the hope of community is leading to buying decisions… Some portions of the market are hungry for community and they can come here and see the possibilities."

By the time he spoke with us, Warren's Pavilion had added a coffee shop and a Bob Evans restaurant had opened off the highway. "The local merchants – the coffee shop, salon, women's apparel – they're easy. They have no problem with the environmental and 'New Urbanist' building restrictions. It's a lot tougher to convert the national companies. Bob Evans almost walked on the deal, but eventually they agreed to most stipulations."

The road to commercial success has been easier for Frank Martin, president of a New Village outside Boise, Idaho. "A developer can't create a community," says Martin, "but in planning and providing amenities, we can set the tone and facilitate people's coming together and taking a sense of ownership of the environment." So at Hidden Springs, set into a view not entirely unlike Andy Toomajian's New Mexico hermitage, a café and a general store were quickly established as gathering places for the residents-to-be. As at Celebration, Hidden Springs residents also bump into their neighbors at the post office.

"On any given day in Hidden Springs, people buy produce grown on the land," writes Elyse Umlauf-Garneau in *Professional Builder*. "Kids skate around the post office and pick out candy at the general store. Friends meet in the café, and a home-based business owner drops off overnight mail at the post office.

"Simple things like a mail service that delivers to a central spot rather than to individual houses create opportunities for Hidden Springs residents to catch up on the day's news and get to know one another in a casual way, not unlike the way socializing was done half a century ago."[81]

At Hidden Springs the environment makes the difference. Facing the Boise Front Foothills from Dry Creek Valley, the residents have unobstructed views of sunrises, sunsets and nature at her most rugged. The village is built around a hundred-acre working farm that sells its sixty varieties of fruit and vegetables right at the Hidden Valley General Store and Farmer's Market, just about all you could ask of a corner store.

Maybe the surest sign of a retail center's success is the readiness of a large retail management company to buy it from the developer. After ten years of managing Celebration Disney was ready to hand over the reins and find a buyer for its Town Center. Metin Negrin, an investor who had been an early consultant on Celebration, brought his company, Lexin Capital, quickly to the table when Disney announced its intention to sell in 2004. By that time Town Center's sixteen retail shops and six restaurants were all going concerns. Lexin, an international company that manages properties throughout the Southeastern and Southwestern United States, also bought 94,000 square feet of commercial office space and 105 apartments, all of them rented. Over the same space of time the average homeowner in Celebration had seen the value of his or her property appreciate at an almost unheard-of rate, as much as thirty percent above the market rate. When a development is zoned to promote community, homeowners can protect their equity and still walk to dinner. Business and the pleasure of life can and do peacefully coexist.

HOUSING DESEGREGATION: A NEW VILLAGE PROMISE.

That commercial success might have proved less convincing had Celebration not broken the second cardinal rule of Euclidian zoning: Thou shalt not mix housing types. Typical builders and developers are aghast at the abandon with which New Village designers, New Urbanists and Smart Growth advocates throw out this long revered baby with the Euclidian zoning bathwater. A bungalow next door to a cottage next door to a split-level is preposterous enough, to their thinking, but a row of town houses across the alley from a Victorian two-story is downright sacrilegious, especially when there's an outright *apartment* building across the street. Who'd want to buy in that kind of development?

It turns out a great many of us would.

In fact, when real estate people talk about types of housing they are really talking about the types of people who *live* in that housing. Like F. Scott Fitzgerald in Hollywood, the savvy realtor can drive into any neighborhood and tell at a glance what sort of people reside within its boundaries. That is, of course, because Euclidian zoning effectively segregates homes by dollar-value. By establishing zones in which single-family homes are permitted but two-family and multiple-family housing is *verboten*, zoning has at least implicitly established a pecking-order in which single-family houses are most desirable. In most parts of the country, desirability is further defined by restrictions on lot size, building heights and the distances homes may be built from the curb (setback) and from each other. The larger the lot, the more the builder has to charge for the house. Thus builders have been encouraged, sometimes forced by law, to segregate their neighborhoods according to the income levels of people who would live in them. The segregation in many instances happens well before the houses are built.

Old-neighborhood estates may bring top dollar and, by extension, a "better class" of people. Overbuilt, monstrous "McMansions" in the far suburbs may be equally expensive as old-neighborhood estates, but the families who reside in those hinterlands are not quite so valuable as neighbors. ("Neighbors," in these cases, should not be thought of in the Biblical sense of the word; "fellow isolates" is more accurate.) Conventional wisdom implies that the lower in price range the homes sell for, the less worthy those who live in them. Ritzy neighborhoods universally oppose the intrusion of apartment buildings, not because of any architectural misgivings but because of the sorts of people they might attract. Ditto the small rental house.

Segregating homes according to dollar value is as blameworthy as racially segregated schools and the effects of both are pretty much the same. We – and our children – begin to define ourselves and others according to stereotypes. We pigeonhole one another according to address. In fact, the address to at least a degree pre-determines the sort of person who will live there.

For all the rhetoric about America becoming a "classless society," evidence suggests the opposite is true. In the spring of 2005 *The New York Times* reported that "Americans are arguably more likely than they were 30 years ago to end up in the class into which they were born."[82] Few factors in American life have perpetuated class consciousness to the degree that zoning has. Today any child of a down-on-her-luck assembly-line worker may come into possession of clothes with designer labels and an iPod equipped with the latest sounds, but if she can't invite her classmates over for a weekend slumber party in the McMansion game room, she may never become their friend. Because she lives in the "wrong" part of town, she has been zoned lower-class.

Surprising to the *Times* was its finding that the United States, cradle of Upward Mobility, actually lags behind nobility-conscious Britain, King Louis' France, Canada and several Scandinavian countries in allowing its citizens to climb the ladder of success. Certain conditions in the United States "gum up the mobility machine," as the report observes. If you start out life in a high-income American neighborhood, you're better off than your counterparts overseas, but if you're born into a poor neighborhood here and grow up looking at all those rich neighborhoods through the schoolbus window, you have disadvantages beyond those of poor kids in a lot of other countries. You are zoned less-likely-to-succeed. That conclusion is bolstered by a recent study that found that within the United States a child's economic background is a better predictor of school success than it is in France, the Netherlands or Denmark.[83] Perhaps instinctively, socially conscious developers of

New Villages in the United States have chosen to mix housing types together.

Indeed, one of the marvels of New Village design is that it not only permits integrated housing patterns, it insists on it and thrives on it. Defying concerns of "diminished property values," it sites apartments next to multi-million-dollar homes, to the benefit of renters and homeowners alike. One encounters a pervasive attitude of equality.

Dawn Thomas, a Trinidad-born Caribbean-American single mother, moved into a Celebration apartment when she was offered a job in the newly-rising village. By working where she lived and living where she worked she would be able to spend more time with her son Eddie. As a "community guide" in the early days, when Town Center was still under construction, she could afford a one-bedroom apartment next to the Celebration Company office. She bought a sleeper sofa for herself and gave thirteen-year-old Eddie the bedroom. Dawn and Eddie were the first and, for several years, the only black family in Celebration.

At Celebration School, Eddie became best friends with Seth, a white boy who lived in a large single-family home down the street. Seth spent time at Eddie's apartment and Eddie spent time at Seth's house. Their parents got to be friends, and when they learned that Dawn would be needing surgery, Seth's mom and dad offered to have Eddie stay with them while she was in the hospital.

"I was just astonished," Dawn remembers. "I said, 'This is too much! I can take him to my mother's over in Orlando.' But they insisted. Eddie would go home after school, then go to their house for dinner and sleep over, and in the morning the two boys would walk to school together. When I came home from the hospital the next week, people would just show up at our house with dinner. They'd call and say, I'm bringing this or that, and I'd have to tell them we hadn't even finished all the dinner from last night." Dawn knits her brow and nods gently. "I think that's when it became real to me, this community thing. I realized, they've got my back. And it continues even now."

And now, with Eddie making plans to start his own business, Dawn is a sales associate for a real estate company whose office is near her old apartment. She rents a small single-family house in the Lake Evelyn neighborhood of Celebration, just a short walk away from work.

That house is owned by Don Rhodes, who rented it out so he could move into a Celebration condo, where he might be nearer the lady he'd fallen in love with. The success of Dawn Thomas and her son, like the romance of Don Rhodes, might never have happened in a place designed under the rules of Euclidian zoning.

RE-ZONING TO BUILD NEW VILLAGES.

At Celebration, there were no existing residents to protest such radical "variances" (as they are known) in the zoning status quo. In older neighborhoods with longtime residents, it is far more difficult to retrofit for housing inclusivity. Most of their residents have lived too long under the assumptions imposed by old-style zoning laws, and few things raise the public hackles like the threat of "down-zoning."

West Seattle, cited earlier in this chapter as a haven of community, nearly succeeded in seceding from Seattle proper in 1995 when city planners announced they would build four New Villages on the West Seattle peninsula. It was not that West Seattle didn't already have a significant mix of housing types, it was that people didn't want to be told where that housing would be built. After all, West Seattle fields an amateur baseball team called the Anarchists. The Washington Legislature actually passed a bill permitting the secession but the Governor vetoed it. At this writing the first of those New Villages, which the Seattle Housing Authority calls "Urban Villages," is renting apartments to former public-housing residents. Lines are forming to buy "market-rate" townhomes and single-family houses going up right next door. Interestingly, the city chose not to start High Point by building grocery stores and restaurants but by building a handsome new library and health center, two institutions that will draw across all income and "class" levels.

In the fall of 2006, we took a walk through High Point. On a sunny Tuesday afternoon, five well-known Northwest homebuilding companies had their crews out working on carriage homes, condos and single-family homes of between two- and five-bedroom sizes. There were many completed houses but only a few "for sale" signs, suggesting that homes were being sold either prior to their completion or as soon as they hit the market. The apartment houses, interestingly, had been completed and occupied earlier, so the presence of a renter population could not have been a surprise to unwitting homebuyers.

Walking down to a little park built around the stormwater runoff pond, where there is a nice view of the city and Space Needle, we met Sheri Moore, a very young grandmother who is raising two of her eleven grandkids. She told us she had lived in High Point a few years back, when it was still a housing project for low-income and welfare families.

"I just love what they've done with this place," Ms. Moore volunteered. "It's unbelievable!" She smiled brightly and gestured back at the park, the pond with its uninvited gathering of Canada geese, to a playground just up the hill. "On Saturdays and after school, the kids are all out playing together, all types of kids. And people are looking out for one another's kids. It was never like that before. People caring about each other." We are struck by the similarity between Sheri's thoughts

Because they are "designed in" from the start, New Village rental properties like these will not devalue their neighbors' single-family homes, townhouses and condominiums.

Photo by George Nemeth for Seattle Housing Authority

and those of Dawn Thomas, the Trinidad-born resident of Celebration, whose neighbors "had her back."

Sheri continued in her effusive praise of the New Village and its housing options. "My next-door neighbors are from Africa. We're learning to enjoy each others' cooking, learning about different places and different kinds of people. Isn't that the way it's supposed to be? Isn't that what a neighborhood's for? Saturday I'm having a birthday party for my two-year-old grandson, and the manager says I can use this park for the party. Like a great big back yard. Ain't that wonderful?"

High Point's liberal approach to rezoning may be a no-brainer in Seattle, where land for building is almost nonexistent and where housing costs are more than twice the national average. In fact, Seattle has been ranked fourth from the bottom in affordable housing. The only worse U.S. cities, in descending order, are Newark, New York and San Francisco.[84] It is more surprising New Village zoning in the desert near Phoenix, where empty land seems to stretch forever and where housing costs are still below the national average. Yet a visit to the New Village of Verrado ("From the airport, take I-10 West and turn right – it's the last thing before you hit L.A.") demonstrates that even when people have a plethora of traditionally-zoned habitats from which to choose, at least some of us prefer living together.

On an unseasonably cool (for Phoenix) February afternoon, we met with five residents at the Verrado Village Club. Bill Retsinas, manager of Verrado's new Bank of America branch, was already friends with his neighbors, Kyle and Melissa Campos, who were getting ready to open a smoothie shop on Main Street. Verrado, created by the designers of Scottsdale's DC Ranch, is zoned like nearly every New Village, allowing housing of all types, office spaces and commercial buildings to peacefully coexist. People get to know one another without regard at what sort of dwelling they inhabit, and often it is the commercial activity and public spaces that draw them together, across nonexistent lines that might be impassable in other places.

"Everything here encourages talking, walking," says Bill Retsinas. "It's great. Being at the bank, I see everyone in the town coming in, every ethnic group, age group, single people, retired people... I kept telling my parents how great it was. They came out to have lunch. When they came into the bank I was opening an account for this older Greek couple, and now they're my parents' best friends: they live across the street from each other here in Verrado. All the people who are buying out here wanted that – to be able to meet people and get that connection. My brother has never lived in Arizona, now he's moving to Verrado."

Melissa Campos married into a Greek family in southern Santa Barbara County, California, where the median home sale price in 2003 was $825,000.[85] Melissa and Kyle couldn't afford to buy in Santa Barbara, but in Verrado they could purchase "a really great house" for $276,000, directly across the street from their smoothie shop in Town Center. Like Bill Retsinas, Kyle and Melissa talked their families into relocating to the desert.

"Both of our families were really close," Melissa says. "We all wanted to move out of Santa Barbara, but none of us had ever been somewhere else we really liked, because Santa Barbara is kind of like paradise." Except for the cost of living. "My parents moved out here, they bought a house two blocks from ours. Kyle's mom is going to rent a loft on Main Street." And Kyle's brother, who sold his Santa Barbara home for just under a million, planned to spend about $400,000 for a single-family home in Verrado that would be twice the size of his California place. The family can be together because different types of housing are allowed to coexist, because Euclidian zoning has been disregarded.

Kyle and Melissa have a little boy named Owen, and besides him their chief topic of conversation was the smoothie shop, which Kyle Campos says they designed "around the community theme." Thus it will be much more a sit-down place than a take-out place. "We have a large seating area, we have wireless, we want to have weekly events at night time, we want to have DJs at night, sometimes have live music – we were heavily involved in the music scene in Santa Barbara – and also we want to let people suggest to us what we should do. We are going to make that space available to the community – we wanted to create another space to congregate on Main Street."

"A hang out place," Melissa agrees. "We are trying to make it comfortable for everyone, intergenerational."

Bill Retsinas, sitting across the conference table, perks up. "Music? I'll go." Bill looks forward to anything that will enliven the singles scene in this part of the Phoenix area known as the Western Valley. He wants his friends to understand what community is all about, to get out of "that mindset that tells you not to help."

"Here I see people inviting people to different things, talking to each other, helping each other out, 'If you need help moving…' Or whatever. Being in this type of community brings that out in you. Here, that's normal; you're not being weird by asking people if you can help them." Bill says that helpful attitude spills over into the bank, where the policy is "lots of personal contact, make people feel welcome."

BANKING ON THE POWER OF COMMUNITY.

Bill's bank, as it happens, is headquartered in Charlotte, North Carolina. It was there, in 1999, that the International Council of Shopping Centers convention was harangued by the man who had bought Bank of America and moved it to Charlotte, Hugh L. McColl.

After opening a British branch of his upstart North Carolina National Bank in 1971, McColl had come home determined to make his "perfectly zoned city" more like London. He proselytized for New Urbanism and Smart Growth long before the ideas had names. No less determined in 1999 – by which time he'd become arguably the most influential banker in North America – McColl spoke to the shopping center developers on "Developing Common Ground." His subject, in fact, was Smart Growth and how retailers needed to get with the program. The then-chairman and CEO of America's largest bank declared that people were on the verge of demanding that their shopping places be within walking distance of their living spaces. The era of insistence on Euclidian zoning, he said, was over:

> "Smart Growth is about families and communities. It's about thinking and acting to create neighborhoods – whether in the city, in existing suburbs or in newly developed areas – with housing, employment, schools, houses of worship, parks, services and shopping centers located close enough together that our kids can ride their bikes wherever they need to go, without asking us for a ride every ten minutes."

McColl told the shopping center developers that the free market is at the point of demanding Smart Growth. In Charlotte, his company was taking the lead by building a "state of the art technology village" on the west side of the Center City to be called Gateway Village. Although this village would be built around office space, it would be like other

New Villages in its mixed-use zoning. Folded into the development would be apartment buildings and condominiums, retail shops, restaurants and open green spaces for public use. It would sit right across the street from the mostly low-income Third Ward neighborhood and its Mount Moriah Primitive Baptist Church.

"Gateway Village is just the kind of development that Smart Growth is all about. It was planned from the beginning to include all the major components any community needs within walking or biking distance," McColl said. "It will be environmentally friendly. And it will be economically robust… It was not mandated by the government. It is being created by businesspeople — bankers, architects and developers — trying to do the right thing."[86] And, to be sure, trying to stay on the profit side of the ledger.

McColl retired as CEO and Chairman of the bank less than a month after that address, but he has continued to write editorials and make speeches about Smart Growth. By mid-2005 Gateway Village ("affordable city living at its finest") boasted 850 upscale condos and apartments, a YMCA branch, several restaurants, a Starbucks and a shopping arcade, plus office space for thousands of bankers and their ilk. Perhaps it was one of those bankers who penned the official village motto: "Located in the heart, possessing a soul."

Charlotte may not yet be London, but for the first time in many decades, its streets are alive not merely with cars but with people. High-rise apartments and condo buildings stand shoulder-to-shoulder with office skyscrapers, thicker than spring dogwoods in the old Myers Park neighborhood. Restaurants and nightclubs stay open late. There are concerts and museums and theater. "Uptown" (so called because it is north of Myers Park and the other earlier suburbs) has an NFL stadium and an NBA arena. Nearly all of this progress has required bending and breaking of Euclidian zoning regulations adopted in 1947.

When Gateway Village residents invite their Third Ward neighbors across the street to dinner – or vice-versa – Charlotte may come to rival an English village or Verrado, Arizona, for classless community. But even then it will be unlikely that a couple living in the sequestered neighborhood of Lansdowne or the distant super-suburb of Ballantyne Commons will be able to experience community as one couple experienced it on a 2005 spring evening in West Seattle…

They walk the five blocks from their condo, past the apartments and private homes and the spa and antique shop and church and day care center, to one of their favorite restaurants, Circa, where big-boned blue-jeaned Judy shows them to one of three vacant booths. "You just beat the crowd," she tells them. Attitudinal Judy, who daylights in public health, wears a smile that suggests something funny has just happened but she is not allowed to tell you about it. She brings the couple a bottle of Washington chardonnay and Caesar salad. The couple toasts their new life. "I love it here," the wife says for the umpteenth time. Then the main course of Dungeness crab cakes, vegetables and mashed potatoes, split into two plates as they have requested, along with extra veggies and mashed as Judy has insisted.

Just over the woman's shoulder in the next booth, a pale little boy asks his mother to pass his basket of toys to a little girl at the table across the aisle. The little girl's face lights up, one mother thanks the other, and it's clear that the families have never met. The little boy stands in the booth to focus his attention on a television at the nearby bar, where the beer-drinking singles are mostly ignoring a Mariners baseball game. The TV sound is turned down and the announcers speak only in captions illegible from the booths. The boy is perhaps three, thin and blond and achingly beautiful; he could play *The Little Prince*. He sees the man watching him. They make eye contact and exchange smiles. The man asks who's winning and the Prince responds with assurance that the Mariners are ahead, though it's not likely he can see the score. The boy shows the man the one toy he has retained from the basket and the man extends his hand across the table to take it, some alien combatant with wicked hooked claws emerging from its elbows. "What's its name?" the man asks. "I think it's 'The Hooker,'" the child says in all innocence.

His mother stifles an embarrassed laugh and turns to speak to the couple behind her. "Is Adrian disturbing you?" (Or does she say "Hadrian"?) Ice broken, conversation ensues. It turns out that the Little Prince is in pre-school and that the older woman is head of a private school in West Seattle and that the younger family is looking for a good school for next year. They have recently purchased a home in the neighborhood. Accidental social contact, business connection, and who knows what difference all this eventually might make to little Hadrian's (or is it Adrian's?) future, or what impact the Little Prince might eventually make on the world at large, that impact influenced in some small way by this small interplay of community?

The family finishes first and goodnights are exchanged. The little girl across the aisle returns the toy basket and Judy makes a fuss over the little girl. Meanwhile, Adrian/Hadrian reaches up on tiptoe to give a parting hug to the old man who smiled at him and spoke to him about baseball and toys and other important things. His mother's blue eyes go wide. "Oh, my goodness," she says. "He's *never* that friendly with strangers."

Living outside the Euclidian zone would seem to have its privileges.

CHAPTER FIVE
Walk, Don't Drive

One December morning in 1995, Cynthia Wiggins, a seventeen-year-old single mother of Buffalo, New York, walked across a street and became a national tragedy.

Cynthia was planning to put in another day at her job in the food court at Walden Galleria Mall, in the Buffalo suburb of Cheektowaga. Then she'd take the ten-mile bus trip home, back to her apartment and her baby boy. But on this day Cynthia was running late. Her workplace – the "International" Food Court, because it includes a Taco Bell and a Manchu Wok along with the Dairy Queen and Arby's – would soon be crowded with Christmas shoppers. She couldn't afford to be docked an hour's pay. Cynthia only made minimum wage, but her dreams were big. She hoped to become a doctor one day, even though she already had a baby to feed and had yet to finish high school.

The Number 6 bus rolled out of Buffalo proper and into suburbs that had grown into cities in their own right, enclaves of middle-class and upper-class homes connected by arteries thick with trade. The bus made its customary stop at the busy three-way intersection of Walden and Woltz Avenues and Genessee Street. Cynthia's mind must have been somewhere else as she started across the seven lanes of traffic, or surely she'd have seen the dump truck barreling down on her.

Three weeks later, Cynthia died in the hospital, but it wasn't till 1999, four years following the accident, that her case came to trial. By then Cynthia had become famous as a symbol of lingering racism in the United States. The Number 6 bus served ethnic minority neighborhoods in Buffalo and it was not allowed to drop off its passengers in the parking lot of Galleria Mall. At the Galleria, most of the customers were white and, by Cynthia's standards, wealthy. Her family sought $150 million in wrongful death damages from the mall owners, the public transportation company and the truck driver. The suit was settled for $2.55 million by celebrity lawyer Johnnie Cochran, who represented football hero-actor O.J. Simpson in his murder trial. In his autobiography, Cochran wrote that in the Wiggins case he wanted to "send a strong message to all businesses that still find indirect means to discriminate against minorities."[87]

But no matter what Cynthia Wiggins' story may say about racial discrimination, it speaks volumes about the need for a different sort of living-working-walking places in the United States. Because as things stand, the suburbia in which the majority of Americans live and where Cynthia Wiggins had to travel to find work, simply is not a place to walk. For the most part, suburbia is and, since its earliest days, has always been a place to *drive*.

Since most middle- and upper-income Americans live in suburban areas like Cheektowaga and most lower-income Americans live in urban centers like Buffalo, the only way for the people who buy the fast food to connect with the people who serve the fast food is by means of the internal combustion engine. Cars, buses, trucks are our engines of social mingling. President Herbert Hoover's Committee on Recent

Nothing accelerated America's suburban sprawl and auto dependency more than the shopping mall. This is Seattle's Northgate Mall in the 1950s.

Social Trends in the United States saw it coming as early as 1933: "The automobile has become a dominant influence in the life of the individual," said that committee's report, "and he, in a very real sense, has become dependent on it."

In an equally real sense, every American lives in a suburb of Detroit, Michigan…

INTERNALLY COMBUSTING.

> *Detroit city, it's one of the finest in this world.*
> *I'm crazy about that city,*
> *And I love its pretty girls.*

New Orleans' Antoine "Fats" Domino recorded "Detroit City Blues" in his first recording session at the end of 1949, expressing a fondness for the Motor City that had been ingrained deep in the Southern black psyche since the early days of the century. In a recruiting drive that carried through a depression and two world wars, Detroit's auto manufacturers lured Southern farm workers to their city with promises of high wages, high living and, no doubt, pretty girls. This was a critical component of what has been labeled the Great Migration of rural Southern blacks to Northern cities. In 1910, the African-American population of Detroit was just 6,000. By the time of the Stock Market Crash of '29, the city had 120,000 black residents. By the 2000 census they numbered nearly one million. Most of those people would be somewhere else today were it not for the automobile industry.

Detroit boasted the first paved concrete road (1909), the first traffic light (1915) and the first inner-city freeway (1942), but its biggest achievement may have been Los Angeles. If Detroit gave America the automobile, the automobile gave America Los Angeles. California opened what would become the suburban Pasadena Freeway in 1940 and Los Angeles business leaders salivated over the prospect of country folk flocking downtown to shop. Instead, Angelenos used the freeway to escape the city and populate the suburbs. Suburban real estate became so hot that developers and builders passionately pushed for more freeways up and down the state, creating what would become the most extensive, notoriously noxious and clogged freeway system in the world, despite the density of Los Angeles proper. California indeed owes much of its identity and anxiety to Detroit. For its own plight, Detroit only has itself to blame.

During World War II Detroit converted its auto assembly-line workers into builders of bombers and tanks, in new factories constructed at great distances from the city. The federal government built expressways from the heart of the city that labeled itself "America's Arsenal," where auto workers lived, to the ever-more-distant suburbs, where the new jobs were. The people with money to buy houses – and these were almost exclusively white people – bought new houses out in the sticks. By 1950, the city Henry Ford built had grown as rapidly as any city on earth, to 2.7 million people. That was a six-fold increase in half a century.

Fats Domino (who 21 years later would change his mind and record "Walkin' to New Orleans") had it right. Detroit City was booming in those days. Dinah Shore was singing her song, too, urging America to see the USA in our Chevrolet. Motor City – or, as the music industry labeled it, Motown – was going like gangbusters in the 50s, even more than it had back in the Roaring 20s. Yet just a few years later, by the mid 60s, the city found itself overwhelmed by poor African American families who'd migrated north looking for jobs. Whites of all income levels began streaming out to ever more distant suburbs. By 1967 Detroit was 40 percent black and black men were more than twice as likely to be unemployed as white men. Meanwhile, the auto factories continued to automate their assembly lines and move production abroad, putting more people out of work. For African-Americans, Detroit City was no longer the finest in the world. The summer of '67, H. Rap Brown, leader of the Student Nonviolent Coordinating Committee, promised that if Motown didn't come around, "We're gonna burn you down."

The resultant five days of rioting in Detroit riveted suburban America to its television screens. We saw burning buildings, National Guard tanks, bodies in the streets. That same summer another city under pressures much the same as Detroit's, Newark, New Jersey, exploded in violence. In 1940 Newark's population had been 85 percent white, with most of them living in the city. By 1967, 55 percent of Newark residents were African-American. White Jews, Poles and Italians had literally abandoned their homes and synagogues and fled to the suburbs of South Orange, West Orange and Livingston.[88] *Life* magazine called Newark's eruption "The Predictable Insurrection."

Indeed, the violence of racial inequity should have been predictable, but in fact, 1967 America had yet to face the truth that community was eroding and being replaced by the isolationism made possible by suburban sprawl. If we lived in the suburbs, behind our shrubs and trees, we could pretend our own social capital was not reduced by what went on in our cities. We could watch our inner cities burn on television from the safety of our suburban strongholds. Between 1950 and 1970, while our total population was booming, 83 percent of that growth was in the suburbs. Over those two decades, suburbs doubled their population, from 36 to 74 million.

In 1971 Detroit lost a piece of its identity when the iconic African American music label, Motown Records, escaped to the car-born smog of Los Angeles. And by 1981, old Detroiters finally understood what blind faith in the motor car had cost them. That was the year the city lost its last great symbol of the glory years, Hudson's department store. The 25-story, city-block landmark, first cousin of Macy's and Marshall Field, put its brass-buttoned doorman uniforms in mothballs to devote all its corporate attention to the stores where the money was, out in the suburbs, where you had to drive a car to shop. Hudson's, in fact, had pioneered the sprawling of America some thirty years earlier by anchoring the nation's first regional shopping mall, Northland Center (see Chapter Two.) The four-level mall in the Detroit suburb of Southfield, Michigan, opened in 1954.

WE ARE WHAT WE DRIVE.

By 2004, Detroit's once-grand population of 2 million would be reduced to only 900,000, and more than a third of those people were living below the poverty line.

In perhaps the final insult added to Detroit's injured pride, foreign auto makers now produce about a quarter of all the cars manufactured in the U.S. and account for nearly half of all car sales. Both those figures are rising, At this writing, the state of Alabama is becoming the New Detroit, with plants operated by Mercedes-Benz, Honda, Hyundai and Toyota, and states such as South Carolina, Arkansas and Texas are staking their claims.[89] The new Great Migration consists of Japanese, German and Korean industrialists swarming to America's Southland.

Thus the automobile continues to define and redefine the places we live and, in the process, continues to reshape our sense of community.

Just as importantly, the automobile today is reshaping our bodies and threatening our health. Our very homes in the suburbs are taking years off our lives, adding inches to our waistline, making us more susceptible to diseases from asthma to cancer. By moving us inexorably farther and farther from the cities into distant suburbs, governments, automobile makers, developers and a host of fellow travelers have helped us forget how to walk. We are literally driving ourselves to early graves.

Start with fat.

In the late 1990s the Centers for Disease Control began warning that the United States was in the midst of an "obesity epidemic." By 2005 the statistics have become too fat to hide: 65 percent of American adults are overweight; almost half of those eligible for the term "obese." Among American children, a shocking sixteen percent are labeled obese, and childhood obesity has more than doubled since 1985. According to CDC director Julie Gerberding, M.D., obesity's cost in health treatments and lost productivity was $75 billion in 2003, having risen more than $20 billion in just eight years. Its estimated cost to business is $13 billion per year.[90] While the CDC was forced to slap its collective wrist in 2005 – it had been using old measuring sticks to overstate the impact of obesity as a direct cause of death – there is no question that the epidemic is quite real and quite costly. Whether or not obesity can be identified as a direct cause of death, it certainly contributes to diabetes, cardiovascular disease, arthritis, stroke and some forms of cancer.[91]

But is suburbia really a direct cause of obesity? Couldn't we simply blame fast foods and slow living? Couldn't we pin it on TV and video games and tuberous roots sunk deep in the divan? We certainly could, but we need to look at the fact that all of those other contributing factors owe their existence, at least in part, to the places where we live. Fast food needs to be "fast," because we are usually in a hurry to be somewhere else, to *drive* to some destination. Wendy's and Burger King have drive-up windows, so we don't even have to walk to the counter. Supersized servings of fried potatoes and high-fructose corn syrup are what goes in; theoretically, we could metabolize even all those carbohydrates and burn up even all those calories if we would seriously exercise. But we don't. We pay the attendant and put the car in gear. Later, those mindless television programs and video games entertain us for immobile hours largely because we have forgotten the pleasures of walking and of evening conversations with neighbors. For children, of course, the loss is unsuspected and therefore all the greater. They don't know what they are missing.

In their 2004 book, *Urban Sprawl and Public Health*, Lawrence Frank, Howard Frumkin and Richard Jackson supply all the evidence we should need to be convinced that postwar suburban development, ever-stretching the distances between our homes and our workplaces and our shopping places, has effectively forced us into total dependency on the automobile and therefore forced us to abandon walking for driving. Streets without sidewalks, large-lot subdivisions, fewer daylight hours spent at home thanks to long commutes – these all discourage walking. One of the collaborators, Dr. Richard Jackson, reports that from his former office – ironically at the Centers for Disease Control in suburban Atlanta – he would watch patients risk their lives trying to cross Buford Highway, where no design consideration at all had been given to walkers.[92]

At this writing Lawrence Frank is an associate professor of community and regional planning at the University of British Columbia, but prior to that he was on the faculty of Georgia Tech in Atlanta, perhaps America's capital city of sprawl. (We note that Houston is America's least dense and fattest city, though Detroit is close on its heels.[93]) Frank published in 2004 a study of nearly 11,000 residents of the Atlanta area. That study demonstrated that for every extra thirty minutes per day of commuting time, participants were three percent more likely to be obese. On the other hand, people who lived within walking distance (defined as a half-mile) of shops were seven percent less likely to be obese than those who lived farther away from commercial areas.[94]

Another author, Joel S. Hirschhorn, takes the argument further with a title that says it all. In *Sprawl Kills: How Blandburgs Steal Your Time, Health and Money,* he writes, "Preventable deaths from the sprawl sedentary lifestyle are five times greater than deaths from microbial agents, like bacteria and viruses, more than two times greater than deaths from alcohol, and two times that of deaths from firearms, illicit use of drugs, sexually transmitted diseases and motor vehicle accidents."[95] That may be stretching the case, but anyone possessed of a quarter-pound of sense should agree that walking half a mile for head of lettuce is healthier than driving three miles for a burger.

Researchers have quantified the poundage of urban sprawl. If we choose to live in one of the less-dense neighborhoods that make up about two-thirds of the populated United States, chances are we will be six pounds heavier than if we lived in a city or village setting.[96] Another Atlantan, Emory University's Dr. Howard Frumkin, who has spent years studying the connection between our modes of transportation and our lifespans, concludes:

> "Low physical activity threatens health both directly and indirectly. A sedentary lifestyle is a well-established risk factor for cardiovascular disease, stroke, and all-cause mortality, while physical activity prolongs life. Men in the lowest quintile of physical fitness have a two- to three-fold increased risk of dying overall, and a three- to five-fold increased risk of dying of cardiovascular disease, compared to men who are more fit. Among women, walking ten blocks per day or more is associated with a 33 per cent decrease in the risk of cardiovascular disease."[97]

To older generations, riding a bike to school is a memory from some distant "good old days," but to kids growing up in village environments, bicycles are preferred over parental chauffeurs. Kid-friendly New Villages may be a cure for the obesity epidemic.

Used by permission of Port Blakely Communities (Issaquah Highlands, Washington)

Another study, this one from Denver, shows that children who live within 250 yards of a road with 20,000 or more vehicles per day are eight times more likely to get leukemia and six times more likely to get other cancers. The authors of the study attribute most of this risk to motor vehicle exhaust. Summing up all these studies, the Sierra Club in 2004 issued a report that declared automobile traffic to be "a unique public health threat."[98]

Pedestrians with a purpose.

The United States has become an unfortunate model for the rest of the world in staying off our feet and putting on the pounds. Although not focusing on suburban sprawl, the World Health Organization (W.H.O.) warns that "globesity" is taking over many parts of the world. New Zealanders are on fat alert. England has its own obesity epidemic, even China has one. (As of 2006, more than 60 million Chinese are considered obese.) "Contrary to conventional wisdom, obesity is not restricted to industrialized societies; in developing countries, it is estimated that over 115 million people suffer from obesity-related problems." If immediate action is not taken, says W.H.O, "millions will suffer from an array of serious health disorders."[99] By the year 2010, health experts predict that China, where the number of obese children is climbing at the rate of eight percent a year, will be home to 200 million dangerously overweight people.[100]

Doctors everywhere are warning us to get out and walk off the fat. But to where shall we walk? Surely walking need not be an end in itself. If we live in the right neighborhoods of big cities, there will be any number of destinations – shops and restaurants and libraries and pubs and bus stops. In those "right neighborhoods" there will be crosswalks and signal lights to help us arrive vertically. But traditional suburbia offers few safe places for walking and fewer walking destinations. And even when all the right conditions for walking exist, the fact that so many of our neighborhoods are designed around automobiles, with little consideration given to the personal interaction of neighbors, makes it unlikely that many of us will choose to walk.

Take, for example, the old, established "streetcar suburb" of Myers Park, one of the first suburbs built in Charlotte, North Carolina, and even today one of the city's most prestigious addresses. In fact, when Todd Mansfield put his Myers Park house on the market in 2001, he got a call from the puzzled real estate reporter of the Charlotte Observer. Why would anyone in his right mind want to leave such a neighborhood? Was the head of the region's oldest established development company getting out of town? As it happened, Todd and Kathy Mansfield were just moving to another, more distant part of Charlotte, where Kathy hoped she reconnect with the sort of community she missed among the majestic oaks and wide spayed lawns of Myers Park.

"I would watch our neighbors leave their garages in the morning and watch them pull into their garages in the evening, and those were the only times I'd see them," says Kathy. "I needed more human contact than that."

The Mansfields moved to Charlotte in 1999, when Todd took over the Crosland Company. Interestingly, Crosland had been responsible for creating many of the post-World War II suburbs that today constitute the city's runaway sprawl. Though not one of its original developers, for a time Crosland actually controlled the latter-stage development of iconic Myers Park. But the Mansfields had lived in Central Florida, where Todd had built Celebration on a foundation of community.

"In Orlando we would see our neighbors at the kids' baseball games, or just out walking," Kathy remembers. "We'd get together with neighbors at least a couple of times each week. In two years in Myers Park we rarely saw any of our neighbors socially. Not that people weren't polite, but sometimes politeness can be a pleasant cold shoulder. We wanted to be able to walk places where we could maybe just bump into people, but there were no places to walk to, no destinations. Except churches on Sunday, and we didn't belong to any of those."

In fact, there are pedestrians on Myers Park's main boulevards most hours of the day. The majority of these pedestrians are running or jogging, often with baby strollers and/or leashed dogs. (A few residents have thoughtfully provided dog-watering stations for hot Charlotte afternoons.) Many of them are students or faculty at Queens University, others just passing through from other neighborhoods, drawn by the stately oaks and grand houses. The majority of these pedestrians are wearing headsets, listening to music or radio talk shows. Greetings are seldom exchanged, especially among people under forty, suggesting that recently-matured generations have been overly warned against talking to strangers. These Walkman-walkers seem just as isolated and insulated from their surroundings as if they were embedded in an air-conditioned

THE STREETS FOLLOW GRACEFUL LAND CONTOURS.

Charlotte's Myers Park was designed by landscape planner John Nolen in 1911 to be a "streetcar suburb." Created from a tree-barren cotton farm, the wide-lawned suburb outlasted the streetcars and became automobile dependent.

Postcards from the early 1900s

A LITTLE BIT OF HERMITAGE ROAD.

PARKS AND WIDE LAWNS ABOUND.

automobile, which is the way most privileged Americans experience the neighborhoods in which we live. Unfortunately, we cannot get to know a place, let alone be a part of it, simply by driving through it, or to and from it. Our sense of place is enhanced, enriched by walking, but for those of us who can afford them, automobiles have pretty much left community in the dust.

That is starting to change.

Inspired by New Urbanism and guided by the principles of Smart Growth, developers of New Villages around the country are building neighborhoods primarily for people, where cars are second-class citizens. These New Village developers – both urban and suburban – are providing bike trails and hiking trails, wide sidewalks and tunnels under busy streets. They are setting aside land for parks, despite the ensuing loss of profits that would come from building more houses and apartments on that land. And they are providing inviting places to walk to – coffee shops, restaurants, grocery stores, post offices. To be sure, New Villages also have their streets, garages and parking lots, but those are primarily to allow ingress and access to the neighborhood. Within the neighborhood, walking and bicycle riding are the most popular forms of transportation, and this makes for interesting neighborhood encounters.

In the Seattle-area New Village of Issaquah Highlands one might meet up with Calm Prince Barkley d'Bouvier, a friendly sort, whose formal name is rarely applied. To him and to his legions of friends, it's simply Barkley. Or Mister Barkley. Like the lady he walks with, Barkley is retired now, his national championship only a sweet memory. Most of his work today is done on the hiking trails in and around the Issaquah Highlands neighborhood. The champ leaves most of the show duties to his young housemate Beau. Born in '02, Beau (full name Cobeauche Beau Cour d'Or) is eleven years Barkley's junior, but Mister Barkley can still give young Beau a run up the hillside.

A big, shaggy bouvier pushing a hundred pounds, bred for herding Belgian livestock, needs to stay active even into dog old-age. So if he could talk, Barkley would probably thank the humans, Bill and Faris Taylor, with whom he shares his home. He might thank them for giving up the city life and relocating to Issaquah Highlands, because the Highlands are built for the active life, the life the Taylors and their pets have always lived. He would thank them for choosing a New Village.

Not only is Barkley fit and trim, so is his 70-something walker, Faris Taylor. She could be a poster girl for a 2005 study conducted by the Research Center for Human-Animal Interaction at the University of Missouri-Columbia, which adds scientific weight to the evidence of experience: walking a dog can help us lose significant poundage. The center's director, Rebecca Johnson, told the Associated Press, "We know that walking is good for people but we don't know how to get people to continue to do it. We wanted to see whether bonding with a dog might be a motivator to continue walking."

Indeed, it might. Participants in the study started walking their loaner dogs just ten minutes a day three times a week. They worked themselves up to twenty minutes a day five times a week. Those who stayed with the program fifty weeks lost an average of fourteen pounds. "That's a better result than most of the nationally known weight-loss plans," Johnson says. The walkers "bonded with the animals, improved their flexibility, balance and ability to walk, lost weight and felt better about themselves so it was a very positive thing all around."[101]

Watching her hike the hills with her big black dustmop dogs, you might notice the twinkle of experience in Faris Taylor's eye, and you'd know she wasn't putting you on if she told you she was a champion once herself, a figure skater ranked number three in the USA. You'd not be surprised to hear she worked as a ski instructor after her children came along. Nor would you blink at her son Billy's skiing for the U.S. in the 1980 Olympics and her daughter Missy's racing sailboats off Rhode Island. So it comes as no shock to find Faris's name in a back issue of the local newspaper, extolling the benefits of walking.

"One of the great things about this community," she told the *Issaquah Press* in 2001, "is we have sidewalks everywhere, and most of the residents are out walking on the sidewalks when the weather is good." The opportunity to move around outdoors is "one of things that gives us the sense of community."[102]

This connection between community and health is critical to understand. By choosing neighborhoods that enable, indeed encourage, the simple act of walking, we become more connected to our neighbors. We meet them out walking, we walk places together. Because it promotes community and enables us to go places we want to go, walking is a means to an end. Because it promotes health, walking is an end in itself.

Obviously, walking is humanity's earliest and still most reliable means of transportation. When we no longer are able to walk, no longer ambulatory, we are considered disabled, crippled. Urban/suburban sprawl has quite literally crippled us. Initially, much of suburbia was built without even sidewalks. Dog walkers and bike riders had to use the streets, which were designed for cars and trucks. Even when suburbs have sidewalks they usually lead nowhere. To live in them is to be utterly dependent on the automobile, much as the physically infirm depend on wheelchairs and life support systems. The analogy is hardly far-fetched, since research confirms what common sense suspects: sprawl is not only expanding America's waistlines, it is damaging our hearts and lungs, our air and drinking water, our psychological well-being and our physical safety.

Sprawl may also be the underlying cause of some other problems. As our bodies are more stressed – from demanding jobs, supersized mortgage payments, pressures of millennial life and long commutes – our adrenal glands release a toxic hormone which kills cells that convert short term memories into long term ones. We are born with a certain amount of an antidote to those stress-killers, but living in a stressful environment can literally cause brain damage. The only way for us to produce more of these antidotes (called BDNF, or brain-derived neurotrophic factor) is to exercise. Through cardiovascular workouts, even low-impact ones like walking, we literally become more immune to stress, and hence, more productive and happier.[103]

CHOOSING A HOME FOR HEALTH'S SAKE.

The authors of *Urban Sprawl and Public Health*, cited earlier, strongly endorse the creation of more New Village-type developments that promote physical activity and offer alternatives to automobile travel.[104] The book argues that "The places we live, work and play affect our health." As Howard Frumkin puts it, "We have choices in the way we design our environment, and those choices matter a great deal to those who care about health." Most of us do care a great deal about our health and especially about the health of our children. As we come to understand that our choice of neighborhood plays a significant role in our health and longevity, we are bound to make more intelligent decisions about where we live.

In the New Village of Celebration, the Disney draw may have been the initial stimulus, but buyers and renters quickly recognized the close connection between walking and community and health. Ann Whelan told us that when she moved from the Walnut Creek suburbs of San Francisco to Celebration in 2002, her most pleasant surprise was that she no longer needed a car, and that not having a car gave her more, not less, opportunity to be with people. In California Ann had managed a dental office, run a clothing business and participated in women's advocacy groups, "but you have to drive everywhere out there. Most of your time was spent traveling to the places you wanted to be." And any time travel involves a crowded freeway, getting there is emphatically not half the fun.

These days, despite her full-time position as caregiver to grandson Brooks, Ann finds herself with "more free time…and it's easier to get involved here. There are so many civic and service groups." She belongs to the Celebrators, a group of about 300 men and women who do charity and civic work both in Celebration and in less affluent neighborhoods of Osceola County. She works with Celebration Republican Women and with the Red Hat Society, which she defines as "a bunch of women over 50 in red hats having lunch." Whether the groups gather in a village restaurant for lunch or at a neighbor's home in the evening, Ann feels perfectly safe walking to the meeting, usually pushing a stroller.

"Little Brooks knows everyone in town," she says. Ann knows the paths by heart, the sidewalks, the parks, the boardwalks that meander through palmetto thickets and wild orange groves, but she can usually count on a surprise. "Walking around with Brooks, there are lots of accidental encounters. Everyone says hello to everyone. That never happened to me in California. We walk everywhere here. It's a beautiful community to walk in, the parks are wonderful, there are great lakes… We do avoid the alligators, though."

Some mornings Ann walks Brooks to breakfast at one of Celebration's restaurants, where she invariably finds herself in conversation with Orlando tourists come to see the Disney version of Utopia. "I think it's funny. The visitors always ask, 'Are you a resident?' as though no one could actually *live* here. They don't think it's a real place. I'm happy to answer their questions."

Reducing auto dependency.

We are not suggesting that ambulatory, or "walkable" neighborhoods will sound the automobile industry's death knell. Few suburban New Villagers are able to get along altogether without their automobiles. However, vehicular downsizing is common. Mary and John Pfeiffer sold one of their two cars when they moved to Celebration. John bought a Segway Human Transport, the scooter made for use in pedestrian environments. "And I walk or ride my bike to work," boasts Mary. "We've cut down on our driving, absolutely."

A step up from the scooter is the Neighborhood Electric Vehicle (NEV) that carries Ike and Alex Eissinmann everywhere in Celebration. Unless, of course, they are walking. Taggert, the big yellow Lab, lolls his tongue and nods to neighbors from the NEV's back seat. Like the $4,000 single-rider Segway, the four-passenger NEV (about $12,000) runs on batteries, rechargeable gratis at one of Celebration's downtown electricity stations. Just plug it in while you run your errands — no gas required. The Eisinmanns also own and operate the Celebration Express, a battery-operated trackless train that carries passengers around the town during the holiday season. Ike plays engineer, Alex loads the passengers. At $3 a ticket, the little train is an "extremely profitable" venture.

"On weekends, it's like a 45-minute wait," Alex beams. "The kids just love it. This past Friday, we did, like, five hundred rides. It's unique, the only electric one in the country." With the train running every night from Thanksgiving to New Year's, Ike and Alex have taught themselves how to maintain and service the engine and its cars, though a good many visitors assume this is all taken care of by higher powers. "People think the train is Disney, that we're insured by Disney. But then they think that about our whole town. They wonder whether it's all a façade, and if the toilets actually flush." Ike jokes about changing his wife's batteries, à la *The Stepford Wives*, when they encounter hard-core doubters.

Like the Eisinmanns, Celebration residents Lee and Sherry Moore also own a NEV. They sold one of their two cars when they moved into the New Village. Lee now works from home, "to spend more time with the kids instead of commuting," driving five-year-old Samantha to school in their NEV each day. "Ninety percent of our lives are spent right here in Celebration," he beams. "The kids go to dance lessons and soccer. Every morning, after I take Samantha to school, sometimes

I swim, or I eat a bagel at the Market Street Café, then I start work around 10.

"I don't stay in this house all day. Just having that opportunity to sit down and interact with neighbors is important. My wife and I do a lot of work with the Home Owners Association. The walking, the family, that's why we're here, even though it's not real easy for us financially. We want to live here, we want to bring up our kids here." Though he cherishes his NEV, Moore is convinced that walkability is one of the most important aspects of New Village life. "The guy down the street feels the same way as I do. He opened up the bike shop. The people who live in this town could be somewhere else, and they are happy not to have to schlep the kids somewhere else."

The fact that they don't need to travel "somewhere else" for activities and companionship makes all the difference for New Villagers. In her former neighborhood outside Scranton, Pennsylvania, Lynn Sands "used to just walk around in a circle" to get exercise and fresh air. In the New Village of Celebration, she can choose from among several different paths from her home to the gathering places of Town Center. And on the pathways, at the outdoor café tables, she inevitably encounters her neighbors.

Free charging stations for battery-operated cars help New Villagers do without environment-crippling gas-guzzlers that are essential to life in the typical post-war American neighborhood.

Photo by the authors

"I used to put twenty thousand miles on my car every year. When we moved here, the fact that I could walk around and just know people…" Sands shakes her head, recalling the astonishment of that discovery. "Now I walk probably about four miles a day. Here you have walking destinations. Or if you don't want a destination, you can just wave at people."

It's not likely that many New Villagers sit around cursing Detroit or Henry Ford. For them as for the rest of us, the car is merely a piece of technology, and technology itself is neither good nor evil. In the 21st century it appears that automobiles, along with suburbia, will be with us for some time yet. But a new suburbia, dotted with New Villages such as Celebration and DC Ranch and Issaquah Highlands, will offer us other technologies to change the way we live once we get there. And along with that technology it will provide both public areas for conversation and walking paths for contemplation.

It was through connecting with people on her walks that Lynn Sands found her way to commitment and public service. In August and September of 2004, Central Florida was walloped by three hurricanes, Charley, Frances and Jeanne. Charley, the first one, did only minor damage to Celebration, but it wrought havoc in the nearby lower-income town of Poinciana. Sands volunteered with the Celebration Foundation to pitch in. "We helped the Davey company to get all the trees back up. We fed a lot of people, and they took food back to their homes. They didn't have any power for weeks. Some of us went out to Poinciana and cleared debris."

Celebration Executive Director Pat Wasson elaborates: "The money that came through our residents for the hurricane relief was incredible. A staff member called in to say that St. Cloud needed ice. One of the other staff members brought so much ice I had to get a truck to take it there. I put out an e-mail after church on Sunday, asking people to meet at three P.M. to bring food and supplies after the first hurricane. We had eight truckloads of food. Our community fed the maintenance crews who were cleaning up our roads." When she asked the county where the most help was needed, Wasson was directed to Poinciana, where 90 percent of the town's twelve thousand homes had serious roof damage. "The Poinciana Fire Department had no roof at all. No one knew what to do." The Celebration Foundation, originally funded by Disney, agreed to match whatever money was raised in the village, which turned out to be $4,000. "We bought hundreds of tarps. The Foundation put together work crews, helping single moms and the elderly first. We called different tree people and they gave us the equipment."

It was all possible, the two women agree, because of the intentional, purposeful sense of community. "People are meant to live in little groups, where you know a bunch of people," says Lynn Sands, "and it's a really nice feeling. You might actually become involved. Or say something bad happens to you personally. You know 25 or 30 people you could just call. But there's no pressure to be involved. It's like a giant summer camp for adults – there are all kinds of people, very talented people here."

And how do those people connect with one another? They take walks, they "bump into" each other. Don't try bumping into someone in a car. Drivers have a great deal of trouble connecting with people when they're behind the wheel. They may lift a finger or even nod at a pedestrian. In Seattle and perhaps in a few other places on earth, they will even stop the car to let pedestrians cross a street, but then they drive away and the possibility of connection disappears in the exhaust fumes.

SUBURBAN AIR QUALITY.

Those fumes appear to wreak more havoc in our typical suburbs that in our crowded inner cities. That, at any rate, is the conclusion of several studies compiled by the National Institutes of Health. These 2004 studies for the first time looked at the effects of living near those crowded roads and highways that accommodate the daily American commute. They conclude that such traffic-related air pollution problems as asthma, cancer, premature birth, low birth weight, and a generally higher risk of terminal illness are more common among suburbanites than among city dwellers.

Donald Chen, executive director of Smart Growth America, a nonprofit research coalition in Washington, D.C., says that while most people expect a healthier, cleaner environment in the suburbs, in fact "sprawl developments actually present a range of health risks including poor air quality from rising vehicle use, watershed pollution, and a built environment that limits opportunities to walk from homes to businesses and schools, thereby exacerbating obesity and related medical problems, such as heart disease."[105]

"You would think you'd have less congestion and cleaner air in the suburbs," notes Reid Ewing, an associate and research professor at the University of Maryland National Center for Smart Growth Research and Education. "But people drive so much more in sprawling areas that they offset the benefits of dispersal. We found ozone levels were higher and congestion was about the same, largely due to these offsetting effects."

Culprit commuters are among the chief victims of suburban pollution, since some of the worst air accumulates inside their cars. Brett Hulsey, a transportation expert at the Sierra Club, notes that people who drive for hours every day "are stuck in a plume of cancer-causing chemicals" that come from the cars around them. "So, what we're saying is that more sprawl equals more driving, and that more driving equals greater health risk. Therefore, sprawl and health risks are related."[106]

So, the longer your commute, the less healthy you'll be and the more you're likely to weigh. To people who design and plan and build the places we live, that would seem to be reason enough to design, plan and build neighborhoods that encourage walking, with shops and offices, parks and schools and houses within easy walking distance and with streets that discourage drivers from mowing down the pedestrians. That was Peter Calthorpe's hope back in 1986 when the California architect and planner proposed that the nation change its way of thinking about suburban growth. "We are still building World War II suburbs as if families were large and had only one breadwinner," Calthorpe wrote in Whole Earth Review, "as if the jobs were all downtown, as if land and energy were endless, and as if another lane on the freeway would end traffic congestion."

Calthorpe's solution was to build what he called "pedestrian pockets," clusters of housing, retail space, and offices, all within a quarter-mile walking radius of a light rail system. In effect, these would be New Villages on a mini-scale. "The convenience of the car and the opportunity to walk would be blended in an environment in which the economic engine of new growth, jobs in the service and information industry, would be balanced with affordable housing and local stores," Calthorpe said.[107]

That is the simple lesson that New Village designers are applying, in both urban and rural settings. Build it close enough and they will walk to it. Build enough dwelling units within walking distance of enough destinations and the dwelling units will be sold and the destinations will be filled. Shops will make sales, schools will be attended, movie popcorn and restaurant meals will be consumed, doctor appointments will be kept. Community will thrive.

Or there is another way.

We can turn the automobile destinations of suburbia into walking places. In the Buffalo suburb of Cheektowaga, as in hundreds of suburbs, we can join the Mall Walkers Club. We are invited to "join your friends and neighbors at Walden Galleria for healthful walking at your own pace in climate controlled comfort." We may take a brisk turn around Gordon's Jewelers and Pottery Barn. We may stroll past the International Food Court where Cynthia Wiggins used to work until she got run over by a dump truck trying to get there.

This is what most of suburbia offers in the way of "walkability" – the shopping mall, the place social critic Carole Rifkind considers "a virtually impervious barrier to social mingling," a non-place in which "consumption replaces community as a means of identification."[108] Indeed, mall walkers like to get there early, before the stores open, so they won't bump into a lot of strangers. It's like walking around in a giant television set that plays only commercials. Dogs and bicycles are not welcome.

Bicyclists bemoan the lack of connectivity in postwar suburban neighborhoods such as these, near Fairfax, Virginia, since their cul-de-sacs are roads to nowhere.

Photo by John S. Allen at www.bikexprt.com

CHAPTER SIX

Parks, Lakes, Greenways and Wary Environmentalists

At Seaside – generally considered the first New Urbanist development – and to a lesser extent at Disney's Celebration, developers assumed that nostalgia would provide an immediate "sense of place," it would thereby serve as a principal selling point for their self-contained living places. Led by the ingenious architectural team of Andrés Duany and Elizabeth Plater-Zyberk, the highly vocal New Urbanist movement has preached a gospel of return to "the good old days." Consequently, the New Urbanists call their master-planned developments TNDs – for "Traditional Neighborhood Developments" – forgetting that for most of us, "traditional neighborhoods" were postwar lawn farms, the very places New Urbanists urge us to reject. What America really craves is not something old but something new to many of us, a brand new day of community.

That craving is like a vein of gold to marketers, and a new breed of land developer has emerged to mine it. Their most powerful tool is not nostalgia; it is the creation of an organized system to get people instantly *involved* in their new neighborhood. Programs already in place – such as sports, clubs, activities, outreach opportunities – spell "community" to a prospective buyer. Increasingly, such programs depend on access to the natural environment, the very environment that a New Village developer must begin by disturbing. Whether it's envisioned as a replacement for an inner-city slum or a start-from-scratch master plan on the outskirts of town, any such development is going to have an impact on the landscape.

BUILDING GREEN.

In the jargon of planners, architects and builders, the shorthand for "environment-friendly" is simply: *green*. If a building or a housing development is "green," it takes advantage of recycling and energy-conservation options, it minimizes water usage, it avoids polluting the groundwater. Its footprint falls lightly as possible on the earth. It demonstrates a profound respect for the land on which it is built and for the waterways which nourish and drain it.

Whether they are built in blue states or red states, as the 2004 election taught us to see ourselves, emerging New Villages are almost universally green. While much of their greenness has to do with technological advances in plumbing and more scientific approaches to land management, New Villages generally intend to help their residents commune with nature in some fashion. New Villages almost always include trails for hiking or walking or biking, along with small lakes or ponds, and lots of parks. Often, the "natural areas" – in which nature is nearly always assisted by the developer – can serve as buffers between the New Village and surrounding property. Even neighbors who do not own or rent within the New Village often feel invited to enjoy the walkways, parks and lakes, and they will become shoppers and diners at the village's commercial center. In fact, of all the amenities they provide, this access to the environment may provide the highest rate of return for developers. From one end of the continent to the other, astute developers are seeing "green" as the color of money.

It is surprising that it's taken most developers so long to figure this out. For decades, contact with the natural environment has been the home seeker's number-one desired commodity. The late Charles Fraser, founder of South Carolina's master-planned resort, Sea Pines Plantation, identified nature as the top attraction for Hilton Head Island as early as 1956. Fraser started The Heritage golf tournament on Hilton Head in 1969, but often told friends that more people came to walk the trails and beaches than ever came to ride the golf carts – though anyone who's ever visited the island during a golf tournament weekend might argue with Fraser on that one.

Hilton Head, twelve miles long and five miles wide, now bills itself as "the first Eco-planned destination in the United States." Its salt marshes alive with fiddler crabs and night herons, its lagoons shaded by moss-bearded oaks, its wild magnolias and palmettos clearly pay their way. Not nearly so much money would be spent in Hilton Head restaurants and on Hilton Head condos if those "amenities" had been traded for more golf courses, houses, condos, tourist shops and tennis courts. At Hilton Head, green is gold.

A developer who visits Hilton Head should have no doubt of the value lying dormant in the environment, especially if trails can be made through land that would otherwise not be developable, either due to environmental regulations or prohibitive cost. As for simple open public spaces, a New Village developer can simply subtract a few square feet of backyard from each home site and add those square feet together in a common greensward, pocket park or playground, thereby sowing the seeds of community. Hilton Head's Fraser was also an advisor to the Celebration team of planners, and Todd Mansfield remembers how much he "challenged and inspired us to work *with* nature."

One of the most aggressive marketers of community, the St. Joe Company, is Florida's largest private landowner. To serve as "the essence of community" in their New Village of SouthWood, located on the (through that time) wrong side of the tracks in Tallahassee, St. Joe created the position of Art of Living Director, hiring Mary Lee Kiracofe, an award-winning teacher of English and student government at a Tallahassee high school and a former organizer of events for the city's Chamber of Commerce. A vivacious and compelling presenter, Kiracofe has duties that range from helping homebuyers close on their property to being the one-woman Welcome Wagon to signing up volunteers for helping-hand projects.

At the New Village of SouthWood in Tallahassee, where Mary Lee Kiracofe plans events to bring people together, Nature-with-a-capital-N is one of the big attractions. "I try to present involvement opportunities simply and in a lighthearted fashion," she says. As an example she cites an upcoming class called "Living with Wild Neighbors," in which wildlife biologists working for the developer, St. Joe Towns and Resorts, "will be here to explain about the coyotes, snakes, hawks, otters, and so forth that people may encounter in the green space around their homes. A local natural history museum is bringing live animals from their traveling exhibit as well."

While Kiracofe is not above playing the nostalgia card, especially to retirement-bound Midwesterners ("It reminds them of where they grew up: sidewalks, houses sitting above the street; alleys, and so forth."), she says the really big draws are nature and community. "The buyers want to know their neighbors," she says, "so they can begin making friends. The best comment I've heard is, 'Our house isn't even finished but we already know more people in SouthWood than we ever knew in our current neighborhood.' …They love the shared green space, which is close to a thousand acres."

Mary Lee Kiracofe's slide program ends with one of her favorite comments from happy SouthWooders: "We could begin with the radiant colors of the sunset reflected on the lakes, or we could speak of the majestic oaks with their cooling shade and myriad wildlife," say Ann and Preston Leftwich. "We could share stories of our wonderful experiences with new friends on the golf course. And we do. But we usually start with the community spirit of SouthWood."

TURNING REGULATORY LEMONS INTO COMMUNITY LEMONADE STANDS.

At SouthWood, as at many other New Village-type developments, community begins in spaces left vacant by the developers, spaces that in times past would almost certainly have been filled by more "housing units." Short-sighted developers have assumed for years that by leaving empty space they would be cheating themselves out of profits. Thanks in large part to the environmentalist movement, many developers are beginning to appreciate the color green.

This appreciation has been a long time coming, and much of the real estate industry has required force-feeding to swallow the idea. It started with the Clean Water Act of 1973, which for the first time regulated what could be dumped into the nation's rivers, streams, lakes and harbors. The CWA regulated what's called "point source" pollution; if you had a factory or any sort of pipe emptying into the water or into the ground, you had to have a permit and were subject to heavy fines for pollution. The Environmental Protection Agency, which administers the CWA, amended the act in 1987 and added regulations covering "non-point source" pollution, meaning anything from rainwater on rooftops to animal waste on pavement that could run off and ultimately make its way to a river, lake or ocean. Those regulations were fully phased in by 2003, requiring stormwater discharge permits for all municipalities, industrial dischargers, construction sites of one acre or greater, school districts and other large property owners. If a developer builds a neighborhood or a shopping center, he or she now must protect local waterways from pollution.

In days gone by, water from heavy rains was generally "conveyed" by a system of impervious gutters and underground pipes to some sort of collection place – usually one of those rivers, lakes or oceans. The environmentalists changed all that, creating new headaches and expenses for developers. But savvy developers have used the environmental regulations as an impetus to create green spaces, oases of one sort or another that cultivate community. Often, especially in suburban New Villages, they build stormwater retention ponds to capture and filter runoff and dub them lakes. Thus at Rancho Santa Maria in Orange County, California, Lake Park surrounds a manmade lake.[109] Thus ducks entertain children at the engineered Lake Kittamaqundi, the liquid heart of Columbia, Maryland.[110] Thus 65 acres of lakes, built over a ten-year period, are one of the biggest lures at Laguna West in South Sacramento County.[111] Thus a lake and wetlands were drawn up by Duany Plater-Zyberk as the defining elements of Kentlands' 350 acres in Maryland.[112]

Baldwin Park, formerly the Orlando Naval Training Center, is a 1200-acre New Village in the heart of downtown Orlando. Developed by Celebration veteran David Pace, Baldwin Park presented an enormous environmental challenge in storm water management. "The Navy was a terrible steward of the environment," Perry Reader, who competed for the development rights, says. "They just buried old airplane parts." The environmental impact statement was the "worst environmental report I've ever seen." The bottom of the existing drainage pond was lined with heavy metals, toxins and PCBs. The toxins are deemed harmless if left undisturbed. However, the developers could not get a permit to haul away the countless tons of concrete from the old base buildings. "It would have taken every truck in Orange County three months working 24/7," says Reader. Instead, the developer buried most of the concrete to form underground drainage streams for storm water runoff, another example of environmental regulatory necessity giving birth to environmentally protective invention.

In Arizona, a neglected, even abused waterway has energized efforts for a park that could eventually connect the cities of Phoenix, Tempe and Scottsdale, offering recreational opportunities and enabling community. The formerly junked and blighted strip of the Salt River bed has found a new life as a 595-acre nature preserve and city park, the

Salado Habitat Restoration Project. By carving a low-flow channel into the riverbed, Phoenix will improve its storm drainage system and flood control, thereby qualifying for a federal grant which funds 65 percent of the project through the U.S. Army Corps of Engineers. Eventually, the former habitat of discarded tires and assorted junk will bring about 75,000 trees and shrubs native to the Sonoran Desert and riparian habitats, attracting more than 100 species of birds, along with lizards, coyotes, javelina and beavers.[113]

Atlanta's reputation for overcrowding, sprawl and ecological rapine has brought the wrath of environmental agencies down hard on would-be developers. Post Properties then-CEO John Williams used the regulations against polluting the air and water as limits within which he could create a New Village called Riverside. Developed on the high banks of the Chattahoochee River, Riverside occupies what was one of the last pristine parcels of land in Atlanta. A conservation buffer along the river's 40-degree-sloped bank assures that the rocky outcrops and thick woods aren't going anywhere, but behind those trees and rocks sits a town square, stores, restaurants, offices, parking decks and a gated residential area of 521 rental apartments and six condominium townhouses.

Riverside might never have happened had not a Post Properties development manager attended a lecture and experienced what he described as an "epiphany" about the tenets of New Urbanism as a cure for Atlanta's sprawl and air pollution.[114] Despite the fact that Riverside is accessible only by car, once inside residents can and do walk within the 49-acre compound. *Atlanta Business Constitution* calls Riverside a working laboratory for residents of the community of the future.[115] Its green border creates an oasis in a concrete desert, and once inside one is reluctant to leave.

Meanwhile, in the far Northwest, Seattle's Housing Authority is breaking new ground in its efforts to improve water quality as it improves neighborhoods. High Point, the 1600-unit urban New Village in West Seattle, has spongey concrete that soaks up rainwater, drainage ditches that look like gardens, and gutters that carry rainwater from rooftops to landscaped park areas. Other city neighborhoods are being retrofitted with everything from recycled-tire sidewalks to cascading artificial streams instead of storm drains, and the positive response from residents has builders and developers spending extra hours at their drawing boards. "Not every builder understands it and not

With its porous pavement, its wide and heavily planted street swales and its carefully designed runoff pond, the 120-acre New Village of High Point has become one of the nation's largest man-made natural drainage systems. Bald eagles and other wildlife feel at home here.

Photos by George Nemeth and SvR Design for Seattle Housing Authority every builder is doing it, but there's interest in the industry," says Tim Attebery of the Master Builders Association of King and Snohomish Counties. "Like anything that is a new development strategy, people are going to ease into it."[116]

ENVIRONMENTALIST VS. ENVIRONMENTALIST.

Human-built or human-enhanced waterholes and streams nearly always suggest land areas for human access, that is to say, parks and walkways and paths and playgrounds. These "greenspace amenities," in builder parlance, are viewed by residents and prospective residents as places meant for recreation and community. What may have started out in the developer's mind as an expensive, government-ordered nuisance becomes the signature marketing piece in his sales brochure. The perceived enemy, the environmentalists, has given him and his homebuyers places for walking dogs, throwing Frisbees, playing with the kids, enjoying a picnic. In the 21st century, "building green" – working with rather than against nature and the environment – is a fact of life.

The Council of Educators in Landscape Architecture (CELA) offers its support. "Socially, ecological infrastructure enhances a community's topographic diversity and recreational opportunities. It connects people to nature by providing evidence of belonging to a larger natural cycle. In addition, wetland vegetation, grassed swales, and increases in green space enhance air quality and can often improve the visual aesthetics of community."[117]

Consider Terramor, the fifth New Village to be developed in Orange County, California's Ladera Ranch. The developers did their homework and found an underserved target market of homebuyers who wanted "tightly knit, socially progressive neighborhoods that have a strong green orientation and that are not focused around automobile use."[118] In Terramor they designed two neighborhoods built around central open spaces, meant for doing things together. The two neighborhoods are linked by an open-space corridor that serves as the "central pedestrian and activity spine of the village." The village is tightly knit, preeminently walkable, and visually stimulating, with a network of arroyos, paseos, courtyards and greens, all landscaped (xeriscaped, actually) with native, drought-resistant plants. The paseos connect to a ten-mile trail that encircles the community and provides access to the 1,600 acres of preserved open space. Other trails allow neighbors to walk together anywhere in Ladera Ranch – to other villages, to community parks, village clubs and retail centers. The continuously flowing Sienna Botanica is built for draining and filtering runoff from Village neighborhoods. But for the Southern California flora, architecture and weather, one might be back in England's Cotswolds. In Terramor as in Minchinhampton, green spaces provide a sense of place.

Rarely does a typical postwar suburban neighborhood provide that kind of green space. In new developments of that size, the economy doesn't work; a builder cannot make enough profit selling a dozen or so houses to justify the expense of holding back a patch of ground for a park or a playground. For this reason, bigger developments are often kinder to the environment than smaller ones. The logic is simple enough and unassailable.

To build a large-scale multi-use project – call it MegaVillage – a developer must win approval of a number of government agencies, often in multiple jurisdictions. Both those agencies and the developer's inevitable opposition will look more closely at its environmental impact than at any other aspect of the plan. Ergo, the developer should be able to convince agencies and the public that his MegaVillage will actually enhance the environment rather than injure it. It will ensure the preservation of wild areas; it will afford the public access to those areas; it will protect rivers and streams… and so forth. Allowing that land to be split up in 50- and 60-acre blocks of Olde Meadows and Garden Gables subdivisions will provide none of the above.

More than a few planners and developers miss the point. And even when MegaVillage is properly designed and presented, the environmentalists and environment-related agencies often make the loudest protests. As CELA puts it, "While considered by many to be an asset to a development, in terms of visual, recreational, and even financial value, such an aesthetic is often resisted by the public, planners, developers, and public works officials."[119]

The fact is that while supersized developments may be kinder to the environment than traditional cul-de-sacs and strip malls, their very size makes them suspect. Consider the fate of Joshua Hills, a New Village cluster intended to create a 9,000-acre self-contained human habitat in California's Riverside County. "Biological corridors" would be dedicated in perpetuity to ensure the connection between nearby Coachella Valley Preserve and Joshua Tree National Park. A university, a trade center, an information technology center, a resort complex, 7,000 homes and all the usual amenities of New Village living were on the drawing board of California Intelligent Communities, headed by long-time Coachella Valley developer and one-time Indian Wells mayor Richard Oliphant. Joshua Hills, Oliphant proclaimed, was sure to be greeted with "widespread acceptance and acclaim."[120]

Less than eighteen months later, those plans all were washed away in a deluge of environmentalist opposition. The bighorn sheep and desert kit foxes would have their habitats irreparably disturbed. Wind-blown sand would be prevented from piling up, thus depleting some of the area's last active sand dunes, which might spell curtains for the Palm Springs pocket mouse and the giant sand treader cricket. Joshua Hills would, "essentially be the nail in the coffin for all of these species," said Coachella Valley Preserve Director Cameron Barrows, who called the plan "a very serious threat."[121] In September 2004, Oliphant sold half his land to The Nature Conservancy and the Coachella Valley Mountains Conservancy.[122]

FOR THE SAVVY DEVELOPER, IT'S EASY BEING GREEN.

Sometimes we want our parks and waterways without the distraction of houses. But when we put them together, we create green and golden opportunities for community. And because community has become a marketable commodity, parks and waterways are being integrated into virtually every new master-planned development in the United States.

When Urban Land Institute member Steven Kellenberg, of EDAW, an international land-planning firm, interviewed developers and builders in 2004, he learned that large-scale developers are "pursuing green" for four reasons. First, because it improves their public and civic image; second, because it speeds up the approval process by government agencies; third, because it fills an unmet market demand; and fourth, because it simply is the right thing to do.[123] Kellenberg's ULI report cites Nevada developer Landon Christopherson as representing the trend. "Green development is appealing because it is development for the future, not just today," says the head of the Landwell Company.

"Many people like to be associated with projects or developments that are forward-thinking and environmentally sound. Indeed, there is satisfaction and value from doing the right thing, both on the part of the developer/builder and the homebuyer."

Often the feared "expense" of green spaces in a new development can be offset simply by building homes closer together than in typical suburban neighborhoods. Certainly in the Southeastern United States, the number of homes per acre increases as the amount of accessible public land goes up. In Celebration, where there are parks, greenswards, playgrounds and ball fields everywhere, the lots average just 40x100 feet. Todd Mansfield is particularly proud of one soccer field that's surrounded by Central Florida scrub.

New Village children learn to coexist with the environment at this wetlands nature preserve in Issaquah Highlands, Washington.

Used by permission of Port Blakely Communities (Issaquah Highlands, Washington)

Celebration's undisturbed wetlands provide buffers against encroaching civilization as well as opportunities for discovery. During the project's early stages, Todd wore night goggles and watched the nocturnal gators frisk. Before the Disney developers arrived, hunting had been the chief interest in the land that became Celebration. Disney executives used it as a private preserve for shooting turkeys, and several of the game enthusiasts campaigned against building the town for that reason. The big turkeys are still there, gobbling and strutting at the edges, but the hunters are gone.

In an entirely different environment, the Arizona desert, John and Robbie Henrickson walk their golden retriever through washes shaded by tall saguaro cactus, thick with scruffy creosote bushes, with desert tobacco and twinberry, all abloom in the springtime. Ironwood trees line the washes, resplendent in their May lilac. Bees work the flowers of the yellow trumpet bush. John and Robbie – whom we met in Chapter One – married after college in Minnesota and moved here from Connecticut, having fallen in love with a "green" place that is rich in color yet far more brown and red and gray than green.

"We were very impressed with the physical layout, the vistas, the lack of walls," says John of the New Village called DC Ranch. "We wanted the space, the walking paths, the bike riding."

"This was our opportunity to live with nature," Robbie adds, "to be in nature."

In the wide Sonoran Desert, Nature can exact a toll. The DMB Corporation, developers of DC Ranch, left lots of habitat for skunks, lizards, tarantulas and javelina, also known as collared peccary. Consequently, the impossibly sharp thorns of the catclaw acacia sink like fishhooks into pants and bare legs. All part of the appeal to the Henricksons. "There's a respect and appreciation for nature here," says Robbie. "We think that DMB did so well with the space here." She points across the road to a more typically suburban development. "Even across the street at Grayhawk, there's the same land, but there's not the openness." In fact, we met several residents of Grayhawk who do their walking at DC Ranch.

"We see the same people walking their dogs," Robbie goes on. "We don't walk together, we meet them on the paths. You don't have to go to the park to walk the dog, because you're living in dog paradise. On Saturdays we go to the market, we see our favorite dog friends. We ride our mountain bikes down here too."

On the outskirts of the New Village, DMB deeded land to the city of Scottsdale, and the Henricksons were working as volunteers to make that land available to the public. "There's a trail being cut," John explains. "Some people from the city of Scottsdale are helping. It's physical work, cleaning land, making sure the land is not being improperly used."

Brent Herrington, Senior Vice President of DMB, came to Arizona after working as Celebration's Town Manager. "If you want to create a vibrant place," he believes, "you need to create spaces that encourage spontaneous interaction with others." Like most of the proponents of New Villages, New Urbanism and Smart Growth, Herrington feels regret, even embarrassment at the way urban sprawl has chewed away both the environment and the neighborliness of the United States over the last half-century.

"Somewhere along the way, the sense of the community got lost, especially with the sterile, vanilla aspect of the sunbelt cities. The great majority of people lived in these tract subdivisions. Driving through them, you saw streets you could fire a cannon down without risk of hitting anyone. I think visually there's this startling sameness – the parade of the garage. In the suburban Southwest, the vogue started in the 70s, the monochromatic color scheme, the same-color stucco everywhere, the vaguely-Spanish style; then came the crushed-granite xeriscape with the objectified cactus and tree. There was none of the physical and social vitality that you would have expected in a well-established neighborhood, just a civic anemia there for anyone to clearly see."

Open, inviting spaces unquestionably foster community. Robbie Henrickson found that out even before she moved in, taking advantage of the DC Ranch "Happy Trails Wagon," a trailer equipped with a large barbecue grill and all the other party amenities, an idea borrowed from Celebration. "You just sign up for it and hook it up to the car. We had a ground-breaking party when our house started to get built, we used the trailer. We had sand candles, luminaries, with the actual ground from the ground-breaking in the bag. Then we did a Lumberman's Lunch when the framing was done, for all the workers, the builders, the architects, the interior designers, everybody."

"At the picnic a year ago," John adds, "we had about 55 families, lots of kids, from all around the neighborhood. The week that we were doing that, Robbie's mother died, but the neighbors were able to take it over really easily. You don't get that in other places. It was a full gathering; the neighbors helped set up, everyone brought something, it was just great."

"That's the village lifestyle." Brent Herrington warms to his subject. "When a neighborhood is big enough, it will create small villages. Villages tend to poly-nucleate. They create many small centers, in addition to the one 'central' center. People will congregate, affiliate with each other in small tight circles, and then radiate outwards from there."

Just another way of saying: Build a park and people will party.

CHAPTER SEVEN
Children in Paradise

"It's the perfect neighborhood – lots of kids!"

In all the sociological treatises on humanity's abandonment of the inner city for its ever-lengthening outskirts, children are rarely mentioned as the root cause of urban sprawl. Yet time and again they have been the reason for our moves. Better schools, safer neighborhoods, more playmates, the "right sort" of families – those characteristics generate desirability in a neighborhood. While we have persistently overlooked the importance of community for us as adults, we seem to have consciously pursued it for our children.

Which perhaps is as it should be. As noted earlier, a preponderance of scientific evidence demonstrates that children are born with a physical need to connect to other human beings. We are "biologically primed" to find meaning in life through connectivity to others. That connectivity forms first of all within the family, our initial experience with what we call "community." Beyond family, children seek connection in play groups and at school. None of that comes as any surprise. The surprising thing is that it hasn't really worked very well. American childhood is in crisis, according to the scientists, doctors, scholars and youth service professionals comprising the Commission on Children at Risk. And they declared in 2003 that the cause of this crisis is "a lack of connectedness… close connections to other people and deep connections to moral and spiritual meaning."[124]

By the time children get to college, suggests the journal *Psychology Today*, "psychological distress is rampant… It takes a variety of forms, including anxiety and depression – which are increasingly regarded as two faces of the same coin – binge drinking and substance abuse, self-mutilation and other forms of disconnection. The mental state of students is now so precarious for so many that, says Steven Hyman, provost of Harvard University and former director of the National Institute of Mental Health, 'it is interfering with the core mission of the university.'"[125]

The Commission on Children at Risk proposed as a solution to the "crisis of childhood" a campaign to renew and build community among "groups of people who are committed to one another over time and who model and pass on [to children] what it means to be a good person and live a good life."[126] Meanwhile, as we saw in Chapter Two, universities around the country are doing their best to convert dormitories into places of community. Rutgers University, for example, has nine of these "living-learning communities" to help students connect on a campus of 35,000 students.

One student at the Rutgers dormitory now called Human Rights House told *The New York Times*, "When you come to a university that is so big, you really need to find people who are passionate about the same things you are... We all try to create a sense of community here." Explains George D. Kuh, a professor of higher education at Indiana University, Bloomington, and director of the National Survey of Student Engagement, "You create pockets all around campus that strengthen social bonds between students, which keeps them in school."[127]

RAISING CHILDREN IN NEW VILLAGES AND BIG CITIES.

The reason commissions and colleges are arguing for community is that as a nation – that is to say, as families – we have failed to provide community for too many of our children. As we moved our homes ever further from our places of employment (to give our children "better neighborhoods"), and as we converted from one-income to two-income households (to afford those bigger houses and to give our children "greater advantages"), we began undermining our children's sense of connectedness. We allotted fewer and fewer hours to family togetherness. Then, with parents spending so much time on the job and on the road, children lost their free time as well, time their predecessors had used to build play-group relationships.

As we agonized over grades and achievement, schools became what *Psychology Today* terms "hothouses" of child rearing. Time together in the schoolyard – where once some of childhood's fondest memories were constructed – became, to a preponderance of parents and educators, time wasted. Consequently, more than 40,000 schools in the United States have completely done away with recess. "Play is all but dead," laments *Psychology Today* editor Hara Estroff Marano. "And what play there is has been corrupted. The organized sports many kids participate in are managed by adults; difficulties that arise are not worked out by kids but adjudicated by adult referees." Marano warns that children denied the basic skills of community-building become ill equipped for normal life. We are raising, she maintains, a psychologically fragile, anxiety riddled "nation of wimps."[128]

Perhaps hard-working parents have too little time themselves to read all these magazine articles and reports, but somehow the word is spreading that children require places to live that they can make their own. Our children need the sort of environments that villages used to provide. The anecdotal evidence available thus far suggests that the New Village movement is indeed providing what children need.

The village life makes parents comfortable with kids getting to know their neighbors, and with walking to neighborhood shops like this one, which specializes in kids' meals.

Used by permission of Port Blakely Communities (Issaquah Highlands, Washington)

As a working mother, Ann Whelan raised her own two children in a typical postwar suburb of San Francisco. Although the kids spent a lot of time in day care, Ann figured she was doing the best she could for her family. Then her son and daughter's nursery became the center of California's largest child-abuse scandal.

Ann's daughter, Jennifer, carried the scars of that experience into adulthood. She promised herself that under no circumstances would she ever leave a child of her own in the care of strangers. By the time that child came along in September 2002, Jennifer had relocated to Central Florida to pursue a career with the Marriott Corporation. Without giving it a second thought, Ann left her West Coast life behind her. She sold her house and moved into a mother-in-law apartment over the garage of Jennifer and husband Max Elson's new home in Celebration. Her new career: full-time nanny to grandson Brooks, in a place very different from where she raised her own kids.

"What will it mean for my grandson to grow up here?" Ann asks herself. "I think he'll believe the world is very safe. Celebration is so low-crime, he'll have the freedom to not lock the door, and he'll grow up being very active as a result of that." Ann and Jennifer and Max chose a New Village for the sake of Brooks's security. What they discovered was community.

Being a part of a place, identifying with the people around her, getting involved in the life of her neighborhood – all these things have taken Ann's mind off the reason she moved across the country in the first place. She has replaced fear with friendship, and it seems likely that her grandson will reap the benefits of her new lease on life. In the farthest corner of the contiguous United States, Ann Whelan's hopes for her grandson are echoed by Sheri Moore, raising her grandson in the New Village of High Point, Seattle. "You know your neighbors here, and you talk to their kids and they talk to your kids. That's what a neighborhood's supposed to be, right?"

Not that New Villages have any monopoly on opportunities for kids. "I thought childhoods should be in small towns or the suburbs," wrote Sally Marshall in an article for *Newsweek*. "I expected that I'd be off to the 'burbs when I had a baby. But my husband believes Manhattan is the center of the universe, and I pretty much agree with him."

Raised in a Midwestern neighborhood where she rode her bike and knew all the neighbors' dogs by name, Marshall is proud that her five-year-old daughter, Coco, spends weekends in the city going to family concerts at Carnegie Hall, zoos, children's museums and the Metropolitan Museum of Art, and that her schoolmates are "an incredibly diverse group of kids."

And what about that sense of place, that feeling of belonging? We asked Sally Marshall whether Coco was really a part of her community. Her answer suggests that children may play a large role in breaking down the walls of big-city solitude, or what we call Community Deprivation Syndrome.

Marshall says that before Coco came into her life, "I was a typical big city resident who disliked talking to people in elevators and would barely break stride to chat with someone I knew on the street. When my mom came in from the Midwest, I found it odd that she'd chat with sales people, cashiers and other strangers." Then, when those same strangers began to stop to look at the little baby with the full head of black hair, "I instinctively thought, 'Why is this stranger talking to me?'"

Sally got over her isolation. "I know how important giving a child a sense of community is and feel a particular obligation to provide that, given that Coco lives in a city of eight million. New Yorkers' apartment buildings are their neighborhoods. Now that I'm a mom and a role model, I make a point of chatting with our neighbors when we see them in the building or on the street. People in the elevator and the doormen always chat with Coco. Coco once asked me, 'Why does everybody know my name?'"

At her health club where, formerly, Marshall might have jogged the treadmill with a blank expression as she listened to the music in her headset, now there is conversation. "I became friends with the parents who worked out regularly and Coco played with the children in the childcare room. My health club was my Cheers Bar where everybody knew Coco's and my names." When Coco got big enough for the playground, she and her mom made more friends. "For city kids and their parents, playgrounds are a community because you see the same kids and their parents or nannies all the time at the playground. I think it's a lot more fun and less lonely to be at a playground chatting with other moms than alone in a backyard watching one's kids on the swing set."

When Coco started school, life changed again for Sally Marshall. First she was elected vice president of the PTA. Then she and her husband joined a church. "By far, the greatest benefit of going to church is becoming part of a community," Sally says. "I didn't understand how much I was craving that."

Now Coco and her parents find themselves spreading neighborliness wherever they go. She says that initially people may be "put off," by her purposeful gregariousness, "but when they notice the pigtailed kindergartner next to me, they get it. Even the most jaded

New Yorker understands the importance of creating a community and being good neighbors when children are involved."

Although Marshall considers herself "a sophisticated New Yorker," and suggests that Coco is already pretty sophisticated herself, "I don't cringe at the Mr. Rogers song about 'Who are the people in your neighborhood?' I know first hand how belonging to a community enriches my life."

CAN TEENS FIND A PLACE FOR THEMSELVES?

Whether we choose a village someone has intentionally planned or make our own village within a big city, our children's lives as well as our own are enriched by community. Yet early in the New Village movement, as critics of every sort descended on Celebration, children, especially teenagers, became the focus of concern. Would a development so carefully engineered prevent teens from just "hanging out," from finding opportunities away from adult supervision to be themselves? The question seemed a good one, so as we visited one New Village after another we talked with teens – and their parents – about whether their chosen environment could be compatible with teen angst.

Tami Jenkins moved to the Orlando area from Pensacola in 2000, "looking for a place that was really a community, not just a busy highway." Tami and husband Michael were looking for "something like the town we grew up in, a place where everything is really close. We wanted a neighborhood, not just some houses."

Most of all, the Jenkinses wanted a change from insular suburbia for their two teenagers, Michelle and Sean. "We wanted the kids to be able to go out on their own, to a theater that plays the latest movies, a place where there are lots of things going on for young people. Sure, they'll still 'hang out,' and the boys will still watch and meet the girls, but they can do all this without leaving the neighborhood."

In her old neighborhood, Michelle Jenkins says, "I couldn't go out on my own. We just hung out at each others' houses. We rode the 'mom bus' to school, because even though school was close, it wasn't really safe for us to ride our bikes." When she moved to Celebration to begin eighth grade, Michelle had "a really easy time of making school friends.

They all introduced each other. Everyone was really friendly." And for younger brother Sean and the rest of the family, involvement in the wider community was just as easy. "On our street, we all do everything," Sean says. "We have street parties, block parties, we all do cookouts. Not everyone in town does that, it's our thing."

New Villages can provide recreation and social opportunities for teens – and make it possible for them to get around without help from their parents and automobiles.

Photo by George Nemeth for Seattle Housing Authority

The Jenkins kids might seem almost too good to be true: no teenage rebellion? No getting in trouble? Not even a bit of mischief? The disbelief is summarized by a twenty-eight-year-old from San Francisco, who identifies himself on his weblog only as "Jamison." While never having actually visited Celebration, Jamison knows it just could never work. "Something about this strikes me as really creepy… a prefab Disney town… Wouldn't this be like living in a tv show? It smacks of artificiality to me. What about crime? Drunk teenagers? Anything? What happens if things go against the cheery plan? Do the Disney bigwigs swoop in & make things right?"[129]

They do not.

Witness the distress of Celebration parents after two eight-year-old boys went at it with a can of bug spray. It was at a weekly Kids'

Night Out in October, 2004, sponsored by the Celebration Parks and Recreation Department. A boy we'll call Child A sprayed Off insect repellent on Child B's sandwich; prompting Child B to aim the spray at Child A's face. One of the four adult chaperones called 911 and a sheriff's deputy sirened up. This is the account one pieces together from angry parental venting on the Celebration Forum web site.[130] A father of one of the boys demanded that the town's Parks and Recreation manager be dismissed over the incident, and so he was. The manager got off his own Parthian shot in the Celebration web forum, regretting that "the situation has been blown into a huge ordeal" and that he had been fired out of "fear of that a parent will file a lawsuit against Town Hall."

By the time of the "Off Incident," the "Disney bigwigs" actually had very little involvement in Celebration. They had sold the town center, including Town Hall and management of its services to Lexin Capital, the private real estate investment firm. Lexin, at this writing, owns about eighteen acres of Celebration, including sixteen retail shops, six restaurants, more than 94,000 square feet of commercial office space, 105 private apartments and three land parcels. Disney still owns the office buildings near the hospital.[131]

For most of Celebration's residents, young and old, the transfer from Disney to Lexin has been uneventful. "Everybody thinks this is going to be a big deal, but it's not," said Heather Clayton, who lives in Celebration and owns the Lollipop Carriage children's clothing store on Market Street. "It's just a different name on the rent check." And no matter who manages the retail buildings, she says, the people who live in the village will be responsible for their own lives and the lives of their children. Most of the residents we spoke with would agree with Heather Clayton that this Central Florida New Village is "a modern-day Mayberry… a wonderful place to raise a family."

But, as other residents point out, not Utopia.

About the same time as the Off Incident, two older boys got into a fight in the courtyard at Celebration High. According to police records, the seventeen-year-old and the fifteen-year-old were smitten with the same girl. One of them sneaked a knife into school and the confrontation ended with the younger boy stabbed in the thigh.[132] Walt Disney was nowhere to be found, but there was a nearby hospital, Celebration Health, to treat the wound, and there was the Osceola

Sheriff's Department to deal with the offenders. Young people may be less likely to encounter crime, violence and other unpleasantness in a New Village, but no matter where we grow up, growing up is rarely a perfect process.

Celebration resident and parent Lee Moore believes the town's planners made a mistake by underestimating the number of people who would choose Celebration as the perfect place to raise their children. When it became obvious that the school-age population would soon exceed the capacity of Celebration School, he says, "Disney claimed to be surprised that so many families with children bought homes in Celebration. I don't know how you sell a town to families, and then don't expect the kids to move in. Disney should have built a bigger school from the start."

As Celebration and its child population matured, town executives met in 2002 with Osceola County school officials and developed a plan for the county to build a large high school inside Celebration. It would be called Celebration High, but it would be open to students from other parts of the county as well. The old Celebration School would restrict itself to teaching children only through eighth grade. By 2005 the high school had more than 1800 students enrolled, teaching English-as-second-language immigrant children as well as Advanced Placement classes.

"That is a sore spot, having all these kids from Osceola," Lee Moore complains. This despite the fact that Celebration High is among the top schools in Florida when it comes to students in a college preparation curriculum (67.3 percent as compared with a state average of 58.6 percent).[133] "Now we've got a mega-school. I am upset, that was an oversight that should never have happened… Obviously, Disney didn't want to run a school. I don't know what the answer was, but this is definitely a problem."

There are plenty of residents who disagree with Moore. Those include parents who fret over the homogeneity of Celebration – a chronic condition among New Villages. One does not require census data to observe the preponderance of the white upper middle class in most of them. At Celebration School, Eddie Smith was the only black kid in his class, though it seems not to have bothered him.

"We lived in several other places before we came here." Eddie sips a December evening beer at Celebration's Market Street Café. "I had friends in those other places, but they were spread out. I never really thought I was part of a *community* until I came to Celebration." His mother, Dawn Thomas, is having a strawberry smoothie. She is the talker in the family, but Eddie's admission is gratifying. After all, Eddie was the primary reason she moved here. Suddenly her son is telling stories she never heard.

"We did all the usual teenage rebellion stuff." Eddie lifts his beer, waving at a pretty white girl across the street, a former classmate. She waves back and tells her friends, "Look, it's Eddie." They all wave. His mother, Dawn Thomas, raises an eyebrow at that reference to rebellion, but she lets Eddie continue. "There was always construction going on back then, you know? We tipped over a lot of porta-potties."

"You did not!" Is Dawn truly surprised? Eddie is twenty-three now and a source of considerable pride to his mother.

"Well, we did other stuff… A couple of times we put soap in the big fountain by the movie theater."

Dawn: "That was *you*?"

"You know, some minor vandalism. Stuff kids do everywhere, we did here."

His mother is surprised that Eddie and his friends ever found a moment for vandalism. They always seemed under the watchful eye of some adult, as she always was growing up in her little village on the island of Trinidad. When Dawn moved at age nine with her mother and her accent to Brooklyn, she was treated as an outsider by African-American girls at her Flatbush school. Like her son, Dawn had found no sense of place in the United States until she moved to a New Village. "I wasn't sure what community meant," she says, "until I lived it."

Mother and son had shared apartments in Miami and in Orlando, but when he wasn't at home or in school Dawn was never sure what Eddie might be up to. In Celebration, Dawn got to meet Eddie's friends' parents for the first time. Moms and dads treated Eddie the way they treated their own kids, and they expected the same respect and behavior from him as from their own sons and daughters. The watchful care of these New Village neighbors reminded her of growing up in Trinidad.

"I could get away with very little back then, you know, with so many pairs of eyes on me all the time. There weren't phones in the village, but somehow if I did something bad, the news of it always reached my mother before I got home. It was the same here with Eddie.

People were always telling me how they had seen Eddie here or there, how they talked to him. And no matter where he went, they fed him!"

While the support of parents is a critical piece of community, no less critical is the willingness of the children themselves to embrace the new, the different, the inquisitive child into their group. As we watch Eddie Smith cross Market Street to reunite with his former school friends, it seems clear that these young adults are linked by a social bond they formed as children. Whether or not that accepting, open behavior was modeled by their parents, the children thrived in it. They grew up in an environment where kids could run around without fear of abduction. They could ride their bikes to school or to a movie theater without being hit by a car or remaining in constant cell-phone contact with a nervous parent. They could knock over portable toilets and put soap suds in the fountain. They could make mistakes and learn from them. They could, as *Psychology Today's* Marano puts it, "forge their creative adaptations to the normal vicissitudes of life," and thereby buck the trend of overprotected, risk-averse childhood, the "spreading psychic fault lines of 21ST-century youth."

If any inherent danger lurks in a village childhood, it is probably not excessive supervision; it is rather that with social networks so easily formed, children who would have a hard time fitting in anywhere may feel all the more isolated. Katherine S. Newman, a professor of urban studies at Harvard and co-author of *Rampage: The Social Roots*, observes that incidents of extreme teen violence invariably occur in relatively small towns where "church is important and everyone really does know your name." Newman cites the 1999 Columbine High School massacre in Littleton, Colorado, population 40,000, as well as Malcolm, Nebraska, population 437, where in March 2004 a seventeen-year-old boy got as far as the school parking lot toting a bolt-action rifle and twenty homemade bombs.

"For all their virtues," she writes, "small towns are hard on misfits. In big cities, oddballs might find like-minded friends, a comic-book clique or a band to hang out with." Such opportunities can be harder to find in villages. "Social networks overlap in small towns: your next-door neighbor is your former high-school classmate, your child's teacher, a church group leader and the fourth-grade baseball coach. If a child gets a bad reputation in one of these arenas, it spreads like wildfire to the others. As a result, misfits can feel like there is no exit from their misery… This means that adults – teachers, parents, coaches, counselors – need to remember that disaffected teenagers who get into minor scrapes or complain about being bullied may be more troubled than they appear."[134]

One possible solution to the problem of the misfit child is a tool being used to build community within New Villages and elsewhere: the internet. A kid who's into 17TH century English poetry or *Tom Strong* comics or particle physics or the evolution of hip-hop will find like-minded correspondents on the web. Even if his friends are not next door, he'll know he's not the only one like himself.

It's hard to overstate the importance of community and connectedness to children. There is probably no single environment that provides community for every child, but parents' willingness to search out that "perfect neighborhood" could be one of the three or four critical factors in their child's eventual success.

CHAPTER EIGHT

Civic Involvement and Following the Rules

When two young, disenchanted Frenchmen, Alexis de Tocqueville and Gustave de Beaumont, toured America in 1831, they visited cities and towns from Boston to Michigan to New Orleans, searching for the essence of the 55-year-old nation. Everywhere they found *engagement*. People involved themselves in village life, ordinary citizens took an active role in government, associations formed for civic improvement. As Tocqueville would later write in his two-volume *Democracy in America*, "In towns it is impossible to prevent men from assembling, getting excited together and forming sudden passionate resolves."

As the 20th century ran down, it seemed that the United States needed to be reminded of its involved, committed past. Consequently, Tocqueville's observations were dusted off by speech and editorial writers across the continent. In 1995, for example, he was quoted (and sometimes misquoted) by President Bill Clinton, House Speaker Newt Gingrich, Senator Jesse Helms and Ross Perot among others. Robert Putnam's *Bowling Alone* quoted the Frenchman in 2000, alerting us to the possibility that we might be losing what Tocqueville had found most valuable in the United States. Putnam's bowling leagues and their diminishing ranks were a metaphor for the country's defining institutions, especially the institution of government of and by the people.

"Towns are like great meeting houses with all the inhabitants as members," Tocqueville had written. "In them the people wield immense influence over their magistrates and often carry their desires into execution without intermediaries." And the lines Putnam loved best: "Americans of all ages, all stations of life, and all types of disposition are forever forming associations... In democratic countries knowledge of how to combine is the mother of all other forms of knowledge; on its progress depends that of all the others."

The ability to "combine" – that is, to build community – is the mother of all other forms of knowledge. While microbiologists, theologians and quantum physicists may take issue with that all-encompassing claim, we will agree that a viable democracy depends on the participation of individuals, and that such participation begins within their neighborhoods. This is what Tocqueville found to be essential and what Putnam entered on the endangered species list.

How we became disengaged from self-government is a complex question that involves perhaps every aspect of societal change over the past century and a half, from recorded music to the Cold War to the internet. Part of the reason is the simple physical distancing of ordinary families from seats of government. As "we" moved ever farther from the centers of city government, those responsible for that government became "they," individuals other than ourselves. ("They're putting in a new sewer line out to Brewston." "They say we're going to get higher electric rates.") As we permitted the federal government to assume ever more control over our daily lives, it became easier to retreat from responsibility. Life in the typical American suburb, as we have seen, became insular.

BUILDING-IN INVOLVEMENT.

The question de Tocqueville and Putnam pose is whether that insularity is *necessary*, or can we somehow regain that knowledge of how to combine? If we can, if it's not too late, then the reconstruction of civic responsibility ought to make its initial appearance at the neighborhood or village level. When the geographical boundaries are daunting – from sea to shining sea in America's case – we tend to feel powerless, but when we think of the town square out to the baseball field we believe we can get something accomplished.

Likewise, living in a changeable environment makes a difference. When our neighborhood consists only of houses filled with families a lot like our own, as in most American suburbs, there's rarely much that requires our concerted attention. But when the neighborhood includes shopkeepers, parks and trails, a school, a hospital and assorted public sites, issues abound. Should the movie theater be required to show only kid-friendly films? How can we get the sheriff to make regular safety patrols? Is the apartment building dumping trash illegally? Can we provide free charging stations for electric vehicles? Can we keep the basketball court open until midnight?

Issues such as those get people to "combine" in the very sort of associations that Tocqueville found so refreshing in America, and those are the sorts of issues rising each day in America's New Villages. Without really intending to – at least in the beginning – the architects and developers of these villages have constructed laboratories of democracy. These small towns filled mostly with formerly apathetic citizens have become Tocqueville's "great meeting houses with all the inhabitants as members."

In prototypical Celebration, this certainly was not a goal early on. Todd Mansfield and his group saw The Walt Disney Company more as a benevolent dictator than as a patron of self-government. Celebration's Uncle Sam wore Mouse ears. In 1994 Disney set the rules and you had to agree that you would abide by those rules even before you put your name in the lottery to buy a house. Later, this became the model for many other New Villages. On its face, that attitude presupposes a degree of passivity among residents, along with their shared belief in the principles behind the rules. In point of fact, the Disney team believed that a majority of prospective homeowners would be grateful to have these rules imposed; many had experienced, as members of suburban neighborhood associations, the frustration of watching weeds grow in the shadow of an RV parked in a neighbor's yard.

Yet as time passed and as Celebration and its emulators grew, several of the Disney rules were challenged, some were changed and others simply went away. Residents of these benevolent dictatorships found that while they may have signed away their independence, they gained *interdependence*. All the members of the community depended upon one another and upon the management company… and the management company depended upon them. Only by working together could they truly maintain the way of life they'd bought into.

"We are aware of one another," Celebration resident Ann Whelan explains. "If you see someone doing something that isn't right, you go up and talk to them. You ask people to their face to go pick up their dog-doo. People are embarrassed *not* to do the right thing here." An appreciation of community, of its benefits and obligations, may spell the end of apathy.

WHEN RESIDENTS TAKE RESPONSIBILITY, EVERYONE IS DRAWN IN.

The nearest thing to a mayor in Celebration is Pat Wasson, the former president of the Community Associations Institute. She left that job in 1997 to become Executive Director of the New Village Disney built. At Celebration, Wasson is responsible for making decisions regarding Town Center and other parts of the New Village not owned by residents. Disney still owns some of the office buildings, but sold the rest to Lexin Capital Consultants, which is now Wasson's employer, not the citizens of Celebration. Yet a large part of her job involves negotiating with the strong-minded residents and business owners, a change she helped engineer.

Wasson says that when she was hired in 1998, the moment was ripe "to really bring the homeowners into the governance. It was time to let the residents start setting up the committees and become involved with the town architect, to establish a covenants committee." The covenants committee is "like a tribunal," says Wasson. While "90 percent of our issues are solved with one phone call" from Wasson or one of her assistants at Town Hall, "if someone disagrees, they have a right to a hearing, and they go before the covenants committee."

Pat Wasson meets New Village neighbors and civic-minded citizens at Celebration's Michael Graves-designed post office.

Photo by the authors

She cites the case of a woman who was operating a hair salon in her home in violation of the covenant she had signed when she first bought her house. Someone filed a complaint, but others came to the woman's defense. "Her neighbors came before the covenants committee and lobbied for her, saying there was ample parking where she was living." The hairdresser received a variance allowing her to continue for six months, "and if no one complained in that time, then she could keep going." Another example of living where you work.

At Scottsdale's DC Ranch, management oversees several residents' and shopkeepers' groups that handle what would normally be government chores. The Telecommunity Council maintains content and quality of the intranet and negotiates with ISP Qwest. The Homeowners' Association gets involved with gardens and lawns and parks, but not with enforcement; that job falls to the Covenant Commission. Those three groups report to the Community Council, on which the developer-paid Town Manager sits ex officio. There is no shortage of residents willing to serve on any of these governance groups.

Melinda Gulick, who took over as management of the triangular Town Center in April of 2004, says her job mostly involves "fostering relationships so you don't get fights." So far, she says, DC Ranch has recorded only two such fights – one involving unclaimed dog droppings, the other involving an "adult entertainment entrepreneur" prone to wild late-night parties. The dog owner was persuaded to pick up after his pet, while the porn merchant was persuaded that he'd moved into the wrong village.

"Our governance model is not one of rules and hierarchies," Gulick told us over lunch at the village's San Felipe Mexican Restaurant. "We get people to deal with one another. We bring them together. If they can build a relationship today, they will avoid conflict in the future. You have to kind of force people and neighbors to talk to each other. We place a real emphasis on relationships. We make relationships with the residents to enable them to make relationships with one another."

That process is not so unlike what happens in any small town or village. It is the way things got done in Jersey Homesteads, New Jersey, one of the "Greenbelt Towns" that grew as social experiments out of the Great Depression. Jersey Homesteads was formed as a "cooperative colony" in 1936 and run by the U.S. Department of the Interior, with strict rules for getting in and staying in, but really it was run by the people who lived there, who called themselves colonists.

The 1938 *Stories of New Jersey* by the Federal Writers' Project says of the town: "The colony is run on the same democratic principles as a club, each member having only one vote. To date only two families have dropped their membership." By 1938 Jersey Homesteads had incorporated as a borough with its own mayor and council. In a later essay, Pearl Seligman, who grew up in the town that changed its name to Roosevelt after the president's death, concluded that it had "proved to be a roaring success as a model for transforming housing into community and thereby transforming lives." Much of that success, Seligman believed, was on account of the unusual level of civic involvement that became possible in a village:

> [B]y far the most dignifying, life-defining occupation the village gave those workers was the responsibility for governing themselves in their own community. That governance engaged them as full people, ennobling them with the activities of citizenship. It is complicated, and it takes a lot of energy, to govern even a small town. Sooner or later, Roosevelt's citizens serve in some public activity: on the school board, the planning board, the borough council, the environmental commission, as a volunteer fireman or on the ambulance squad, in the PTA, the art association, the senior citizens club, the nursery school board, the food co-op, the historical commission, a political action group, the Little League. Eventually, everyone is drawn into active town life by anger, gregariousness or conviction of how things should be done. And, eventually, argument and ideology wind up in the town's budget and its taxes, yes or no to a new well, water-tower, sewage plant and road repairs, school administration, zoning ordinances, master plans. It's just a matter of scale from the politics of a village to that of a city. [135]

MAKING THEIR VOICES HEARD.

But the difference in scale as one goes from neighborhood to city and state governance can prove daunting. To whom, for example, would a resident of Cincinnati complain about the lack of a grocery store to walk to? Even in New Villages, that is the sort of complaint most common and most frustrating for developers and managers. Their residents clamor for a grocery, a hardware store, a pharmacy, but mom-and-pop enterprise has been all but exterminated by big chain operations, for whom the village market is too small for consideration. Consequently, many New Villages struggle to build enough commercial destinations for a determined walker.

"I'd like a hardware store," sighs Lynn Sands of Celebration. "Maybe a nice bakery, some Chinese food." In addition to a deficiency of shopping opportunities, New Villagers sometimes lament the limited opportunities for social engagement. While a few civic and social organizations may be established from the outset by management, others are left to the resident to organize and maintain. This was how the Celebration Garden Club took root and eventually blossomed into the Celebration Library Committee.

As the garden club's second president, Akron transplant Mary Pfeiffer was "trying to think of things that the club could do to promote community." An advocate of inter-generational activities ("Kids need adults to help them, not just build teen centers."), Mary hit on an idea for Mother's Day: the club bought plants for all the members of the village Girl Scout troop, charging the girls to distribute their plants to mothers in Celebration who were not their own mothers. Sophie Miller gave a flower to Dorothy Johnson, who told Sophie's mother how touched she was, and that she would be delighted to read to Sophie some time.

Whether in suburbs or inner cities, New Villages are rich in "third places" where neighbors can get to know one another without regard to such differences as age and income. After a chance meeting, Mary Pfeiffer (left) and Dorothy Johnson became friends and discovered a mutual love of reading, which led to building a new library.

Photo courtesy Celebration Associates

Mary Pfeiffer had not met Dorothy Johnson, though she had seen her around the village. Dorothy is hard to miss: an octogenarian African-American retired teacher who rides her three-wheel bicycle everywhere. Mary invited Dorothy to dinner. This often is the way things happen in New Villages, where people are not only open to unplanned encounters but often go out of their way to find situations where they're likely to happen. White homeowner Mary Pfeiffer and black apartment-renter Dorothy Johnson "discovered we had a lot of common interests." Among those interests, a love of literature and reading. "We started reading to grade-school kids on the weekend, and we realized that we really needed a library."

Despite its cornerstone of education and its appeal to the intellectually curious, Celebration's designers had attempted unsuccessfully to secure a library branch from the county. White's Bookstore had opened near the inn, then gone out of business. Mary Pfeiffer and Dorothy Johnson took matters into their own hands. They expanded their group and became the West Osceola Friends of the Library, collecting donated books and operating out of a 14x14-foot maintenance room in Town Hall. By the end of 2004, Friends of the Library had collected five thousand books for its one thousand patrons and they were offering regular story-reading sessions for preschoolers. Their goal was to establish a full-service library in Celebration Town Hall. Mary Pfeiffer believed that as a citizen she and her friends had power, and that it would require smaller numbers to make things happen in smaller and more unified towns.

In August, 2006, the West Osceola Branch Library opened – not in the center of Celebration but at its edge, in Water Tower Place, the strip shopping center at the corner of Celebration Avenue and Highway 192. The new, fully equipped library is within bike-riding distance for older children, but younger kids have to be driven there. In the town center, where Pfeiffer and her committee had hoped the library would go, condominiums are going up instead. "I think you might say the new urbanism has been abandoned here in Celebration," says Mary Pfeiffer, who describes herself as "bitter…We're more than a little discouraged." On the other hand, they did succeed in getting a library built.

While the lack of certain amenities and conveniences bothers some New Villagers, others are bothered by the plethora of regulations. The Celebration management team, encouraged by Charles Fraser, convinced itself that its residents would prefer top-down rules to protect their investment. However, once the homes began selling, a few voices complained that they were forced to sign unwanted and unnecessary covenants.

Pastor Pat Wrisley of Celebration Presbyterian Church blames former Disney CEO Michael Eisner for the regulations, although in fact Eisner never got involved in the specifics of covenants. "This was Michael's little Lego-land," Wrisley insists. "The micromanagement of those kinds of decisions – I understand the community and covenants – you do that for a reason – but the minutiae of those things are frustrating."

Pastor Pat, whose e-mail handle is "disneypope," is not known for compromise. When he first moved to the neighborhood he argued that

Reverend Pat Wrisley preaches the community benefits of New Village life, but chafes at the "minutiae" and "micromanagement" of non-resident master planners.

Photo by the authors

Celebration should carve a sixth cornerstone into its mission statement. In addition to Place, Community, Education, Health and Technology, Wrisley "stridently challenged" the Celebration Company to add Faith. Todd Mansfield and his cohorts steadfastly held the cornerstones to five. (On this issue, Eisner did weigh in, letting his people know it was inappropriate for a public company to engage in faith-related discussions. He also insisted that Celebration Health, operated by the vegetarian Seventh Day Adventist Church, serve meat in the hospital for non-vegetarians.)

Pat Wrisley's church benefited from a gift from a Disney family member, which may have suggested a divide within the company, but when the minister headed up an effort to build a cemetery inside the village, The Celebration Company once again held its ground, permitting only a memorial garden. Wrisley took umbrage and went on the offensive.

"In 1996, as the holidays approached, Disney said, 'When you decorate, be tasteful.' The next year, they reminded people to use white twinkle lights. One of the things I did was to say to folks, 'In order to remind ourselves to pray, we are going to violate the codebook.'" Wrisley bought a crate of pink flamingos, prototypical Florida kitsch, and passed them out in church. He asked members to anonymously plant a flamingo in the lawn of anyone who might benefit from the congregation's prayers. "And when you see a pink flamingo planted in your yard," he smiled, "you will know that someone is praying for you."

YOUNG ACTIVISTS MAKE THEIR POINTS.

There will be rules no matter where we live. Yet in a village, where the central authority figure is usually a close neighbor, it's unlikely that a reasonable request will go unconsidered. That's what ten-year-old Alyssa Rexford discovered when she got fed up with having no place to ride her skateboard – no place really *fun* – in her picturesque little village of Scotia, California. So one boring summer day she just walked across Main Street and knocked on the door of the man who ran the town. He wasn't in, but his wife directed Alyssa to his office, just a block away, where she could make an appointment with his secretary. The girl got her appointment the next day and made her point rather eloquently.

"This town is being very oppressive to skateboarders," Alyssa said. At least that's the way the head honcho, Robert Manne, remembers it. Scotia is a company town owned by PALCO, one of the West Coast's largest lumber companies (and you may read more about Scotia in the following chapter.) As president and CEO of PALCO, Manne is also Alyssa's father's boss and ex-officio mayor.

"She wasn't at all intimidated," Manne recalls. "All the kids in town know me. They call me 'Mister President.' The first thing I did was investigate putting in a skateboard park, but I found out that would be a huge liability for the company."

Instead, Manne decided to create some options for kids. "That encounter was what prompted us to start our Summer Fun program. I got eight sets of parents together and held a meeting. They said they would find volunteers to run the program and I said, 'Okay, then I'll fund it.'" Presto: organized bike riding, fossil hunting, dances, swimming classes, basketball, soccer camp and more, for kids from age five through grade eight. As for skateboarding in town, Manne decided the PALCO policy might be just a mite Draconian, so he eased up. In a village, sometimes a ten-year-old can get the rules changed.

In most government bodies it would be difficult if not impossible for kids to get involved. Not so in New Villages, where rules are often written on the fly. When two high school freshmen learned that Washington's Issaquah Highlands had its own Parks and Trails Committee, they started attending meetings, because "we wanted to make sure the trails were kept clean and clear." That explanation from Corbin Credelle, who goes mountain biking with his buddy Brandon Gaytan on the county trails that connect with the Highlands' path system. "We pretty much go out every day," says Brandon, "even if it's raining or snowing."

The committee quickly signed up the two young men, and on their recommendation added a few bike jumps along the trails. Community Association Executive Director Vicky Steir then sought Brandon and Corbin's input in planning new playgrounds. "They researched different equipment," she says, "and came up with a list of suggestions. As a result, our equipment is much more unique than what is typically found on a playground."

Corbin and Brandon, who met when their families moved to Issaquah Highlands, have become involved in dozens of community events and regularly help entertain younger children at "Kids' Night

Out." Having gained the trust of parents, children and civic leaders, it was only natural that they start their own babysitting business. They are, says Vicky Stier, "near and dear to my heart."

As further evidence of New Villages re-engineering themselves to suit the needs of children, consider the case of Baxter Village, in South Carolina just south of Charlotte. There, what had been designed as an adult-oriented sports bar and grill has been remade into Beef O'Brady's Family Pub, catering, as its name suggests, not to the singles scene or to rowdy guys, but to tables filled with moms and dads and kids. "It's great," says Baxter Village CEO Don Killoren, a veteran of the Celebration management team. "On Sundays in football season you get practically the whole town down here watching the Panthers." Another Baxter feature is cleverly designed street signs alerting drivers to the presence of children. "The only problem with these," Killoren says, "is that people from outside the village like them so much they steal them to put on their own streets."

NEW VILLAGE CRIMINALS.

While many New Villages lure families with gathering places and amenities, equally dear to parents is the relative absence of crime in their neighborhoods. When people know each other as well as villagers do, uncivil behavior is easily discouraged… although it must be stated that New Villages do occasionally make the police reports. In January 2004 a live-in nanny at DC Ranch went to jail for drug possession – but it turned out to be a case of mistaken identity and she was released.[136] That one made the news, as did the Celebration vandalism of a car owned by a highly visible supporter of Democrat John Kerry in the impassioned presidential race of 2004, when Central Florida voted famously GOP. However, such negative publicity is rare.

Because they are relatively small, most New Villages fly under the radar of the Federal Bureau of Investigation's crime statistics. An exception is Rancho Santa Margarita in Orange County, California. In 2003, the FBI reported a total of 514 crimes in Rancho Santa Margarita, including one forcible rape, six robberies, 27 aggravated assaults, 78 burglaries, 355 larcenies or thefts, 43 car thefts and four cases of arson. That sounds like a lot for a city of fewer than 50,000 residents. However, this New Village has grown into an incorporated city, and crime rises with the population.

The chamber of commerce was quick to compare their crime rates with those from elsewhere in the county and proclaim Rancho Santa Margarita as "Orange County's Safest City." The most frequently reported crime, larceny or theft, is still only a quarter of the national average on a per capita basis.[137] "Despite our tremendous population growth," brags City Councilwoman Christy Riley, "the [civic] participation by our residents certainly makes the difference!"[138]

The expectation of a lower incidence of crime is planted by virtually every New Village developer, builder and real estate salesperson. Those who buy in New Villages are rarely disappointed. Diane Musick, who'd been married and living on Navy bases for 28 years until her divorce, found it "a little scary" to be suddenly on her own. "As a single woman I felt vulnerable," she says, until she moved to Celebration in 1997. "Here I immediately felt very safe."

That feeling persisted even when Celebration's celebrated First Crime was committed just two doors down from her new house. The robbery has achieved almost legendary status in Celebration, the New Village equivalent of an urban myth. One expects to see a statue erected to commemorate it one day. According to Diane Musick, a couple with two children were confronted inside their home by a young worker at one of the village construction sites. According to others, the attacker was unemployed. In some tellings, he was wielding a gun, in others a knife. You might hear the confrontation happened in the front yard in broad daylight, or you might hear it happened in the alley garage at night. "Whichever way it happened," as Tom Lewis notes, "we went two years before we had our first crime."

Lewis, one of the original residents and an early executive of The Celebration Company, says, "People always seem to be surprised about crime here. There's a huge drug challenge with the teenagers. Wealthy teenagers." Still, he says, New Villages are poster children for Neighborhood Watch programs. "Everybody's watching out for everyone else. It's hard to get away with anything."

Monitor the Celebration online Residents' Forum (www.34747. org/forum) and you'll see that while there is the occasional wrongdoing, someone is nearly always taking names. Feed the alligators in the lake or let your dog run without a leash and you'll find an angry neighbor on your virtual doorstep: "What happened to the sign in the downtown lake about not feeding the alligators? ...Last week some real estate agent was feeding bread to an alligator saying that her clients could come down and feed him everyday!" "Last week, right in front of the owners, I almost hit a little fluffy dog a few blocks from here. I took down the address and was going to call animal control." "Is there a leash law in Celebration? ...I worry for the children who might be playing in the area and possibly startle a dog and be bitten." [Someone responds:] "The leash law is a *county* ordinance."

"Sadly," sighs Diane Musick, "this is not Utopia."

On the other hand, Diane reflects on what made her feel safe in all her years as a Navy captain's wife. "There's community in the military; you have a core of friends. You all move together. You keep the same friends for 30 years. I had this protective family in the military, and now I have it here. When I moved here, no one locked their doors. My neighbor came in one day, just walked in until she found me – said the front door was wide open. I remember going walking, and out in front of Gooding's [the onetime grocery in the village center] were two pairs of rollerblades, a couple of bikes. Nobody bothered them."

ONCE IT'S BUILT, THE CITIZENS MUST TAKE CHARGE.

"But it's not one-hundred-percent perfect," Celebration's Lee Moore cautioned at the close of 2004. "We have growth issues like anyone else. We have a developer [Disney] who did a great job, and now the process of transition to government by the Home Owners Association is kind of a scary thing for a lot of people." Moore smiles. "I am enjoying that process. People here are very passionate. They are passionate about what they're doing, why they are here. In other towns, the HOA is probably not as much work. But you sign on for some responsibility when you come to this town. We have real issues. There's billions of dollars in assets here and we want to ensure that it all works. We have people on all sides of any issues. If it is a county issue, we are the most vocal people in the whole county."

Among those highly vocal people, Pastor Pat Wrisley believes "the town is at an interesting place. We live in a benevolent dictatorship here, not a democracy. When people bought in, they bought into the town mentality. Now the question will be, will the sludge rise up to fill the gaps in leadership? Or will the leadership fall? Lexin Capital bought downtown from Disney. If it's just an investment, if it's dollars and cents rather than about community, then the bar has been adjusted down."

"There was that early idea that Disney was going to make everything perfect," muses artist Lynn Sands. "There was earlier a cadre of people that thought Disney should fix everything. Mostly, those people didn't stay. By the time we got here, they had got the kinks worked out. We viewed it as an opportunity – they made a great physical place, now *we* have to make it work."

Lee Moore, who once worked taking pictures of visitors to Disney World, sees Disney as having set a hopeful pattern for New Village developers, that of seeing the project to its completion, then getting out. "Now it's our responsibility to continue Disney's vision," he says. "There are incorporation issues. There is a group of people who are researching how we can incorporate, how to be autonomous – we are funding a study to find out how. The residents have come out in favor of incorporation, but we are doing a study through the University of Florida."

Shared greenspaces become gathering places for neighbors to plan civic improvements, and Seattle's High Point has found a way to do that while providing fenced backyards for individual homes.

Photo by George Nemeth for Seattle Housing Authority

The pitfalls of political involvement can be dug in the most devious spots. When some residents requested regular patrols of Celebration by the Osceola County Sheriff's Office, they were turned down. "It seems we don't have enough crime," laments Tom Lewis. "We need crime to get police. The county says that we don't need police, so we hired our own security guards. So the crime stays low, so we'll never get police."

New Villages around America have a variety of governance structures. Some choose to incorporate separately from any municipality or county near them; others function within the local governance; still others yet operate on different principles, with laws and governing bodies closer to the structures found in board rooms than in the customary chambers of government.

Whichever governance model they select, the planners of New Villages have one enormous advantage over most municipal planners: they can hand-pick their citizens. It happens not through any ham-handed screening process but through clever marketing strategies and self-selection of homebuyers. By selectively marketing certain features of Celebration – education, technology, health and fitness, a true sense of place – Todd Mansfield, Don Killoren, Charles Adams and Tom Lewis believed they would attract people who were "highly engaged."

It was, Todd Mansfield unabashedly admits, social engineering, though it was billed as "community building." By soliciting people from out of state, people who were in the Orlando area on vacation, Celebration would draw transplants who would arrive without pre-existing social networks, who would be inclined to quickly embrace and become highly involved in their new home. Those more comfortable in typical isolationist suburbs were neither sought nor wanted. The result of such market selectivity is an advantage for residents over their people moving to new homes in other geographic locations: instant community, instant civic involvement.

Yet that New Village advantage may be receding, thanks to the internet. In larger towns and cities and in rural America, people are connecting with their governments as never before and creating citizen networks with the potential to alter the course of government. The movement surfaced in 1997 with MoveOn.org, founded to block President Bill Clinton's impeachment. In the 2004 election, MoveOn raised $60 million for liberal causes. Not to be outdone, one twenty-five-year-old architecture student from Boston, Matt Margolis, started Blogsforbush.com, and by Election Day he had nearly 1,500 conservative bloggers raising money for Bush and writing letters to editors.

The true power of cyber-civic involvement may be realized at the local level. In Spokane, Washington, Shannon Sullivan, a single mother inspired by her nine-year-old son, decided to use the web to start a recall drive against Mayor James E. West, who had admitted using a city hall computer to solicit sex in online chatrooms. Though she had no experience in politics and little enough with computers, Sullivan organized rallies and media events and eventually collected 17,000 signatures for a special recall election in December, 2005 that drove West from office. Elsewhere, the internet helps voters stay in close touch with elected officials, such as Iowa Governor Tom Vilsack, who takes citizen e-mails on his Blackberry.

"People are just beginning to realize how much power they have," Democratic consultant Chris Kofinis told the Associated Press. "At a time when we are craving community and meaning in our lives, people are using these technologies to find others with the same complaints and organize them. They don't have to just sit in a coffee shop and gripe about politics. They can change politics."[139]

Whether in villages designed to foster civic involvement or in cities fallen victim to unwieldy government, Americans have the opportunity to return to that time observed by Tocqueville when all inhabitants were members of a "great meeting house," where they might once again "carry their desires into execution without intermediaries."

CHAPTER NINE

Company Towns and Hard-Wired Community

St. Peter, don't you call me, 'cause I can't go...
I owe my soul to the company store.

When Merle Travis wrote the lyrics to "Sixteen Tons" in 1946 and finger-snapping Tennessee Ernie Ford recorded them nine years later, they were reminding postwar America about a kind of village still very much alive in those days, the company town.[140]

Muhlenburg County, Kentucky, where Travis grew up, was home to dozens of small towns wholly owned and operated by coal-mining companies. The companies provided whatever necessities and amenities they believed their employees required – usually the barest necessities, like food and shelter, and often even those were at a hefty price. Hence a resident living in one of these towns might run up a considerable IOU at the company store. Sometimes, employees were paid in scrip that was legal tender only at that store. There were company towns all around North America, and in other countries of course. Mines and logging camps generally operated at good distances from centers of civilization, so if you wanted to be in those industries, you had to bring workers to wherever the gold or silver or coal or trees happened to be. You might well have to provide for their families as well.

In Hershey, Pennsylvania, everybody worked for the chocolate company, either making candy or at one of the company's auxiliary institutions – the school, the hospital, the post office. During the last two decades of the 19th century, if you built Pullman Railroad Cars, you could live in "the world's most perfect town," where company-owned stores and stylish townhomes were the envy of your neighbors in their squalid Chicago tenements. In Kannapolis, North Carolina, everybody got free garbage collection supplied by Cannon Mills, the sheet and towel manufacturer, and lit up their mill village with lights and power also courtesy of Mr. James William Cannon. In Alcoa, Tennessee, you filled up your truck at the aluminum company's gas station. If you lived in Port Gamble, Washington, you were almost certainly an employee of the Pope & Talbot sawmill and lived in a little house furnished by the company and built of Pope & Talbot Douglas fir.[141]

By the end of the 20th century, most company towns had either disappeared – gone with the companies on which they'd depended – or been absorbed into some larger municipality. One notable exception is the northwest Washington town of Newhalem, on the Skagit River, populated entirely by workers at the area's hydroelectric plants.[142] If you or a member of your family doesn't work at one of those three plants or for their owner, Seattle City Light, or for some other government agency, you are not welcome as a permanent resident.

SANTA WEARS LOGGING BOOTS.

But perhaps the ultimate example of a thriving company town is one we visited in the preceding chapter, Scotia, California, about 250 miles north of San Francisco in booming Humboldt County. If Celebration is a Disney movie, Scotia is a postcard painted by Norman Rockwell. On the banks of the Eel River, framed by stunning redwood ridges, its 276 houses (front porches, manicured lawns, flower beds, etc.) are all within walking distance of a daycare center, a grade school, a grocery, a deli, a bank, a hardware store, a beauty shop, a post office that closes for lunch, a recreation center, a medical center, a combination movie theater-playhouse, a museum, an aquarium, a picturesque inn that features its own resident ghost, a playground and a world-class soccer field. People stop and talk to one another. They look out for each other's kids. The catch is that you can't live in Scotia unless someone in your immediate family works at one of the aforementioned establishments. Or at the world's largest redwood sawmill down the street.

Scotia started out as a logging camp in 1863, two years before General Lee surrendered to General Grant. In those days, that camp was the only place you could live if you wanted a job with the new Pacific Lumber Company. If you wanted to make a living felling the giant redwoods and Douglas fir that would go into the construction of California's cities, you high-tailed it to that faraway logging camp. The company would supply your bunk and your blankets and your breakfast. Nearly 150 years later, Pacific Lumber is officially PALCO, owned by a Houston outfit called Maxxam, and the logging camp is the town of Scotia. Billing itself (with perhaps pardonable exaggeration) as "the last company town in the U.S.," Scotia is still owned, every square inch, by the company.

Robert and Donna Manne moved to Scotia in 2001 when Robert accepted the position of president and CEO of PALCO. They had lived in big cities like Philadelphia and Seattle, or in suburbs of those cities, and weren't sure how they would react to living on the main street of a village. "It was amazing," says Manne (pronounced "Manny"). "We didn't realize how much that 'community' thing was going to suck us in."

There are few if any secrets in Scotia. Neighbors all know their neighbors and their neighbors' children. Robert Manne is not only the boss of nearly every adult in town, he is the de facto mayor and town manager. Kids treat "Mister President" as though he were their rich uncle. Donna is first lady. "When people need something, they come to us," Robert tells us. "They come to the company. There's this feeling of family that we've lost in much of America. You couldn't ask for a better job."

Scotia provided earlier an example of how children in villages have easier access to the movers and shakers. The other side of that coin is that, for better or worse, the movers and shakers can have enormous influence on the children. Consider Christmas in Scotia, when Santa and Mrs. Claus – portrayed by PALCO employees, of course – arrive in a parade of volunteer PALCO fire engines. The town is all lit up with lights (and electrical power) provided by PALCO, with the company's huge live redwood and its 800 colored lights glittering up the hill. The kids follow Santa into the Winema Theater for a party, during which the jolly old elf distributes gifts to each and every child. Santa PALCO hands out not lollipops and candy canes, but gifts that cost $40 to $50, personally selected by Mister President. The Christmas party has been going on since 1926.

When the company recognized a need for a good soccer field, it tore down the old abattoir, where hogs and cattle were once butchered to feed the loggers and sawyers, to build a state-of-the-game field. Now teams from all over the area travel to Scotia for their games. PALCO changed its babysitting service into professional, educational daycare, and provides it free to employees' children. It built and maintains a top-rated elementary school which it leases to the state for $1 a year;

PALCO technicians, engineers and scientists regularly donate their time to augment the curriculum. Over the years, employees' teenagers have received more than $5.5 million in PALCO college scholarships.

The chief disadvantage among all these advantages is that Scotia residents tend to miss out on many of life's adversities – the challenges Americans like to believe go into making us tougher, stronger, better citizens. Many Scotia families have gone through four and five generations of village isolation without experiencing much of the "real world," beyond what they only half-jokingly call the Redwood Curtain. Since the scholarship program began in 1964, the majority of its recipients have attended schools close to home.

Access to the internet has reduced the concerns of isolation and insularity, but Robert Manne wants to do more. So he has created a new scholarship program he calls Expanded Horizons. Based on a program created by President Dwight D. Eisenhower, in which Manne's own children participated, Expanded Horizons selects four high school students each year to become "student ambassadors" to Europe, Australia and Asia. "I grew up in a tiny house in Cincinnati," Manne smiles. "My sister, my mother and father and I lived in three rooms separated by pocket doors...Now I've done business on every continent...I know how education changes lives." His hope is that these students will sufficiently expand their horizons to study farther from home and to one day return with their knowledge and experience to Humboldt County.

After nearly a century and a half, Scotia has survived fires, earthquakes, devastating floods and, perhaps worst of all, the wrath of radical environmentalists. Earth First!, California Forest Defense and other activist organizations have made PALCO the chief target of eco-terrorism since the late 1980s. At the start of 2006, Manne was dealing with a petition to delay cutting of an old redwood stand at Nanning Creek, about a mile east of Scotia. If you live in a company town you may have to endure whatever publicity attaches itself to the company.

For that reason and others, chances are that a good many of us would not choose to live in a true company town like Scotia. Something about owing our souls to the company store, perhaps. But what Scotia demonstrates is that there are clear benefits to living in a town where nearly everyone participates in an *esprit de corps* built around the workplace. The more we have in common with our neighbors, the more likely we are to socialize with them and to assist them in times of need. Just as obviously, there is a downside. Diversity, cultural opportunity, opportunities to expand one's horizon – all these will likely be in short supply in a place where everyone is so much like everyone else. When the company controls the flow of goods and, at least to some extent, information, the quality of both may be questioned. Yet despite these apparent shortcomings, the notion of the company town is being revived in the 21st century.

TWENTY-FIRST-CENTURY COMPANY TOWNS: WALKING TO WORK.

At the heart of this revival of business interest in the neighborhoods we inhabit is the response by corporate America to the gorgon they helped create, the beast we call urban (or suburban) sprawl. In many companies, employees are spending almost as much time getting to and from work as they are working, and that is taking a toll on their health and productivity. How much better if they could walk their kids to school on their way to work and walk home for lunch, the way people in Scotia do? It is interesting to note that of the several master-planned developments that sprang up after World War II, the one that has become most economically self sufficient is Reston, Virginia. More than likely, this success stems from the fact that developer Robert Simon failed in his attempt to get an on-ramp connecting Reston to the highway between Washington, D.C. and Dulles Airport.[143]

As of 2004, according to a report by the Transportation Institute at Texas A&M University, the average American motorist was spending 48 hours – two full days – idling in rush-hour traffic each year. The average Los Angeles driver was sitting for 93 hours, the average Seattle commuter 46. Nationally, rush-hour idling is wasting 5.7 billion gallons of fuel each year, the report goes on to say, and the annual financial cost of traffic congestion in wasted fuel and lost productivity is estimated at $63 billion, four and a half times what it cost twenty years ago. And all those grim figures were before the Iraq War pushed petroleum prices even higher.

Greater than the financial cost, however, is the cost of stress associated with long commutes. In an article on the subject, *HR* magazine quoted Boeing senior manager Steve Stephenson of Greenbank, Washington, as saying, "People come to work jangled...

a 15-second (traffic) episode can cause hormonal changes that last for six hours. That infects the whole day." On the other side of the continent, Anita Caggiano, Marketing Administrator of W&M Properties in Stamford, Connecticut, says, "During rush hour, I-95 is a nightmare… people without alternative commute options arrive at work very stressed and upset."[144] Both companies are seeking options to that nightmare, hoping to add years to their employees' lives and incalculable hours of productivity to their careers.

By rejecting the daily commute, many are joining the ranks of community builders. When Michael Jenkins took his job in Disney's Information Technology group, he started thinking convenience. His new job just happened to be located in the Celebration office complex, so he and wife Tami decided Celebration was where they wanted to live. They started by renting a house, then bought a townhouse. Within a few months, Mike realized he could get in shape by biking to work. "I just ride my bike to work, then come home for lunch. It's nice having lunch together with my wife every day. We only need one car in a place like this."

The second car was passed on to teenage daughter Michelle, who, wheels or no wheels, finds that there's plenty for her and her friends to do right in the neighborhood. "We all do everything," she says. "We have street parties, block parties, we all do cookouts."

The Jenkinses' son Sean, still awaiting the rite of passage that a driver's license represents, was just as delighted with the bike-ability of their New Village. "We liked it here right away because of the bike trails. Instead of taking the main avenue to go downtown, you can go through Lake Evelyn. There are all kinds of different ways to get to town."

In Northwest Landing, a New Village just south of Tacoma, Washington, Intel and State Farm employees regularly walk or ride their bikes to the office. Some go home for lunch and others simply work from home. Like Issaquah Highlands further north, Northwest Landing is the product of a tree farmer-turned-developer, in this case Weyerhaeuser. Fittingly, it sits adjacent to the old company town of DuPont, where for nearly 70 years the chemical corporation of the same name manufactured and tested explosives used to blast stumps, clear roadways, and fight two world wars. In days gone by, DuPonters shopped at the town butcher shop, held their picnics on the village green and walked to work – living much as their modern counterparts live in Northwest Landing today.

When Intel brought five technicians from China for a project at its DuPont chipset facility, the company put up its guests at Northwest Landing's Guesthouse Inn. To travel back and forth to work, the Chinese received bicycles, along with lockers in the employee fitness center. Intel's Commute Reduction Program encourages employees to bike, walk or run to work and provides bike racks, showers and lockers for those who do. The world's largest computer chip manufacturer is one of a growing number of employers who preach the benefits of walking to their employees.

That was part of Microsoft's decision to announce it would build a new office campus in the New Village of Issaquah Highlands, long before the streets were laid out, and the reason a number of Microsoft employees bought up Highlands homes as soon as they went on the market. When the giant among techno-giants staked its claim to become the town's new chief employer, Port Blakely Communities looked as though it might be developing the 21st century equivalent of a company town there in the "Issaquah Alps," the coal-rich mountains at the western base of the Cascade Range.

In the 1860s the region's earliest settlements were true company towns, with simple cabins and company stores clustered around mine shafts. A century later, coal mining had long given way to tourism, with urbanites drawn by Issaquah's small-town charm and the easy access it afforded to fishing, hunting, skiing, skydiving and other outdoor activities, right in Seattle's eastern backyard. A nice place to visit soon established itself as a great place to live, and the Issaquah Alps became the eastern outpost of the city's suburban sprawl. Microsoft moved to nearby Redmond in 1986 and the Eastside population explosion began. The dot-com boom of the 1990s made Issaquah residents wonder whether there would be anything left of their once-idyllic landscape. The hills were alive with the sounds of bulldozers. Herds of SUVs had replaced the deer and cougar. How long before concrete condos outnumbered the Douglas fir?

Britain's *The Economist* called Issaquah and its environs a "wildly growing part of the country." In its 1999 article on King County's ultra-sprawl, *The Economist* identified as chief culprit "an exploding high-tech industry powered by Microsoft." Issaquah is located near the southern tip of Lake Sammamish; Microsoft has its headquarters in the city of Redmond, about a 30-minute drive away, near the northern tip of the lake. In 1997 Microsoft announced it was buying 150 acres of Issaquah Highlands. There it would build a satellite campus for as many as 12,000 employees. The company refused to say which employees those might be, but the land rush in Issaquah Highlands was on.

"Home sales have been much faster than anticipated," Judd Kirk, president of Port Blakely Communities, told *The New York Times* in December of 2001. Despite Microsoft's continued reluctance to commit to a building date and its announcement, in the summer of 2004, that it was building a new campus in Hyderabad, India, Microsoft people remained willing, even eager, to take their chances on Issaquah Highlands. Among the earliest Microsoft arrivals in the New Village were Joseph and Vanessa Cusimano. He is a Microsoft software tester in the e-Home Division, where the company designs and tests the programs it hopes will eventually turn everyone's home into a computer-controlled environment.

"One of the main reasons we moved into the (Issaquah) neighborhood," Joseph Cusimano told us in early 2005, "is because we have the new Microsoft campus coming. There's kind of a betting pool going on, which division actually gets moved out here. Everybody kind of prays and hopes… I don't know if we can bribe or somehow manage to influence the powers that be to have our division move out here, but it would be nice. It would be good to be about 300 yards from the campus."

Just a few weeks after that interview, things changed. Redmond, Washington, Microsoft's hometown, lifted its moratorium on new building. Suddenly the company had the option of expanding its current office campus. Microsoft ended up buying only 63 acres of the Highlands, just a little over a third of the originally planned 150 acres. Since the developer, Port Blakely Communities, had already benefited from Microsoft's well-publicized interest, it was delighted at the turn of events. "When Microsoft let their options lapse," explains Port Blakely's Judd Kirk, "we expanded the town center and put in some office buildings. We were happy, since we weren't really looking forward to putting all our eggs in one basket."

"At first I thought, 'Wow, that's a bummer,'" says Mike Krassner, who has lived in the Highlands since mid-2001, "but when you think about it, it's an opportunity for a mix of employers. Instead of it being dominated by Microsoft, we could have a full-fledged emergency hospital and other companies here. It could be a really good thing."[145]

Though it likely will never be their "company town," Issaquah Highlands has become home to more than a few Microsoft employees. They meet each other on the Highlands playing fields, they push baby carriages together along the wooded paths, they relax together over caffè lattes after work. And it is more and more common for them to forego the half-hour (on good days) commute to Redmond to do their work from home. They may do that easily, because the developers of Issaquah Highlands laid fiber optic cable down every street, requiring builders to connect that cable to every home. And inside the houses and apartments, jacks to "category 5" (Cat-5) cables are implanted in the walls of every major room. Those cables make it possible for anyone in Issaquah Highlands to send and receive data at up to one gigabyte per second. Microsoft's dream of global connectivity, if not the company itself, is coming true in this New Village.

"Being able to not go in to work when I don't feel like going in to work, and working from home, that's just life's simple pleasure," says Microsoft's Joseph Cusimano. "I don't want to go to work today? All right, I'll log in and work from home." And perhaps walk out for a cup of coffee or lunch. As it turns out, more hours spent around home, right in the neighborhood, can help build community far more than driving to the office can. Oddly enough, hours spent on the internet can also feed the hunger for community.

THE VIRTUAL COMMUNITY, THE VIRTUAL COMMUTE.

Earlier we met Faris Taylor and her dustmop bouviers hiking the paths and trails of the Highlands. It was hardly surprising to find Mrs. Taylor among the champions of "walkability." Less predictably, this woman who loves the outdoors and staying fit shows up on an Issaquah Highlands marketing video, praising high-speed bandwidth, connectivity and internet chat rooms. This technology she proclaims to be "one of the key things that makes Issaquah Highlands the community that it is… It's really the glue that holds the community together."[146]

Computer technology equals community? Web surfing a walker's best friend?

Wasn't so long ago those thoughts spoken aloud might draw snickers. In the early- to mid-1990s it was considered chic in some circles to rank the personal computer and the internet somewhat ahead of suburban sprawl in the category of community arch-enemy. Out in society's mainstream, millions were learning to ride the new wave, but in university lecture halls and psychiatric offices, concerns were mounting. Academic hand-wringers fed the media stereotypes of lone wolves crouched late over keyboards, gaunt faces lit by their monitors' flicker. Behavioral scientists saw personal relationships wrecked, human communication disemboweled by the technology intended to enhance it.

In fact, nervous futurists had been warning about the arrival of the computer since the 50s; forty years later, their worst fears had come to pass. While the media hyped the information highway, Studs Turkel took a closer look and wrote, in "The American Prospect," that community was nowhere to be found in the black hole of cyberspace. Clifford Stoll, a Berkeley astronomer and a pioneer of the world wide web, wrote an entire book to warn us that the technophiles were selling us a bill of goods. "Few aspects of daily life require computers," Stoll wrote in *Silicon Snake Oil*. "They're irrelevant to cooking, driving, visiting, negotiating, eating, hiking, dancing, speaking, and gossiping. You don't need a computer to… recite a poem or say a prayer." [147]

A group of Carnegie Mellon scientists from the Human Computer Interaction Institute published "Internet Paradox: A Social Technology that Reduces Social Involvement and Psychological Well Being?" The question mark may have been added by an editor, since the team of scientists, headed by Robert Kraut, had erased any of their own questions with solid research. Their paper's conclusion brooked no doubt: "Greater use of the Internet was associated with declines in participants' communication with family members in the household, declines in the size of their social circle, and increases in their depression and loneliness. These findings have implications for research, for public policy, and for the design of technology." [148]

As the millennium drew nigh, Neo-Luddites seemed to emerge from behind every tree, whispering that the end was surely near. Technology was the antichrist. The Year 2000 Bug was going to drag us over the edge of the flat e-universe. The very word "community" had been hijacked by America Online and web gamers, defining "neighbors" as the code-named, faceless people with whom they played EverQuest online.

A beyond-bleak future was glimpsed in a 2000 report for the Stanford Institute for the Quantitative Study of Society. We were on our way to hell in an electronic handbasket built for one. "The more hours people use the internet, the less time they spend with real human beings," prophesied the report's co-author, Stanford Professor Norman Nie. "The internet could be the ultimate isolating technology that further reduces our participation in communities, even more than television did before it."[149]

The millennium arrived without significant catastrophe – that awaited us in September of 2001 – but the experts were still worried about what the internet (still spelled with a capital "I" then, as though it were something to be worshipped or shunned) could be doing to us. "What excites me and at the same time troubles me," said Stanford's Phillip Zimbardo, "is the Internet and the electronic technology revolution. I think the growing epidemic of shyness is fueled in part by so many people, so many adolescents and adults spending huge amounts of time relatively alone, isolated on e-mail, on video games, in chat rooms, watching television, all of which reduces their face-to-face contact with other people, making social connections simply more awkward and thus avoided." In his clinical studies, Zimbardo said, "We are finding that the level of shyness has gone up dramatically in the last decade, and so I think shyness is now an index of social pathology rather than a pathology of the individual."[150]

Could be. But there were others who believed that this technology might make us more human rather than less.

Just two years after that Stanford report, Basic Books published Richard Florida's *The Rise of the Creative Class: And How It's Transforming Work, Leisure, Community, and Everyday Life*. In a book that quickly created a buzzword, urban theorist Florida suggested that technology and easy access to it was one of the key reasons that the people who make things happen resist living in typical suburban neighborhoods. He insists that creativity and the creation of "social capital" both require density. "You sprawl, you die," is one of Florida's mantras,[151] and one of his "three keys to economic growth," along with talent and tolerance for diversity, is: technology.

The developers of New Villages across the land were inclined to agree. By the time the creative class theory took hold, several of its members already had relocated to high-density, hard-wired New Villages from one side of the country to the other. From the results of early trials, such as those in Blacksburg, Virginia, in 1993 and Celebration, Florida, in 1995, it had begun to appear that technology just might be the critical factor in moving the quest for social capital to the tipping point, that point at which scarcely anyone will think to challenge the preeminence of community as a driving force of the nation's lifestyle choices. We had begun to demand community and we were beginning to recognize that one important tool for building community is technology.

New York University's Mitchell Moss certainly believed that in 2000 when he wrote, "In the near future, a house may be judged by the speed of its telecommunications service and the quality of its information structure, not just by the number of bedrooms or proximity to a good school system."[152] Moss was incorrect only in that by 2000 hard-wired connectivity had already become a criterion for the seeker of community. Certainly it was one of the attractions that lured community seekers to Florida in 1995, where Amy Westwood was in charge of The Celebration Company's "technology cornerstone." No matter that at first, Westwood wasn't quite sure exactly what she and Disney meant by "technology."

"Remember, we were in the land business, the entertainment business, not the technology business. We know what 'place' is, and how it depends on architecture and style, we know what 'health' is and 'education' – but what is technology?" Developers in her experience had never looked at technology as an amenity, or as something to integrate into their homes and offices.

"We didn't want to create it just for technology's sake – just to run around saying we had the fastest technology, or the latest and greatest technology. We wanted to use it to add meaning to people's lives." Rather than going on "a bandwidth hunt," Westwood reflects, "we had to define what connectedness meant, and what would be valuable and meaningful to the community." The light bulb went on, "when we realized it wasn't purely about technology, but about how people used it. It wasn't about getting one gigabit of bandwidth to the home, it was about the connectivity, which was facilitated through the technology but driven by the people."

Thus, among the critical services Amy Westwood and her team provided to Celebration residents were "community network training classes, giving everyone their own email address, making sure the school and the health campus and the businesses were all on the community network… and kind of serving as the evangelist for it all."

This proselytizing was no mean feat at a time when the internet was in its infancy. On hearing the word "mouse" in Celebration, Florida, most people assumed Westwood was talking about Mickey. "But once people started using it, they created the content and the input, and it became theirs." Turning homeowners, a good number of them seniors, into computer whizzes was a social experiment that deserved study. Could connectivity really enhance community? But there was no time for study; in Celebration they were selling houses and managing real estate and building schools. The study would have to be done elsewhere.

THE NETVILLE EXPERIENCE.

About the same time as construction reached a frantic pace in Celebration, crews on the fringe of Toronto were getting started on a neighborhood with the less than endearing name of Netville. Visitors to this new suburb encountered a billboard depicting the excited face of a young girl lit up by a computer screen. "Life has changed," the sign proclaimed, "Experience it." Motorists were urged to turn left into "The Smart Community." Further in, an old chuckwagon proclaimed across its canvas: "Canada's First Interactive New Home Community – Welcome."

In Netville, homes were equipped from the get-go with a high-speed local network, supplied and operated free of charge by a not-for-profit consortium called "Magenta." While Netville was not the first community in North America to be hard-wired for connectivity, it may have been the first in which high-speed connectivity was the main, highly marketed attraction. Technology was not one of five cornerstones in Netville, it was the only cornerstone. More importantly, Netville appears to have inspired the first study of whether this sort of technology brings people closer together or if it pushes them further apart. "Living the Wired Life in the Wired Suburb," was written as a 2001 doctoral thesis at the University of Toronto by Keith N. Hampton.[153]

Hampton moved to Netville in 1997 to study what he calls CMC, or "computer-mediated communication," a techno-label that mercifully has not caught on. Comparing the wired residents of Netville to a group of non-wired residents of a nearby suburb, Hampton found that the internet, community discussion forums and e-mail lists greatly facilitated the exchange of information and resources, serving as "a bridge between network members, providing access to information and resources while increasing connectivity and community solidarity." In his thesis, Hampton gives examples of messages posted on the Netville electronic bulletin board to support his contention that connectivity nurtures community:

"I have walked around the neighborhood a lot lately," one resident writes, "and I have noticed a few things. I have noticed neighbors talking to each other like they have been friends for a long time. I have noticed a closeness that you don't see in many communities."[154] Another message says, "I would love to see us have a continuation of the closeness that many of us have with each other, even on a very superficial level. Do not lose it, we know each other on a first-name basis."[155]

In a neighborhood wired for broadband communication, Hampton concludes, people who have not yet formed personal ties with one another show little hesitation in posting personal information to the local computer network, and this becomes the first step to forming social ties. People more quickly recognize common traits and common interests. They seem to do this in Netville far more easily than do residents of typical suburbs, where the spread of acreage and the dearth of public spaces limit chance encounters. Yet but for its high-tech communication network, Netville is identical to one of those typical suburbs. Unlike Celebration, Florida, or Issaquah Highlands, Washington, the Toronto suburb is not engineered to encourage those chance meetings. Nevertheless, writes Hampton, "use of computer-mediated communication in Netville facilitated recognition, individual introductions and the sharing of personal information."

This has proven to be the case in the South Carolina New Village of Baxter, where in 2004 WiFi "hot spots" were added to enhance the already significant investment in fiber-optics connectivity. Laptops have become common sights at neighborhood restaurants and at the community pool, where parents can manage to work while they monitor the kids' swimming. "It has really increased everyone's mobility," says Michael Hunt of Beef O'Brady's Family Pub. Business at Hunt's place and at the Baxter Starbucks has also increased, thanks to the ability to enjoy lunch or a coffee break away from the home office without losing touch.

Of course, a neighborhood need not be wired – or wireless – when the majority of its residents are internet-savvy. In Seattle's South Park, Joel Clement's blight-fix happy hour has been facilitated largely through an informal neighborhood listserv. Every Sunday, he writes other South Park residents to remind them of the upcoming event, then every Tuesday morning, he recaps it virtually for those who were unable to be there. As was posted in November 2005: "We had a great crowd from all over town to celebrate the Happy Hour's six-month anniversa-…wait a second, we've been drinking on Monday nights for six months straight?"

Robert Putnam in *Better Together* seems to caution against holding out hope for these electronic handshakes: "It takes person-to-person contact over time to build the trust and mutual understanding that characterize the relationships that are the basis of social capital," he writes. "So we see no way that social capital can be created instanta-neously or en masse."[156] Yet Netville's Hampton has concluded just the reverse. "Contrary to fears that living in a neighborhood of smart homes where work, leisure and social ties can all be maintained online would lead people to become increasingly privatized, the results from this analysis suggest that new home-based communication technologies do much the opposite… Rather than isolating people in their homes, [technology] encourages visiting, surveillance, neighbor recognition, and the maintenance of local social ties."

HANDS ACROSS THE ETHER.

While examples of the internet's community-building possibilities abound, none makes the point more forcefully than the phenomenon known as Craigslist. What began in 1995 as a free San Francisco posting service had become by mid-2005 what *The New York Times* described as a major web site with a triple-digit annual growth rate, in fourth place among all general-interest internet portals, drawing 10 million visitors each month without spending a penny on marketing. "Craigslist thinks and acts locally," commented Silicon Valley writer Randall Stross, "organizing listings city by city for merchandise, jobs, real estate, personals, events, volunteer opportunities and discussion forums… Today, it has sites for 120 cities in 25 countries."[157] That was in June of 2005. By November 2006, it's expanded to over 300 sites, in more than 50 countries.[158]

The founder of Craigslist is Craig Newmark, an approachable, non-entrepreneurial computer programmer-sort who oversees his virtual domain from San Francisco and travels around encouraging people in other cities to commune and commingle online. We caught up with him as he was returning from New York, where he had what he calls a flea-market epiphany. "I realized this [the flea market] was set up to be a place of commerce," said Newmark, "but in reality it's a social thing. It's about people hunting for things *together*. It's a place of community." And so, he believes, is his craigslist.org. Postings on Craigslist are about jobs, housing, items for sale, personal interests and discussion forums. "One of the reasons people like what we do," says Newmark, "is that it's random. This is not a department store."

But does it really help build community?

"In the beginning, I was not thinking about such lofty things. People just needed a way to get the word out." He was working at Charles Schwab when he "saw that people were starting to use the net, back in 1994-95, to help each other. In the beginning, we were just giving people a voice, giving them a break. But it works beyond that." He cites a San Francisco food forum that started out on craigslist.org, with people getting together to eat out. "Eventually, some of the people in that forum got together and started a restaurant, called A16."

The A16 Restaurant is the product of a virtual meeting on the Craigslist "San Francisco Food Forum" between Victoria Libin and Shelley Lindgen. After several trips to Naples, Victoria was using the forum to lament the lack of "authentic pizza" in the city. Shelley commiserated and the two women met for the first of a series of "pizza crawls." Sadly, their particular palates went unsatisfied. Back to Craigslist.

"We found this pizza thread," recalls Victoria. (A "thread" is a conversational string devoted to any specific topic.) "And through that we found this guy who knew *everything* about pizza." The "guy," Christophe Hille, joined the two women in a partnership that became the A16 Restaurant – named after a highway that runs between Naples and Bari in southern Italy. Then they found a line cook on the internet... but they weren't finished with Craigslist.

"We announced our opening on the Food Forum," says Victoria, "and people showed up. People told other people. Maybe the most important thing was the honest feedback we got from those customers. They told us things online that they might not have been comfortable telling us face-to face." For instance? "Well, our coffee is better now, for sure. And one person suggested that we do a better job attending to the needs of people with children."

Victoria Libin, the deep-voiced, rapid-fire, behind-the-scenes business manager of the A16 partnership, says the internet is the perfect tool for building community. "Take the Food Forum. People who share a passion for something congregate online. Somebody has a party idea. Online becomes off-line. Faces become attached to e-mail handles. A lot of us become close friends." She pauses to catch her breath. "Of course, sometimes we forget each other's real names and just go by our handles."

Across the country, a group of New York Craigslist devotees formed The Lunch Club. Their raison d'être – "because eating alone is boring" – became the slogan of their web site, TheLunchClub.net. The stated purpose of the site is to promote "gatherings that build community." Lunch Club founder Jared Nissim tells us that after he used NewYork.Craigslist.org to find the perfect East Village apartment, he decided the web service could help "fulfill my need for having a greater sense of connection to the world around me. People were using Craigslist not only for finding jobs and apartments, but also for meeting and connecting with people on a community level. I had always felt that New York was a very difficult place to have a community, which is something that is very important to me. This is a city where most people don't know their next-door neighbors. Yet here was something new – people using the internet to meet and connect in real life for purposes other than dating!"

Boasting more than 5,500 members at this writing, The Lunch Club supports itself by charging small fees for its events. "We bring together people from all walks of life who might not otherwise meet, to sit down and get to know each other," says Nissim on his web page. "We connect people and remove the barriers that keep us from speaking to one another. New friendships, relationships, ideas, actions and endeavors are the result… new endeavors, new horizons, mutual benefit, help in time of need, late night conversations, job connections and life-long friendships!"

MEET THE NEIGHBORS, ONE MOUSE-CLICK AT A TIME.

So successful was Jared Nissim's foray into meeting people for lunch, he decided to expand his community at other hours of the day. The annoying fact was that despite his ability to meet people from all walks of life and from all parts of the city and its suburbs for lunch, after two years he still did not really know any of his apartment building co-dwellers. In the summer of 2002 he disobeyed the unwritten commandment of life in New York City, Ignore Thy Neighbors, by slipping flyers under every door in the building, inviting people to join him first online and then at a party in the building's backyard. When the event got rained out, everyone showed up at Nissim's apartment and MeetTheNeighbors.org was born. "My building became very social and a true community developed in time," he says. "We even joined forces to turn our backyard patio into a garden oasis where we all took up headquarters to help each other through the blackout of August, 2003."

When you sign up your apartment building at Meet the Neighbors, you get a "lobby bulletin board," on which you may encounter such postings as "I made *brownies* – Anyone want to come by?" or "[I] Need a sparring partner for my Brazilian ju-jitsu class" or "Whoever spat their gum out in the elevator, I'm going to find you out." or "Who the hell listens to heavy metal at 4 a.m.?" This is, after all, New York. As one participant in a MeetTheNeighbors event told a reporter, "Normally we don't talk to each other unless somebody's apartment is robbed."

Meet the Neighbors, a direct descendant of Craigslist, has itself been featured in a number of national media, yet the prophet of internet-as-community-builder, Craig Newmark, remains sanguine about his accomplishments. "I grew up as a true nerd," he says, "socially dysfunctional. But I do think that lack of human contact is bad. Lack of community resources is a problem. There are a lot of ways we're involved now in building community. A lot of our users are engaged in acts of goodwill. Maybe you're just unloading a sofa, and the person who comes to pick it up turns out to be someone like you. We help people interact with other people."

Another enabler of e-community is internet-advocate Keith Hampton. After completing his University of Toronto thesis on Netville, Hampton in 2004 built a web organization called I-Neighbors to enable people who share nothing more than a zip code to discover what else they just might have in common. If you register at I-Neighbors.org ("Your Neighborhood's Home on the Internet"), you can post notices about pool parties and car pooling, block parties and yard sales. You can add snapshots to the neighborhood photo album. Before it celebrated its first birthday, I-Neighbors.org boasted more than 3,000 neighborhood sites up and running in the United States and Canada. *The New York Times* called I-Neighbors "a one-stop shop where people can exchange e-mail with their neighbors, find information about them and be matched to those with similar interests."

Hampton started up the program on an experimental basis in a suburban neighborhood of Boston. There he found that 46 percent of those who used I-Neighbors believed the program increased their sense of community, and 40 percent reported that the web site improved their neighborhood's ability to react to an emergency. "One of the strongest criticisms of urban life is that you know very few of your neighbors," Hampton told an Atlanta *Journal-Constitution* interviewer. "This is a way to break down some of the barriers."

Hampton argues for the internet as a community-building tool. "The internet is just another communication medium that any of us use to communicate with friends and family," he told the BBC News in May, 2002. "If you look at it as just another technology that provides you with access to people, you see that communication online leads to more communication, in person or on the phone."

Yet Hampton is curiously skeptical about physical place-making that might promote community. New Villages, specifically designed to enable and promote community, are to Hampton a New Urbanist fiction. "Design does not encourage community," he tells us (ignoring the fact that considerable "design" has gone into his I-Neighborhood), "but merely attracts people who are already community oriented." To our argument that vast numbers of Americans appear to be craving community, Professor Hampton replies: "There are no longitudinal studies to suggest that. It's simply a process of self-selection."

Of course, this is the very point. Given a choice of places to live, many, perhaps most people will select a place that most nearly provides what they desire. Yet Hampton insists there is "a lack of ethnographic studies to support the thesis that a place designed to encourage community can actually promote community." Our own research convinces us otherwise. As Michael Chabon has observed, people bought houses in Columbia, Maryland in the 1960s simply because of the vision that James Rouse articulated.

In Celebration, Florida – a place Hampton has never visited, by the way – we encountered everywhere individuals who had consciously relocated there to find community, which they felt was lacking or undernourished in their former places of residence. Those people, Keith Hampton maintains, are merely pre-conditioned to the sorts of civic activity we associate with community.

"People who live in suburbs are more likely to be community-engaged," insists Hampton. Could it be that suburb dwellers are, in fact, suffering from community deprivation? Not so, he says. "Typical suburban sprawl is not that isolating." New Villages, as he sees them, are merely better-built suburbs, wherein these already engaged people "latch onto places where they can become even more engaged. Residents of apartment buildings are less interested in building community." This last despite the evident success of Jared Nissim's MeetTheNeighbors. org and other inner-city community-building efforts. Dismissing the fact that Nissim and even Craig Newmark have begun to earn a living from community building, he says, "My hypothesis is that those are not going to be successful. There is no profit model in this."

Hampton, whose salary, when the above interview was conducted, was paid by the Massachusetts Institute of Technology and whose research has been underwritten by NEC Corporation, the National Science Foundation and others, uses students to perform much of the actual research he publishes. (Beth Yockey worked on his Netville research when she was a sociology student at the University of North Carolina, Charlotte.) In the summer of 2001, Hampton assembled a small army of students from universities in 77 cities in the United States, Canada, Europe, Africa and Asia, in order to test the "helping behavior" of people in different environments. To do this, Hampton used the famous "lost letter technique" devised by psychologist Stanley Milgram in the 1960s. He instructed his student brigade to carefully "lose" more than 5,000 letters on sidewalks, in public places and in telephone booths. Each envelope bore an address in Iowa and contained the proper amount of postage to get it delivered there. The technique is meant as a way to measure the attitudes of people towards other people who are strangers to them.

Of all the envelopes mailed by their finders, the highest percentage came from Celebration, Florida. Fifty-one of the sixty letters "lost" in Celebration got put in mailboxes and delivered to a stranger in Iowa. (Close behind in second place, by the way, was Vancouver, British Columbia, a city rich in community involvement, apartment dwelling, and opportunities for meeting strangers.) Did the neighborliness of those 51 New Villagers exist before they moved to Celebration, or did the neighborliness of Celebration make them more inclined to help a stranger? Our own experience suggests that living in an atmosphere of community, we are more inclined to be community-minded ourselves. Anecdotal as the evidence may be, there is no lack of it. Just as contact leads to contact, neighborliness certainly leads to neighborliness. The places we live and the actions of others who live there can affect our behavior.

Keith Hampton, despite his sociologist's predisposition toward academic acronyms and obfuscating syntax, believes we can engineer community not by building more walking paths, parks and coffee shops, but by clever use of the internet. As he writes in the journal *Planning Theory & Practice*: "The introduction of ICTs [information and communication technologies] specifically designed to facilitate communication and information sharing in a residential setting could reverse the trend of neighborhood noninvolvement. Local use of CMC [computer-mediated communication] might improve the flow of information and serve to expand local social networks, generating high levels of social capital, reducing the cost and increasing the speed of community involvement."[159]

Not only "might" they; clearly they do. Technology is bring us together in cities and suburbs and villages around the world, contributing to community just as surely as do front porches and neighborhood meeting places and walking trails and public parks. As *The New York Times'* Randall Stross observes, "the success of Craigslist shows an enduring public appetite for online offerings that closely complement life lived off line."

THE INTERNET ICE-BREAKER.

Robert Putnam, disparager of our communal future, does devote an entire chapter of his second book, *Better Together*, to the internet's promise for promoting community. However, he comes away dubious. "Our investigations strongly suggest (as we have indicated) that trust relationships and resilient communities generally form through local personal contact." Putnam somehow fails to notice the ice-breaking power of the internet as means of instigating those "local personal contacts." Beth Yockey, a longtime Craigslist aficionado, has used the internet to acquire a new place to live, a roommate, two healthy cats and research opportunities galore. She stays in touch via e-mail and instant messaging with friends, whether they happen to be right upstairs or on the other side of the globe. And she uses it to make and keep friends right in her block.

Computer contact leads to personal contact. And in New Villages, where streets, sidewalks, pathways and common areas are all laid out to encourage such personal contact, the computer and its offspring have demonstrated their value in the quest for community. New Villages as a rule intend to build community and they embrace the technology as a perfect tool for the job. We have been unable to find a development we would identify as a New Village that does not rely heavily on some variation of the internet for keeping residents in touch with one another. From its prototypical inception, Celebration provided a community intranet called Front Porch. At DC Ranch, RanchNet "creates opportunities for residents to get involved in clubs or sports leagues, connect with neighbors and self-publish based on their hobbies and interests." Residents of Indiana's Coffee Creek Center get their homeowners' association news, vote on government issues and learn about their environment by way of their computers.

On their web site, www.issaquahhighlands.com, the Highlands marketers have put together a video testimony to the satisfaction of villagers with their neighborhood network, prosaically titled IHwebsite. com. "The community web site is becoming a really good tool for communicating," says resident Lacey Leigh. "It's really interesting, the comments that people post. You know, comments about the ponds, whatever." Michael Rubbinaccio says, "We have e-blasts that go out weekly to update the residents on community activities – concerts, picnics, that sort of thing. We're all wired, connected. It's part of being a community."

"It can be something as simple as a new mother wants to organize a Boy Scout troop, and she sends an e-mail out to everyone in the neighborhood," adds Port Blakely Communities' Judd Kirk, "or it can be the community sending out an announcement. And they do that every Monday... People here are so well informed about what's going on in the community as a result of our network." Faris Taylor's video sound-bite sums it up: "It's really the glue that holds the community together." The woman who walks her dogs three miles a day and who in her spare time promotes the cause of Washington's Sound to Mountains Greenway makes the causal link from technology to community indisputable. "It's how we communicate on issues and find out what people are thinking."

HIRING BRAINS, NOT BODIES, FOR THE "DISTRIBUTED WORKFORCE."

As the century's second decade approaches, it's very likely going to be how many of us work. George Mason University's Richard Florida, formerly of Carnegie Mellon University, MIT and Harvard and author of *The Rise of the Creative Class*, argues convincingly that the day of the big office-based corporation is coming to an end. Instead, companies will hire not bodies but brains, allowing their employees to work when, how and where they are most productive.

Cleveland-based developer Albert Ratner, CEO of Forest City Enterprises, hands out copies of Florida's book by the hundreds, hoping to lure the best and the brightest from New York and San Francisco, L.A. and Boston to his new virtual company town, Mesa del Sol. Sitting on the edge of Albuquerque, New Mexico, Mesa Del Sol is a 25-square-mile plateau that Ratner hopes will eventually become "one of the largest planned – and technologically tricked out – communities in the nation," as *Business Week* describes the dream. Just starting construction at this writing, Mesa is designed by West Coast New Urbanism guru Peter Calthorpe. It will be a collection of New Villages, where houses and apartments will come equipped with up-to-the-minute connectivity options in lush, sequestered home offices. Videoconferencing with Europe and Asia – and anywhere else – will be available 24 hours a day at village center compounds, just a jog or bike ride away from the breakfast table. Actual office staff and meeting rooms will be available for renting by the hour. Mesa del Sol, as Michelle Conlin writes in *Business Week*, will be "the first place of its kind built from scratch and targeted at the creative class" in a "post-geographic, location-independent, office-agnostic" world, a world in which many of us find the internet an indispensable tool for daily living.

If Florida, Ratner, Calthorpe and Conlin are correct, the era of the "distributed workforce" could be the beginning of the end for our much-discussed urban sprawl. When people live independent of centrally located office buildings and corporate headquarters, they can forget about daily commutes, spending more time in their neighborhoods with family and friends. Already perhaps twelve to fifteen percent of the United States workforce qualifies as "distributed." As with the number of New Villages under construction, that number is climbing steadily. IBM claims 40 percent of its workforce has no company offices. Sun Microsystems boasts that nearly half its employees have the flexibility of working from home. A third of the managers at AT&T are office-less. At Agilent Technologies the company is saving 60 percent on "virtual workers," which constitute up to 70 percent of its workforce.[160]

From his home office in Central Florida, Lee Moore does business with clients around the globe. New Villages encourage the demise of daily commutes and enable residents to spend more time with family and friends.

Photo by the authors

When New York City's transit workers went on strike in the week before Christmas 2005, about four million bus and subway riders had to find other ways to get to and from their jobs. Smart companies told their employees to stay home and get on the internet. As train stations turned into mosh pits and police turned back drivers attempting to enter Manhattan with fewer than four passengers, ABC News showed lawyers and investment counselors avoiding the pandemonium by working from their city apartments and suburban houses. According to one estimate, the city was losing $100 million a day, but for companies with instantly distributed workforces the economic impact was negligible.

As other businesses, both small and large, look to the future, they will be considering all these trends and events. It seems quite probable that more and more of them will seek ways to diminish or eliminate the real bottom-line impact of home-to-work commuting. For companies that depend on the whereabouts of employees' minds rather than their bodies, an obvious choice will be encouraging them to live in places where the necessities and pleasures of life are close at hand, where the world is easily accessible from desktop, laptop and palmtop computers. Other companies, those whose functions require the physical presence of a workforce, will be seeking settings in which their employees' needs for community and family can be met at minimal cost to the company. Meanwhile, an ever increasing percentage of the population will be leaving the corporate world entirely, forming their own small companies and creating their own work environments. The new model for a "company town" in the United States, and perhaps eventually elsewhere, will be the New Village.

PROPINQUITY MATTERS... BUT IT'S NOT THE ONLY THING.

In his alarm-sounding *Bowling Alone*, Robert Putnam reminds us of an early caveat by a communications pioneer who, back in 1891, prophesied that the newfangled telephone was an insidious wrecker of community that would bring an "epoch of neighborship without propinquity." In other words, our "neighbors" would no longer be the folks next door or down the street, but those in faraway places at the end of the phone wire. Yet, Putnam is forced to observe, when the first comprehensive study of the social impact of the telephone was conducted in 1933 – predating by decades the first broad awareness of urban sprawl – researchers concluded that this communication technology actually worked more to reinforce existing *local* ties than to build distant relationships. The phone gave us a new way to communicate with our shopkeepers, our co-workers, our friends around the block. The internet is simply the next generation in that advance. On a recent weekend, neighbors in Ross Yockey's condo used e-mail to borrow an electric screwdriver, to ask for help changing outdoor floodlights and to seek contributions for a memorial gift of flowers to a bereaved resident. Each of those internet contacts led to a face-to-face contact.

Whether one embraces the technology or watches it from a wary distance, we can all agree that to write about technology as a fixed point in time is to hold oneself up to ridicule. We may be sure that, just as the wall-mounted crank telephone has evolved into the Blackberry, the technology with which we communicate tomorrow will be something very different from the technology we use today. Coffee-shop tables may become WiFi isolation booths. Katrina-wrecked, technology-poor New Orleans could become a showcase of wireless communication. No matter what, communication of whatever type will beget more communication, and communication is the very foundation of community.

For those who earn their livings by creating the places in which we live, the message seems clear. In the future, access to both communication and community will be critical marketing messages, because they will play significant roles in our deciding where to live, either as renters or buyers. Hardwiring every house and apartment for broadband, setting up neighborhood WiFi networks, hiring community organizers, sacrificing salable land for the sake of parks and paths – these are things developers and builders will have to do in order to add value (i.e., profitability) to the places they build. They will do it because they see New Village homes, with rare exception, bringing higher prices than nearby houses in ordinary subdivisions.

And this raises the question as to whether homes designed for community will be inevitably unaffordable for those at the lower end of the income scale. Will New Villages serve to deepen the so-called "digital divide," ensuring that fewer low-income children and adults will have access to the tools of technology?

Perhaps.

In 2004, the University of Southern California's Annenberg Center for the Digital Future (CDF) released a study of the internet's first ten years of public access. The report, "Ten Years, Ten Trends," said that while more low-income Americans have access to the internet through libraries, school, work and other locales, a "new divide" was emerging between those who have broadband access at their homes and those who don't. The discrepancy is in what we are able to achieve with the internet and how fast we can achieve it. So, at first glance, greater access to faster connection for the haves creates greater distance from the have-nots. [161]

Or perhaps not.

At the West Seattle New Village of High Point, the Seattle Public Library has built a spanking-new facility that provides free WiFi and computers for public use. The Seattle Housing Authority is, at this writing, completing a Neighborhood Center that will house a computer room for young people. And that, says the Housing Authority's Tom Phillips, will be in addition to youth tutoring, Safe Futures and Jobs Connection programs, each with its own computer bank, as well as an evening Neighborhood Networks computer program for adults at High Point Elementary School.

A Pew national survey completed in February, 2006 concludes that while education levels and household income still play a role in Americans' ability to access the internet, web usage by African-Americans and Hispanic-Americans had made huge gains in that regard in the past eight years. In 1998, Pew found that among Americans eighteen and older only 23 percent of blacks and 40 percent of English-speaking Hispanics were using the internet, compared to 43 percent of whites. By 2006 those numbers had jumped to 61 percent of African-Americans, 80 percent of English-speaking Hispanics and 74 percent of whites. [162] If the Pew study is to be believed, whites are no longer the most internet-savvy demographic. America's so-called minorities may well be better connected than anyone would have thought possible just ten years earlier.

Even real estate developers and homebuilders driven by the profit motive are recognizing our urge to connect with the world and with one another. For the last hundred years, most of the products they've provided were designed to supply one of our most basic needs. They have given us, as the Rolling Stones so urgently requested, shelter. Now market pressure for satisfying what Maslow identified as "higher needs" has arrived. The new demand for technology is at least in part a demand for community. As that pressure rises, developer resistance will fall.

The building-in of internet connectivity at most New Villages means that nearly everyone who lives in one will have equal access. And, as we'll see in the following chapter, some New Villages include not only those who can afford top-of-the-line single-family homes, but apartment dwellers as well, and, in a few cases even those who live in Habitat for Humanity homes.

CHAPTER TEN
Technicolor Dreaming

We used the phrase "the American Dream" earlier in this book, suggesting that it has meant different things to different people at different times – disembarkation at Ellis Island in the mid-nineteenth century, a house in the suburbs in the mid-twentieth. In the 21ST century, we have postulated, the American Dream is a dream of coming back together, a dream of reuniting our disparate population, a dream of community. Forty years prior to this writing, that same idea was eloquently expressed by Dr. Martin Luther King, Jr. On Independence Day of 1965, King preached to his congregation in Atlanta's Ebenezer Baptist Church on "The American Dream:"

> It wouldn't take us long to discover the substance of that dream. It is found in those majestic words of the Declaration of Independence, words lifted to cosmic proportions: "We hold these truths to be self-evident, that all men are created equal, that they are endowed by God, Creator, with certain inalienable Rights, that among these are Life, Liberty, and the pursuit of Happiness." This is a dream. It's a great dream.
>
> The first saying we notice in this dream is an amazing universalism. It doesn't say "some men," it says "all men." It doesn't say "all white men," it says "all men," which includes black men. It does not say "all Gentiles," it says "all men," which includes Jews. It doesn't say "all Protestants," it says "all men," which includes Catholics. It doesn't even say "all theists and believers," it says "all men," which includes humanists and agnostics.

Dr. King's eloquent sermon – punctuated by congregational shouts of Amen! Yes, sir! Preach it! – went on to lament the racial segregation of America's cities, towns and suburbs. He spoke of "twenty million of my brothers and sisters... still smothering in an airtight cage of poverty in an affluent society... still by and large housed in rat-infested, unendurable slums." Three years after that sermon, the Housing and Urban Development Act and the New Communities Act began eliminating many of those rat-infested slums, helping to finance the private development of new neighborhoods for low-income families, and in 1974 the Housing and Community Development Act provided "block grants" to redevelop existing neighborhoods. Yet, at the headwaters of the new century, no matter how nearly "equal" our monochromatic, income-specific neighborhoods become, it seems difficult, in many parts of the country, to make them anything but separate. And for all their efforts to create community, the dream of inclusion remains elusive for the planners of America's New Villages.

Developers' disappointments.

Spend a few hours in Celebration, Florida, one of the prototypical New Villages, and you may assume that it is inhabited solely by relatively affluent white people. While this is not precisely true – there are a handful of minorities, as well as some renters and owner-families struggling to meet their mortgage payments – it is close enough to the truth to embarrass those who would wish it otherwise. For Todd Mansfield and many of the other planners of Celebration, the absence of visible diversity is a lingering disappointment.

In the early days of Celebration, ethnic diversity and affordable housing were high on the list of goals for the ambitious Disney developers. Todd and many of his Disney management team envisioned their New Village as a peaceable kingdom in which families and individuals of many races, creeds and experiences would settle down side by side. They saw a chance to use tax credits as a means of subsidizing housing that would be at once low-income and profitable for builders. They believed that as the village grew there would be jobs enough at the lower end of the income scale, and that the people who would fill those jobs deserved a chance to be a part of the community.

Ultimately it was the fears of Disney marketers that defeated this line of reasoning. The marketing team argued that buyers would be frightened away by the thought of sharing their village with low-income wage earners. Potential buyers would expect their property values to diminish on account of low-end housing nearby. Perhaps because there were so few models of successful mixed-income developments at the time, Todd yielded to the marketers, a decision he regrets to this day. Todd had worked on a plan to incorporate affordability into subsequent phases of the development, but left before the plan was realized. At Celebration, where Disney's pockets hung deep, he believed there was a chance to "do it right." But it would happen only if diversity were built in from the beginning. As time passed, although rental apartments continued to become available, significant diversity among homebuyers became unattainable.

"One of my disappointments in Celebration is that it is such a wealthy place," says Tom Lewis, former Vice President of the Disney Development Company and the initial leader of residential planning for Celebration. "There is no economic cross section. I helped create that."

Lewis looks around the Barney's Coffee Shop courtyard, where a group of well-dressed architects pull three tables together to talk about the new section ready to build: rich white people building for rich white people. "This is starting to become an elitist place," Lewis sighs. He explains that in Celebration, as in most master-planned developments, the individual builder buys the land and builds on it; naturally, that builder is driven by the profit motive. The more a builder puts into a house, the more he can charge for it and the greater his profit. The greater the profit potential, as demand rises, the higher the asking price.

The number-one problem in achieving New Village-diversity may be their almost instantaneous market success, from the perspective of developers and homebuilders. As more and more people discover their amenities, New Village homes escalate in value far more rapidly than their counterparts in typical postwar neighborhoods. In Celebration, Drew and Kimberly Locher bought one of the new batch of bungalows constructed in 2000. "The people lined up overnight, for maybe eighty or ninety homes." Kimberly remembers. "Drew got there about 6 p.m. the evening before and stood outside with all the other people all night long. And we got one! As soon as we moved in, we realized it was too small." So, as soon as they could afford it, the Lochers moved up from a bungalow to a cottage. They decided to hold on to the bungalow as an investment, renting it out in case the values went up. The bungalow they bought in 2000 for $168,000 was appraised in 2004 for $374,000, more than double in four years. The cottage may be an even better investment: they paid $325,000 for it in 2002, and, according to the appraisal, its value had more than doubled in just two years, to $695,000.

"Our home values in Celebration have been artificially inflated," agrees Mary Pfeiffer. "They are selling the lots by lottery, they are just selling and getting the value up. There are renters, a lot of great renters, but they all want to be owners, and they are locked out of being full participants in the community. The young families are the ones who are being priced out of the market." The surge in home values has caused some of her friends to take the money and move out, but "there are always new people coming in. They all come with that excitement, even eight years later."

"Yeah, we tried to bring in an entry-level product." Tom Lewis can only shake his head. "We had cottages and we had townhomes. We tried to bring in entry-level. But the pricing never got low enough. The escalation came too fast." When Lewis himself decided he needed a smaller home, his best option was to leave Celebration. "I was going to downsize, and, I was not going to pay two-and-a-half times what I could find elsewhere in the Orlando market."

New Villages can break the pattern of single-ethnic-group neighborhoods when builders find ways to include homes of varying price ranges.

Photo by George Nemeth for Seattle Housing Authority

Yet other Celebration residents are convinced that the New Village has a significant degree of income diversity. Ann Whelan, who moved from the San Francisco area to start a new life with her daughter and grandson in Celebration, suggests that the apparent prosperity of people in this New Village prototype is a bit of an illusion. "A lot of people have sacrificed a lot to live here, they can afford the house and maybe not furnish it, or they have to give up their second car. They are really the people who give a lot, who volunteer a lot."

A more obvious form of diversity among New Village residents is social diversity, especially that of age. In contrast to retirement communities – and to typical new suburbs filled with young families – most New Villages boast a population of as many as five generations. In Celebration, fifty-something Ann Whelan has friends in their thirties, her daughter's age, as well as friends much older. "Some of my best friends are in their thirties," she says. "You meet people across the age range, and we all do things together. I think it's because there is this *community.* I'm friends with the seventy-year-olds, I play *pétanque* [or *boules,* the French version of lawn bowling] every Saturday, and there's this opportunity to meet people who are as young as thirty and as old as eighty. Sometimes the kids play too. Everyone has opportunities to meet people of all ages. We know our neighbors, and we talk to our neighbors. The schools also provide a lot of volunteer opportunities to bring people together. Because you have this place in common, you have reasons to get together."

Certainly some developers of New Villages recognize a need for diversity, if for no other reason than to ensure obtaining all the necessary rezoning permits. Among those cognizant development companies is Rancho Mission Viejo in Orange County, California. At its Ladera Ranch, 44 apartment homes have been made available for families who earn less than half the county's median household income. According to the 2000 Census, that median is about $57,706.

In a March, 2004, interview with *OC Metro* magazine, Rancho Mission Viejo's vice president of community development, Paul Johnson, called the issue of affordable housing "very complex." Johnson argued that when the master-planned development's Rancho Santa Margarita opened in 1986, the so-called "urban village"[163] had a number of homes priced under $60,000. "When we opened Ladera Ranch [in 1999], we had homes priced under $200,000." In order to build these relatively low-income units, the developer put together a $1.7 million loan from the California Housing & Community Development Department and more than $25 million in partially tax-exempt bond financing from the county.[164]

This sort of public-private venture could well become standard in New Village development, where a developer's design restrictions force builders to provide high-quality housing regardless of the ultimate residents' income levels. "The architectural execution is at such a high standard that the term 'affordable' carries no stigma," says Paul Johnson. "In fact, Ladera Ranch is one of the few places in Orange County where the range of housing is still the broadest – from the $300,000's (which is below the average price of a new home in the County) to over $3 million. The real issue today regarding affordable housing is building homes for all types of people, from teachers, firemen, single parents, active adults and young professional couples to growing families and empty nesters."[165] As Johnson suggests, there is only so much a developer can do to stimulate economic inclusion. Local governments must see affordable housing for teachers and firemen, as well as office workers and sanitation crews, as being in the community's best interest.

The need for affordable housing is no less urgent in the metropolitan Phoenix area, where DMB Associates has built the New Villages of DC Ranch and Verrado. Architecturally, the two developments are not all that different, save that DC Ranch hews more closely to the regionally ubiquitous desert-modern look. But while DC Ranch is North Scottsdale, near the built-up shopping and office complexes on the northeastern end of the valley, Verrado is long dusty miles on the other side of town. Both New Villages are in Maricopa County, where the population topped 3 million in the 2000 census and may well be pushing 4 million by 2010, and just under a quarter of the county's residents are Hispanic or Latino. The median household income in 2000 was $45,358. In the town of Buckeye, where Verrado sits, the Latino population is even higher than in the county as a whole, 36.65 percent, and the median household income significantly lower at $35,383.

DC Ranch is surrounded by developments built around golf courses, and it has two courses of its own, but developer Brent Herrington says DC Ranch is not all about golf. "That 'lifestyle segmentation' option is like catnip to developers – it's very attractive, because you can say this one group will give you the edge. It's an attractive concept, but it's terrible for community building. Research shows that only a small fraction has an interest in living in a restricted community, whether it be a golf lifestyle village or a retirement village. All of those groups like to network with other sorts of people – if you're a golf nut, you don't want to only hang around other golf nuts all the time."

DC Ranch residents bear out Herrington on that point. "There are so many different things to do here," says Ohio transplant Sheldon Rubin. "You participate, you start to meet other people. This is a real community; that's not just an advertising word." Sitting down with strangers at Market Street Coffee, Sheldon and his wife Jane do not exude wealth. "We bought a house here for, like three-hundred thou," Sheldon says, "which for us was a lot of money. There were all income

New Village designers encourage the chance encounters that build friendships and community across age, race and gender differences. Some days the outdoor chessboard at Issaquah Highlands attracts much younger players.

strata, from all over the country. South of Thompson Peak Road, we call it 'the ghetto,' because the houses started in the mid-two hundreds."

Yet the Rubins have become friends with people in other parts of the village, even in the dazzlingly expensive, gated Silverleaf section, where every home is custom-built. "Some of them have diamond rings like plates, enough to blind you. But they are all super nice. There's no stigma attached to us from not being the richest people here. Our neighbors are very active in the country club, but they are great friends of ours nonetheless."

"When we plan district cores, we are mixing incomes," says Brent Herrington. "We try and plan in diversity, we believe most people like an economically- and age-diverse community. We used to say that we wanted to build a place where the partner in the law firm could live next to his kids' teacher." Herrington says builders would have bought up all the lots in DC Ranch for top-of-the-line custom homes, but DMB turned them down. "Custom housing makes the most money. But we wanted to do a full-spectrum planned community – from apartments to condos to patio houses to single family production houses, all the way to high-end custom homes."

SHOCKING ESCALATION, DISAPPEARING AFFORDABILITY AND THE FULLNESS OF TIME.

Herrington was town manager for Disney in Celebration before moving to Phoenix as vice president of DMB. By that time, 1998, construction had begun at DC Ranch. Houses were selling faster than they could be built, and prices were rising even faster than the frames.

"The market went nuts," Herrington recalls. "I couldn't get a house when I came on board, I had to wait. The houses escalated at a shocking rate." By the spring of 2005, mid-size single-family homes that started at a price-point of $220,000 were selling for more than $600,000. "One of the condos went on the market for $650K. The market reacted dramatically. We're building 200 more apartments to keep up and try and continue to provide affordable housing."

The Rubins consider themselves lucky. By 2005 they would have been priced out of the community they have found at DC Ranch. "When we moved in, we had neighbors from all income levels," says Sheldon in his clipped Cleveland accent, chuckling at the fact that he could now get something close to double the price he paid for his house just five years earlier. "The inflation has been insane." His wife, Jane, gives him a gentle poke in the ribs. "Did you ever think we'd live in a $600,000 house?" The question is rhetorical. Sheldon answered, "Only after we won the lottery!"

Noteworthy is the fact that while the Rubins and Herrington speak of diversity in DC Ranch, they make no mention of ethnic divergence. In our two days there, the only recognizably Latino people on the Ranch were waiting tables or gardening. On the other hand, this was anything but the case on the far side of Metro Phoenix, where it was still possible in 2005 to buy a small house for $250,000. In DMB's Verrado, many, perhaps even the majority of shoppers at the home sales center had dark complexions and Hispanic accents. In the still-building town center, it was obvious that Latinos were both welcome and comfortable.

Bill Retsinas, whose heritage is Greek, moved there when he was named manager of the new Bank of America Verrado branch. Retsinas is naturally gregarious. "Everything encourages talking and walking here," he tells us. "It's great! Being at the bank, I see everyone in the town coming in, every ethnic group, every age group, single people, retired people."

To Kyle and Melissa Campos, formerly of Santa Barbara, California, their new banker knows whereof he speaks. No sooner had they settled in Verrado than other members of their family moved out to join them. "The house was the last reason we moved here," says Kyle, who works for a software company. "The house alone didn't sell this place, it was the way that the community was set up and the relationships."

Brent Herrington is bullish on the subject of diversity in New Villages, but he says it's not going to come about overnight. "I served on something called the Underserved Borrowers Outreach Group," he says. "That's one of the challenges, figuring out why minorities don't borrow. The Hispanic community has a stigma against indebtedness. In Phoenix, it's difficult to foster diversity. We have a Caucasian population in the development industry – white men building subdivisions for white men. But with Verrado, we are taking the long term perspective – 100-plus years. In the fullness of time, the balance will come. We are building for the next generation. Our robust hope is that diversity increases with every passing year. The first generation will probably be commuters. We can create a sufficient core, bring the employment, then the stabilization will come. We are trying to encourage diversity, but we're taking the long view."

Yet even in the long view, one cannot help but see that the more desirable "community" becomes, the more people will want it and the more they will be willing to pay for it. Until it is viewed as a prerequisite, community will remain an amenity, like a golf course, which creates above-average price acceleration.

Around the country, several developers in search of diversity have taken the unusual step of including in their New Villages homes constructed by Habitat for Humanity, the worldwide ministry that enables low-income renters to enter the arena of home ownership by means of "sweat equity" and low-interest mortgages. Because Habitat chapters are held to the same rigorous standards as other builders, New Village Habitat houses are the same as those of more affluent neighbors. And in the Phoenix area, Habitat for Humanity Valley of the Sun has leapfrogged developers by creating their own master-planned neighborhoods.

The first of these, South Ranch, opened in 1994 and quickly became a model for other Habitat chapters. While not quite a New Village – there are no shopping, office or entertainment spaces – South Ranch does have a homeowners association, covenants, front porches, a park and sidewalks. Its twin, Villa Esperanza, is going up not far away, scheduled for completion in 2006. Because Habitat for Humanity has no prohibition against resale (though the organization retains right of first refusal), homeowners are able to get good prices when they decide to sell and to move up to more upscale neighborhoods. This, in turn, has raised the value of all the homes in South Ranch, so that more affluent white families are moving in among the largely Mexican immigrant population. Another way to achieve economic and ethnic diversity.

For most New Villages, however, whatever level of diversity they can muster is usually achieved by inclusion of rental property, by building apartments over shops or garages or in the midst of single-family homes. Since those options are anathema for strict adherents of old-school zoning and building codes, even they can be a struggle for developers. Dawn Thomas believes they are worth whatever struggle they take, because if not for the affordable apartments, she and her son might never have found community in a place like Celebration.

GETTING PAST THE SKIN COLOR.

In the Disney version of Community, planners and architects designed a place that would have great nostalgia-appeal for many Americans. Streets resembled those of the *Dick and Jane Readers*, the town center seemed a bit like Mayberry from *The Andy Griffith Show*. In the ads and promotional materials, the Disney team depicted a diverse community, and they made sure ads appeared in magazines that had ethnic readership. Yet the neighborhoods on which their designs were based – places like Augusta, Georgia and Charleston, South Carolina – were historically all-white. African-Americans lived on the other side of the tracks in those towns. There were no blacks in *Dick and Jane*, and only a few in the background on later editions of *Andy Griffith*. The nostalgia card did not play well among ethnic minorities. Yet the Celebration managers were determined to convince home seekers that this would be a place friendly to people of all colors. As part of this effort, the company hired sales people of varied ethnic backgrounds. One of them was Dawn Thomas, the black mother from Trinidad whom we met sipping a strawberry yogurt smoothie at Celebration's Market Street Café.

After her divorce, Dawn and son Eddie had moved from Miami to Orlando, where her mother worked for Florida Hospital, the company that was building the Celebration Health center. She began hearing about "this great new place" first from her mother, then from friends who worked for The Walt Disney Company. In 1995 Dawn landed a job with The Celebration Company as a "community guide," providing pre-sales information to curious visitors. It meant a cut in pay, but she saw potential for advancement. "A leap of faith," she says.

Dawn began to think of herself as Celebration's staff ambassador. "This was while the town center was just being built. The minute you'd open your mouth and you sounded like you knew something about this place, you'd have a crowd. There was excitement all the time. I would orient the people, talk about the 'Five Cornerstones,' then funnel them to an agent. Sometimes people came in and asked me a lot of racial-type questions. I tried to be honest, but there was always a 'thresholding' concern for some of the ethnically non-white people. 'How many of "us" are there?' I tried to get them to look past the skin color, and ask,

'Does this place meet your criteria? If it does, then this place will work for you. If you find that skin color is more important to you, then that changes everything.'"

For Dawn, with her memories of being snubbed as an island outsider in a black New York City neighborhood, there was at least one criterion more important than skin color: a good environment in which to raise her son. "I had always worked two jobs year-round, three during the holidays. I never got to go to any of Eddie's school events. It was hard. I had to experience Eddie's childhood vicariously, through my mother. My mother would go to the basketball games, the plays, the band concerts, the track meets. I would get home at night and my mother would tell me, 'You should have seen what Eddie did today!'"

Previously, much of her time had been spent traveling between home and work. In the New Village, Dawn could reclaim those hours of her life. She moved into an apartment next to the Celebration office. She got a fold-out couch for herself and gave Eddie the single bedroom, because "a growing boy's got to have some privacy." As Celebration flourished, Dawn was promoted, but never into the lucrative sales position she saw for herself. She worked as apartment manager, as secretary to the Town Manager, then as assistant Town Manager. "Whenever I told them I was considering moving, they made a place for me. They wanted me to stay."

Eventually, Dawn Thomas made a place for herself at Frontgate Realty, one of the independent real estate companies in Celebration. She now sells and rents property inside and out of the New Village. For herself she rented a bungalow vacated by a Celebration resident who moved in with his girlfriend (and that happens too in New Villages) and still was able to walk to work. With Eddie enrolled in Celebration School, she also could walk to many of the sports events.

Eddie became a standout in high-school sports and nurtured dreams of winning a sports scholarship to college until he hyper-extended a knee in his senior year. Around the house, Eddie took on the cleaning work so his mom could enjoy more of her time off, but she never trusted him with the cooking. Eddie decided he could manage that and one afternoon he let the housework go, and "intentionally messed things up." When his mother came home, she was mad until she went into the kitchen and saw the balanced meal – chicken, rice, peas, corn – Eddie had prepared.

"She said, 'You did this?' I said, 'I did.'" Eddie, a young man built to play either defensive back in football or power forward in basketball, developed a passion for cooking. He attended Orlando Culinary Academy to pursue a degree in *Le Cordon Bleu*, working a house-cleaning job in Celebration in pursuit of his new dreams, first an MBA then a bed-and-breakfast establishment of his own.

While there are not many stories of racial diversity in Celebration, the story of Dawn Thomas and Eddie Smith, to this point at least, must be classed a happy one.

Village diversity, U.K.-style.

Interestingly, ethnic diversity is even rarer among the oft-cited models for America's New Villages, the rural villages of Europe. Out of England's 354 districts, the Cotswold District, which includes the village of Minchinhampton, ranks 285th in ethnic diversity. According to the 2001 U.K. Census, nearly 99 percent of Cotswold citizens are white; 0.2 percent are South Asian, 0.1 percent Afro-Caribbean, and 0.2 percent "Chinese and other." That fits resident Katie Jarvis's description of her village of Minchinhampton, home to about 5,000 people. "In Minchinhampton," says Jarvis, "I can think of one family with a white British father and a black African mother; and one other child of mixed race, who lives with his white mother and white sibling from a different father. But that's about it."

In the United Kingdom, the subject of ethnic and racial diversity is much in the news at the mid-point of the century's first decade. In 2003 the Home Office conducted a Citizenship Survey that asked questions about perceptions of racial discrimination and the impact of diversity on community participation and cohesion. From a sample of 15,000 people in England and Wales, the survey concluded that in England there was "no significant relationship" between a town's degree of diversity and such "social capital" measurements as civic participation and volunteering. But, according to the report published in 2005, "the more ethnically diverse an area is, the less likely people are to trust others within that area."[166] Significantly, that level of trust had nothing to do with socio-economic diversity, only with ethnic diversity.

For the most part, that mistrust exists in the cities, where the overwhelming majority of England's ethnic minorities make their homes. In the relatively small Cotswold District, the big city is the southern port of Gloucester. There minorities generally live within their own neighborhoods and poverty is no stranger. Further north is the city of Stroud, with a thriving Muslim minority, including shopkeepers and town council members. And there is Cirencester (Siren-sess-ter), "a million miles away socially from Gloucester, but 22 miles in reality," as Katie Jarvis puts it. Princess Diana used to shop in Cirencester, while Gloucester is known for its "chavs" – a derogatory term for those who are both tasteless and possibly on public assistance (etymologically, it derives from being "on the chav"). Outside the cities, in those

Common, accessible spaces – rather than private closed-in backyards – draw people together. So an age- and income-diverse volleyball game can be played in the shared "front yard" of people who live in townhomes, condos and single-family houses.

Used by permission of Port Blakely Communities (Issaquah Highlands, Washington)

picturesque little villages that white Americans cherish in our photo albums and our hearts, the question of racial diversity rarely comes up.

"Diversity in the English countryside, on the whole, has nothing to do with race," Jarvis assures us. "It means different ages in the same village (not just a retirement enclave), different income brackets (not just the wealthy) and different reasons for being there. Some work nearby; some commute; some were brought up there; some move in for the schools; and a very few are weekenders. But mainly all are white. There is no issue with this; it's just how it happens to be, mainly because people who live here either have a long-standing connection with the countryside or are rich enough to move into a very high-price area and be able to commute to jobs."

Jarvis has written of the Cotswolds' mounting concern over gentrification. In a 2002 article for *Cotswold Life*, she interviewed the Reverend Graham Martin, pastor of a little church in Bibury, where the population is just over 500 souls. "One of my biggest sadnesses is the way high house prices mean there's a noticeable turnover in people," said Rev. Martin. "Young couples I marry can't live here — and it's the same at the opposite end of life. When it comes time to live in a nursing home, or sheltered accommodation, people in their 70s and 80s have to grasp reality and go to live in Cirencester or Fairford, or leave the area altogether to live with relatives."

By the arrival of the 21st century, Jarvis writes, the ancient little village of Bibury had developed a tri-layered population: "those who are resident permanently; about one third of the houses are weekend lets and retreats; and then there are the 'seriously rich,' who have a house in London, one abroad and a yacht!"

Like Katie Jarvis herself, Reverend Martin has no plans to leave. "What I enjoy about village life is the fact that there is a relatively small number of people: it gives an opportunity for intimacy. I took my dog out early this morning and, in half an hour, I'd been spoken to or tooted at by over twenty people... There's still a wonderful community spirit – it's changed, but it exists."[167]

A HABIT OF HOMOGENEITY.

Back in the United States, Ike Eissinmann believes it's that very community spirit that enables a New Village to transcend differences that might otherwise keep people apart. "We have as many different sorts of people living in Celebration as you could find anywhere,' he says. "We have just as many gay families, just as many people living together that are not married, we had just as many people wearing Kerry buttons as Bush buttons."

Ike and his wife Alex might overestimate the political mix in Celebration, yet both Republican and Democratic viewpoints certainly were represented – and vigorously argued. In New Villages, as elsewhere, diversity stimulates conversation. Sitting around their dining room table, the Eisinmanns' neighbors, Larry and Terri Haber were asked, "When you think of this place, would you describe it as diverse or homogeneous?" They answered in chorus:

"Diverse." (Larry)

"Homogeneous." (Terri)

"Well, it's not *racially* diverse," Larry hedges. "It's diverse because we have people from all walks of life. We have the international couple in our Rotary, someone from India, someone from the Netherlands, from the U.K. It's the background. It's definitely not racially diverse, because it is so expensive." (Larry fails to note the error in his assumption that Florida contains no African Americans or Hispanics who are also wealthy.)

"I wish it were *more* diverse," nods Terri. "I have that same selection of people in my groups, but I don't think that that makes us diverse, because we are all the same types of people, with the same desires and wants, and how we like to live. I think that the similarity of the people who want to live here and the economic status of all the people who live here make it not diverse."

So, it all depends on your definition of "diversity." Terri Haber's point is that, for all the assurances that mixing ages and occupations constitutes diversity, perhaps the real test for a 21st-century American neighborhood is ethnicity. Does it provide homes for brown- and black- and yellow-skinned people, not just for whites? Can we tell by walking the streets that a place is diverse? If we are going to create diversity that is visible to the naked eye, we may require more than good intentions by planners and developers and builders and real estate agents; we will likely require a break with tradition by buyers and renters of property, because most Americans, whatever their ethnic background, have grown used to living in largely segregated neighborhoods.

As we have seen, segregation was written into law in the early days of the Great Depression, when the Home Owners' Loan Corporation and then the Federal Housing Administration red-lined neighborhoods that were mostly poor or mostly black as being unworthy of government-backed loans. Even earlier, in 1926, the U.S. Supreme

Court ruled that while blacks had the right to own property, whites were not obligated to sell to them. These two events ushered in the age of restrictive covenants, contracts among land speculators, homebuilders and homebuyers to ensure that neighborhoods would remain closed to "undesirables." By 1968, when Title VIII of the Civil Rights Act finally outlawed housing discrimination, the nation had grown accustomed to segregated neighborhoods. That was the year Martin Luther King, Jr. was assassinated, prompting racial violence in more than 100 cities. Some cities, such as Seattle, quickly passed their own open-housing ordinances in hopes of calming the outrage. But the vestiges of restrictive covenants and the reality of neighborhood segregation are still with us.

In 1988 George W. Bush bought a house in Texas that was restricted by its original deed to "white persons only, excluding bona fide servants of any race."[168] And in 2005, embarrassed residents of an upper-class Seattle neighborhood called Innis Arden were signing a petition to remove from their 60-year-old deeds the very same covenant.[169] Our prejudice is historical, and perhaps not so easily confined to the history books.

REJECTING ISOLATION, FORMING TRIBES.

Let the authors confess to a prejudice of our own: a prejudice against prejudice. And not merely against the prejudice that underlies conscious discrimination, but against the sort of comfortable homogeneity whose inevitable spawn is an attitude of either superiority or inferiority, depending on your end of the social ladder. If we surround ourselves exclusively with people who are like us in some important way, then our neighborhood becomes the "right" place to live, a place inhabited almost exclusively by wealthy white boaters or golfers or corporate executives or retirees. In such ghettos of privilege it is all too easy to believe we have arrived in the promised land of *community*. After all, we have so much in common with our neighbors in a place like that. It seems to fit our very definition of "community": a place to live not in isolation but in the company of other people who share some values and interests and who interact for mutual benefit.

What's wrong with that? Maybe only the isolation part.

That word, isolation, at its root, means "island," and in fact every New Village, like every "golf community" and "retirement community" and "singles community" has the potential of drawing in on itself, becoming an island of self-sufficiency and self-interest, to the point of dismissing the rest of the world as unnecessary. If the danger in that is not self-evident, we need only consider the famously-named "golden age of fraternity" that flourished from the end of the 19th century through much of the 20th. This was the time of joiners and secret societies, the time when men felt obliged to belong to something like the Masons, Odd Fellows, Knights of Columbus, Lions Club, Orangemen, Knights of Labor, Hibernians or Royal Black Knights. Women joined their auxiliaries and other organizations of their own.

In the oft-cited *Bowling Alone*, Robert Putnam argues that the decline of membership in societies such as those indicates an alarming rejection of community in the United States. However, a less-heralded book by another Harvard Professor, Jason Kaufman, throws cold water on Putnam's theory. Those fraternities actually split us up into fractious interest groups, Kaufman insists, and – despite the fact that surely Masons and Elks can be personally inclusive of others – he believes that if we hope to have a more equal and harmonious society we'd be better off without their societies.

In *For the Common Good? American Civic Life and the Golden Age of Fraternity* (Oxford), Kaufman writes, "This period in American history was unique not because Americans suddenly turned to one another for faith and succor, but because faith and succor were suddenly turned into matters of organizational self-segregation." Organizations (and neighborhoods) with restrictive memberships are "not endorsing the commonweal, they're endorsing what's good for them."

The golden age of fraternity may be, as one reviewer has concluded, in fact responsible for "a tradition of racial prejudice and interethnic hostility, a fear of government, half-hearted attempts at public social services, and even a political system dominated by special-interest groups."[170] When we self-select ourselves into societies or neighborhoods where people unlike ourselves are unwanted, we are violating the non-isolationist principle of community.

A better option is explored in Ethan Watters's 2003 book, *Urban Tribes*. Watters tells us than in many American cities young adults are encouraging community to develop not merely despite diversity but on account of it. He provides example after example, such as that of a woman identified only as Heather, whose "urban tribe" consists of blacks, whites, Hispanics, gays and straights, immigrants from Germany, Afghanistan, Korea, and Portugal. "Because of the diverse nature of our group we have a range of opinions on the issues of the day," Heather says. "But we are like family. We give each other rides to the airport, we cover each other's shifts, we care for those who get sick and give each other money when we're in a pinch. We feed each other - every meal I eat is with at least one member of this group - and we cut each other's hair." More community than some of us might desire, certainly, but it illustrates that group support can flourish in an inclusive environment.

Yet, as we've admitted, one may also find that support on islands of exclusivity. Differences of opinion may be shared on the golf course or at the health club. Families from different backgrounds may come together at the members-only swimming pool.

New Urbanist guru Andrés Duany has considered this conundrum, rationalizing his passion for incorporating inclusivity into New Villages, frequently against the objections of developers, builders and buyers. In *Suburban Nation*, Duany and his co-authors write: "Building social ties among people who already share a reservoir of cultural referents, family history, or personal experience is qualitatively different from building ties among those who do not—different in how it gets done, how often it gets done, and what happens as a result."

Thus Duany distinguishes, as have others before him, between "bonding social capital" – linkage among individuals or groups with much in common – and "bridging social capital" – connection among individuals or groups across a greater "social distance." Both kinds of connections, says Duany, are valuable to us as individuals, but "bridging" is the thing that reconciles democracy and diversity. "A society that has only bonding social capital risks looking like Bosnia or Belfast," he writes. "Yet bridging social capital is intrinsically less likely to develop automatically than bonding social capital—birds of a feather flock together. Social-capital strategists need to pay special attention to the tougher task of fostering social ties that reach across social divisions."

In Seattle, the notion of injecting poor people into wealth-heavy new developments has been turned on its head. The city's Housing Authority has chosen instead to tear down the ghettos and build New

Villages in their place, to let the privileged into what were distinctly un-privileged neighborhoods. In places now called NewHolly and Othello Station and Highland Park (cited in earlier chapters), the Authority has razed blocks of substandard housing and created self-contained live-work-play neighborhoods that attract upscale homebuyers. And their neighbors are the relocated poor, living in subsidized but new upscale housing.

Here, in the first new large developments in Seattle proper in fifty years, families of many different backgrounds share apartment and townhome complexes, share medical facilities and libraries, share playgrounds. They shop together, walk together, board the bus together. Festering centers of unemployment, crime and drug use have become true neighborhoods, where people of different colors, from different countries, in different sorts of jobs, can work together to build community. No one seems to be worried about their property values plunging.

In fact, when the developments' first market-rate houses and townhomes went up for sale in 2005, builders opened their doors to long lines of would-be buyers who had camped out on the sidewalks the night before – just as in Celebration and Verrado. The first five single-family homes were bought up almost instantly; townhouses sell before the interior walls are up.[171] Considering the cost of housing in Seattle – as high as $469,000 for a single-family home in NewHolly – this suggests a sea-change in the way Americans will be selecting the places they choose to live. Community – along with proximity to work and entertainment – is superceding class or race distinction.

It is critical for developers, builders and the rest of us to make this commitment to community. We all need places to live in which families and individuals of diverse income levels can feel welcome. Without such places, our cities will become simply too expensive for people of even moderate income. Consider what's happened in the Washington, D.C. area in recent years. Between 1997 and 2005, the price index for housing there rose 153 percent. In suburban Fairfax County, Virginia, the median sales price for existing homes rose 129 percent between 2000 and 2005. In 2000 you needed to spend about 48 percent of your income to buy a single-family detached house; by the end of 2005, you might spend as much as 89 percent of your income – nearly everything you earned going into your home. If you bought a townhouse in 2005, it would have cost you 61 percent of your income, just 44 percent for a condominium. One result: today about half the people who work in Fairfax must commute from outside the county.

These numbers, in the opinion of George Mason University housing expert John McLain, add up to a housing affordability crisis. "Labor shortages and the resultant wage inflation caused by housing supply shortages and the lack of affordability," McLain warns, "threaten the region's economic health." And beyond economics and the chamber of commerce's tooth-gnashing, consider the cost in social opportunity. Buying a home has long signified the first step in one's admission into the social mainstream. As more Americans are denied that opportunity, we can expect to pay a steeply rising price. To a degree, the New Village can address affordability, provided developers and governments are willing to subsidize the cost of some units, as has been done in the Seattle Housing Authority's New Villages and elsewhere.

CAN SOCIAL ENGINEERING MAKE A DIFFERENCE?

All in all, we are seeing a remarkable rise in social engineering. Planners with the best of intentions are trying to put people together in combinations that might not occur if these people were left to their own choices, or, perhaps more accurately, to their own resources. Though it isn't always easy, they are finding ways to mix black, Latino and Asian families in with whiter families, mixing economic groups as well as ethnic groups. But will they stay mixed? Will they truly *integrate*?

Science is still working on that one. In fact, the science of "artificial societies," as it's called, is very much in its infancy, but in university labs and think tanks around the country, researchers are creating cyber-models that will help us understand the possibilities. Using what has been called "agent-based modeling," some researchers have concluded that left to its own devices and unmanipulated, society tends to organize itself around certain commonalities, just as our ancestors did in the era of fraternal organizations. Among social scientists such as David Goldfield, history professor at the University of North Carolina Charlotte and author of *Cottonfields and Skyscrapers*, the belief is that this tendency has resulted in neighborhoods that, no matter the "equal opportunity" signs posted everywhere, are "self segregated."

Simply and obviously put, Armenian people tend to associate with other Armenian people, Bolivians with other Bolivians and so forth –

which is what we all might have told the researchers without benefit of any grant money. "We tend to live in neighborhoods where the people around us look like us racially and are in our same economic class," says Georgetown law professor Sheryll Cashin. Discussing her 2004 book, *The Failures of Integration* on NPR's *All Things Considered,* Cashin said that despite the hopes and dreams of equality and integration, "in terms of who we spend intimate time with on a day-to-day basis, most of us are spending time with people who look like us and are in the same class."

This, Cashin believes, is "the black middle-class dilemma." In order to provide a better life for their children, financially successful African-Americans "move into an area that is overwhelmingly white and affluent. For black people, what tends to happen, in realistic markets, is once you get a critical mass of black people, white people flee, and that depresses property values in the neighborhood. And then the next lowest rung on the income ladder of black people comes in to try to take advantage of the depressed housing markets. And so within a decade the… affluent or middle-class or upper-middle-class black people who sought to create a suburban enclave find that the social distress that they thought they were escaping has migrated right up to them."[172]

Yet there is a sort of chaos-theory aspect to all this social engineering. So many factors can and do come into play when members of society are moved from one locale to another that the effects of racial and ethnic mixing are not always easy to predict. In the realm of artificial societies, scatter a few "blue" families in among a cluster of "green" families and any number of combinations is possible.

Writing of such research in *Atlantic Monthly,* the Brookings Institution's Jonathan Rauch argued in 2002: "Artificial societies suggest that real ones do not behave so manageably. Their logic is their own, and they can be influenced but not directed, understood but not anticipated. Not even the Olympian modeler, who writes the code and looks down from on high, can do more than guess at the effect of any particular rule as it ricochets through a world of diverse actors. The diversity of individuals guarantees that society will never be remotely as malleable or as predictable as any [single] person."

At least in the laboratory, computer models hold out the hope that putting people into unlikely situations, or unlikely neighborhoods, can produce healthy changes in the individuals, in their neighbors and even in the neighborhoods themselves. "To me," Rauch writes, "the early results of this work suggest that social engineering can never be as effective as liberals hope, but also that it need not be as clumsy as conservatives insist." [173]

Social engineering has been at the heart of creating new towns and villages from the beginning, because most of the people who planned them were dreamers of one sort or another, dreaming of making places that were somehow better than the places they knew. In the late 1960s James Rouse, talked about his dream of Columbia, Maryland to the United States Commission on Civil Rights. If a place was built from scratch, he said, on a large enough scale to permit "a wide variety of housing and activity and uses, so that it was truly a town or a community or a city or whatever it might be, then there would be absolutely no problem to a completely open policy regarding race in housing." Indeed, as Rouse biographer Joshua Olsen points out in *Better Places Better Lives*, the first child born in Columbia was to a white wife with a black husband.[174] At the end of his life, Rouse was prouder of this feat of social engineering than of anything else he'd achieved.

Todd Mansfield led a group of Disney executives to Baltimore for a consultation with Rouse in 1993 to seek his input on their plans for Celebration. (This over the objection of Michael Eisner, who wondered why his team would bother spending time with "that old man.") Rouse was nearing his 80th birthday and would shortly learn he had not only lymphoma but Lou Gehrig's disease. He had lived a full life, turned around the economic fortunes of large cities, championed affordable housing, built untold shopping centers. Yet when Mansfield asked what he considered his most important achievement. Rouse took only a moment to consider. A few years earlier, he said, he had gone back to Columbia and met a young man and a young woman who were about to get married and start a family. They had met as children at a Columbia playground, had grown up together in the 1970s, had fallen in love in that place he had built. "One of them was white," he said, "and the other was black. Without Columbia, those two kids never would have met."

Back in the 1950s, when all television and most movies came in dreary shades of gray, children used to ask each other, "Do you dream in Technicolor?" In Maryland, James Rouse was dreaming in Technicolor. Further south, in another state of the old Confederacy, Martin Luther King was having Technicolor dreams of his own. The American Dream has never been black-and-white.

CHAPTER ELEVEN

No Developers Allowed

So, if what most of us really want is to live among friends and neighbors in peaceful coexistence with the environment, to be able to walk when we choose not to ride, to be within a stroll of the destinations we require, to have a sense of place rather than of displacement, why is it that most of us don't get what we want? The simple answer is that we have not been making enough noise about what we want. We haven't demanded it. But simple answers are rarely sufficient in a complex world.

To really get to why we continue to embrace isolation in our culture, let's watch a video shown to students of family-run businesses at the Harvard Business School. Early on in the video, a mature, sophisticated San Franciscan named Eddy Starr Ancinas faces the camera and tells us that when she was younger, she used to have deep reservations about her family's participation in the timber industry. "I would say to my father, 'Tell me some good things about cutting down trees, so I can tell my friends in California we're not raping the forest. And then we got into real estate development, and in California that is even worse."

Real estate development: *even worse*. About the worst business a thoughtful young woman could imagine. The company in question is Seattle's Port Blakely Tree Farms, today considered one of the most environmentally sensitive of all major timber companies, and parent company of Port Blakely Communities, developer of the New Village of Issaquah Highlands. While Eddy Ancinas has learned that all developers (and all timber companies) are not alike, she is probably ahead of many Americans on that score.

BULLDOZING THE COUNTRYSIDE.

For those who care about the places we live, the word "developer" is enough to make us throw up our arms in a sign of the cross, hoping to ward off these evilest of spirits. Word of their approach turns local activists into Paul Reveres: "The Developers are coming! The Developers are coming!" And why should it be otherwise? Look what most land developers and public policy have given us over the past half-century and more – insular subdivisions, strip malls and several thousand acres of parking lots. Some legacy. No wonder most of us hear the word "developer" and conjure up images of bulldozers ravaging the countryside. Dissatisfaction with suburbia is written into our cultural muscle-memory. Even if we live in it, we really don't want more of it right next door, because it might lower our property values. We tar all developers with the same brush, and the developers own the brush.

It is time we learn that all real estate development is not alike and that all developers are not equally unlikable. In fact, as we have seen, there are companies building places such as Issaquah Highlands and Baxter and DC Ranch and Coffee Creek, developers who respect the land and who value community. They build their village-like neighborhoods in such a way as to profit by conscience-driven development. They often do this in spite of the fact that it would be quicker and easier and at least in the short run more profitable to develop land in the traditional way: buying up large plots and selling it off in pieces to individual homebuilders, apartment builders and shopping-center builders. Instead, this new breed of real estate developer takes the long view, often in the face of fierce resistance from the people who would stand to gain the most from their success and from government agencies who ought to be their staunchest allies.

It is time we learned to differentiate.

It is time too for the majority of real estate developers to see that they cannot continue turning quick profits on the sorts of non-places they have been making for us. There is simply no future in it, not for the long term. The longer they persist in pursuing sprawl, the more resistance they are going to encounter, the louder the cries of "No developers allowed!"

Even the developers in the white hats need to think more carefully about the deep and largely justified bias that rallies a populace against them. New Urbanist and Smart Growth literature abounds in condescending, even adversarial references to opponents of "good" development. People who have learned over time to be wary of builders bearing promises of prosperity are disparaged by developers as NIMBYs – Not In My Back Yard – or BANANAs – Build Absolutely Nothing

Anywhere Near Anything. Even preservationist Jane Jacobs called the anti-development people "squelchers." The danger of putting simplistic labels on one's opposition is that the label may become a badge of honor, as the British monarchy discovered to its chagrin in the 17th century when it went down to defeat at the hands of the Puritans they had derided as Roundheads, because wore their hair cropped close.

It is not the NIMBYs or the BANANAs or the squelchers who keep us from getting the community we want. The blame, by and large, falls on the building industry itself, partly due to its prolonged resistance to change and partly due to the failure of those who have changed to educate the public about those changes. When the industry satisfies those two conditions – changing its own attitude and educating the public as to what is possible – it goes a long way toward gaining the approval of government, without which change is all but impossible.

Tom Lewis helped Disney "work within the system" to create the New Village prototype of Celebration. Ten years later, with housing prices risen drastically, Tom sits at Barney's coffee shop, wondering if he was too successful. In the background, a group of developers plan additions to the town's retail core.

Photo by the authors

Working within the system.

Lee Constantine was chair of the Regional Planning Council for Central Florida when Disney proposed the huge development that would become Celebration. He felt it was "extremely important" for the council to stay very close to the project since, as he puts it, "Disney had their own arrangement with the state" and whatever Disney wanted Disney was likely to get. Constantine became almost a partner in the process, agreeing that trees could be moved from one side of the site to another and that apartments could be built over storefronts. "They had a new idea every week, a new plan almost every month," he says. "They would ask me to come out and take a look." The Celebration Company understood from the beginning that they could only succeed by working within the system.

Disney had been dealing with Florida governmental agencies since the early 1970s and they knew success in building a New Village would depend on their ability to make it through or around the mined quagmire of the state's recently adopted Growth Management Act. The Disney team gave itself an advantage by hiring the man who'd been largely responsible for getting that law passed in 1985, Tom Lewis.

"They wanted to bring in someone who understood the growth-management process." Lewis, a lanky, slow-talking Georgian leans back and sips his latte at Barney's on Market Street in Celebration. "One day I was enforcing rules, the next day I'm trying to figure out how to get around them."

"We went through three phases," says Lewis. "Phase One: 'You're crazy. People want what we're giving them now – curvy streets, cul de sacs, etc.' Phase Two: anger [on the part of homebuilders]. 'You're going to do this, it's not going to work, but it's going to be mandated in all the localities, its going to be put into ordinances.' Phase Three: adoption by many of the doubters. Now they're all using the same language we used to sell Celebration."

Florida's Growth Management Act seeks to encourage compact development and limit urban sprawl. In Osceola County, adjacent to Orlando's Orange County, urban sprawl was not high on the list of governmental concerns. In a relatively low-income area, county commissioners readily saw the economic potential of any large development. "The price of houses was the thing that got them on board," says Tom Lewis. "The Osceola County people did a study, and calculated, at what price level does a house pay for itself? That is, at what point do the taxes on that property pay for the typical government services it will require?"

The break-even sales price for a new home, the county concluded, was about $145,000, nearly twice the value of the average Osceola County home at the time. Lewis reported to others at Disney that the starting price for homes in the New Village could be no lower than $145,000. It would take a price that high to win county approval.

Unfortunately, a price-point that high augured against the developer fulfilling one provision of the Growth Management Act, that of providing low-income housing that would be priced below one-half the county's median household income. Eventually, Disney had that GMA requirement "mitigated" by writing a check – actually several checks totaling $300,000 over three years – to establish an affordable housing office in the Osceola County. While this so-called "payoff" became a public relations liability and a weapon in the hands of Celebration's opponents, it was welcomed by county officials who felt they already had more than their share of "affordable" housing; what they want was some less affordable housing to stimulate growth and shore up the tax base.

Tom Lewis's government connections proved invaluable in these negotiations. He was able to go over the heads of low-level bureaucrats whenever he deemed it necessary, but satisfying governmental demands beyond the county level proved more challenging. "The Regional Planning Committee [RPC] had quite a vendetta against Disney," he says, because all Disney's earlier projects had been grandfathered into existence, using planning regulations that were written before the RPC was formed. "So the RPC took about two years to study this new project," Lewis says. "They had been handed a stack of plan books about eight to ten inches high. That was the first regulatory step towards Celebration, it was also the toughest."

Once Celebration cleared the initial state and regional hurdles, it came up against what Lewis calls "the typical bureaucratic challenges – changing ordinances, getting bureaucrats to give up control. We had to create new sections for several ordinances. Our alleys were disallowed at first. The county wanted eighteen-foot alleys, and we did real-time tests to prove that the garbage trucks could work in much narrower spaces. We ended up with eight-to ten-foot alleys."

Environmental challenges at first seemed insurmountable. There were rules against removing trees – and the developers wanted to keep whatever native trees it could, in what was mostly a scrub-and-marsh terrain – but most of the existing trees were in the wrong places. "We had to basically strip the land, because it was going to require so much fill dirt. We moved several hundred trees." Lewis points to a large oak, the base of its trunk perhaps three feet in diameter, at the center of Barney's patio. "Like that tree. It was moved here from somewhere else. The tree mover looks like the rocket mover down there at Cape Kennedy. I looked at this huge machine, and I said there's no way these trees are going to live. But we didn't lose one of them."

OLD HABITS DIE HARD.

Lewis believes the Celebration negotiations will one day provide a case study in compromise between developers and governmental agencies. "Today, the elected officials in Central Florida love it. They are proud of it, they take credit for it when they go anywhere."

Lee Constantine, now a state senator, supports Lewis's claim. "This was Walt Disney's real dream," he says. "It's part EPCOT, part Wally Cleaver-ville. I look back on it and remember what a great deal of fun it all was. With Disney's resources they could produce these great, lifelike models and we could move them around and try new things. We were like kids playing with blocks."

If the living, breathing example of Celebration can make New Village believers out of career politicians, one would think that might be the end of it. But perhaps no one is more inflexible about the way neighborhoods should be built than the people who plan most of our neighborhoods. We toured Celebration with a group of real estate developers, most of whom had been involved in real estate businesses for twenty years or more. To a man (and they were all male) they simply could not fathom why anyone would want to live in a place like this. It made no sense to them. The yards were too small, the streets too narrow, the mix of building types simply inexcusable.

"I can't see people using those front porches."

"Imagine having to walk out to the park to barbeque instead of doing it in your back yard."

"It seems like a real pain in the butt to drive into an alley to park your car instead of just pulling into your garage off the street."

"If I'm gonna pay two-fifty for a house, I'll be damned if I want a condo right down the street."

"Let alone an apartment building."

"You mean people don't mind looking at the golf course across the street like this? I'd want it to be right off my back deck."

It was eye-opening to hear their resistance to even the simplest alterations in neighborhood design. It made no difference to them that the restaurant at which we'd all feasted the night before was only a short walk from these houses, or that our van stopped to let a platoon of children cross on their way to school, or that a square foot of a Celebration home was worth considerably more than a square foot in a nearby traditional subdivision. When it comes to reaching accord with the community-seeking population, one might suppose that developers are their own worst enemies.

But no; that distinction probably belongs to homebuilders – the companies that buy the land from the developers and then hire or assign contractors to erect homes, apartments or shopping strips.

"Builders are definitely our worst enemies," says Kevin Warren, developer of the Indiana New Village of Coffee Creek near Chicago. "People talk about the hurdles of doing developments like this – the zoning boards and negotiating with the fire departments – but those aren't hurdles. The real hurdle for us has been reluctance in the builder market."

What this means is that the companies that erect our houses and apartments and shopping centers have sets of plans they build from – and usually each design comes with a catchy name: The Fauntleroy, The Oakwood, The Cloister – and they tolerate little if any deviation from these blueprints. Developers of New Villages, however, cannot allow "The Oakwood," probably designed with a two-car garage to fit on a half-acre lot, to be erected in the middle of a village block.

Whether the village is inner-city or suburban, the master plan will necessarily call for alterations in any pre-existing building plans. Garages generally must be moved to the rear. Set-back, or distance from the curb, will likely need to be drastically diminished. Porches may be *de rigueur*. Fiber optic cable may need to be built in. And commercial builders may even need to do the unthinkable, putting residential units above storefronts. This is not the way they're used to doing business. This is not how they've gotten rich.

"It's slowly starting to change," Coffee Creek's Warren tells us, "but builders in our area are busy and don't want to be bothered with all these stipulations. So we mostly bypass them. We get the buyers hooked and send them to the builders and they say, 'We want a house built like this.' And the builder reluctantly agrees to build it, because it's what the buyer wants, not what we want."

Once that message is delivered by buyers, it can do wonders for a builder's flexibility. Consider the case of the national home building company, David Weekly Homes. One of the largest builders in the country, David Weekly was at first very reluctant to build a house the way The Celebration Company wanted it built. Celebration's demands were unlike anything the Houston builder had ever dealt with. They were ready to walk away from the deal, until they realized they would certainly be walking away from a lot of money. Some company was going to build these houses, because these were the houses people moving to Celebration *wanted*. The builder caved in. Now Weekly enthusiastically markets its Celebration-design houses all around the country.

More often, in a typical subdivision or city pocket, builders have their way in the early stages. Thus cookie-cutter homes continue to proliferate, with one or two builders taking a relatively small area of a developer's total holding to create a so-called "neighborhood" or "community" of look-alike houses. After that area is nearly "built out," as they say in the trade, the developer will look for another builder to start work on the neighborhood next door, as he, the developer, goes through the next round of street grading and pipe laying that provide the requisite infrastructure.

RETHINKING THE ECONOMY OF HOMEBUILDING.

If those developers and builders would open their minds to the possibilities, they might see that their way is not the best way. Because they do their building in such a piecemeal fashion, they miss the economies of scale. Developing an entire village at once eventually makes for larger bank deposits. But by building small, they are able to come under the radar of some governmental regulations and avoid stirring the NIMBY passions. This makes their path through the bureaucratic quagmire a relative walk in the park. The traditional developer and builder (and we do not mean the "Traditional Neighborhood" developer of New Urbanist terminology) is happy to encourage the anti-development credo that Big is Bad and Bigger is Worse.

In fact, as we have seen, it is the large-scale, more dense, self-contained new villages and towns, that preserve at least some of the natural environment, that hold down air and water pollution, that contain sprawl. If more homeowners and the governments that represent them would come to grips with the truth of this statement, we might go a long way toward a more sustainable long-term development pattern on the growth edge of cities in the United States. Take the cases of Brentwood, Tennessee, and Bainbridge Island, Washington.

Brentwood is an incorporated city just outside the southern boundary of Nashville, a place with the feel of country, not city. Its broad-lawned country manor houses – McMansions to some Nashville neighbors – nestle against former horse pastures. Folks in Nashville consider Brentwood a suburb, even though most of them can't afford to live there. Until recently, whenever land went up for sale in Brentwood it came with a price tag of $200,000 an acre and up. Most homes were priced in the range of a million and up. Brentwood incorporated in 1969 so it wouldn't have to take any advice or interference from its big-city neighbor up the road. Were that not the case, Nashville Executive Director of Planning Rick Bernhardt would have had a very different opinion to share with the Brentwood commissioners when they took up the issue of master-planned development.

Before returning to his native Nashville in 2000, Bernhardt had spent seventeen years as director of the Planning and Development Department of Orlando. There he watched Celebration come to fruition and then engineered the conversion of Orlando's former U.S. Naval base into the New Village of Baldwin Park. He saw what could happen when city government and developers worked together to create community, and he knew he was looking at the future.

"We're beginning to see the same push for community in Nashville as we saw down there," he told us in 2005. "Though so far most of it here is infill, because there are not so many large tracts of land as there are in Central Florida. We've started changing some of the old zoning laws to make things possible. My experience as a planner has convinced me that this approach is the way to build sustainable communities, great communities where people want to live." In 2002, Rick Bernhardt had great hopes for a New Village proposed for nearby Brentwood.

The founder of Dollar General Stores, Cal Turner, had the biggest chunk of privately owned land in all incorporated Brentwood, a horse farm of 579 acres off Interstate 65. Cal and his wife Margaret wanted to use their land in a way that would provide something special and lasting for the people of Brentwood, Nashville and middle Tennessee. They wanted to build a New Village, something along the lines of Letchworth in England. But rather than force his idea on Brentwood, Turner invited the public to a meeting where they could consider a lot of ideas – maybe a village with trails for equestrians rather than bicyclists, maybe a commercial-residential cluster where people could walk to work, and some way to highlight the natural beauty of the area, with small streams featured in the design.

What the Turners did not want was to sell off their land in pieces, to be nibbled away by builders who would happily hew to the current zoning restriction: single-family homes on lots of at least one acre. Brentwood and Williamson County had been growing that way for at

Multimillion-dollar McMansions define the coastline of Palos Verdes, about thirty miles south of Los Angeles.

Photo by Philip Greenspun at http://philip.greenspun.com

least 33 years, and the Turners wanted to stop that mindless sprawl. They hired South Florida-based planning consultants Dover, Kohl & Partners, whose slogan says the company is "focused on revitalizing traditional towns, growing neighborhoods and fixing sprawl – by design."

About 200 Brentwood residents showed up at the town library meeting (which in New Urbanist jargon is called a "charrette") to share ideas on what the Turner farm might become. Meeting leader Victor Dover challenged the citizens to "think big and think grand."

The people arrived having thought; they spoke loud and clear. The people at that meeting wanted a real town center, with small shops and offices and restaurants, something that did not then exist in Brentwood. They wanted residences of different sizes and prices, not more exclusive, look-alike palaces. They wanted a park the whole town could use. They did not want more subdivisions of cul-de-sacs and one-acre lots. One participant heard Victor Dover say afterwards, "We held a 'blank-sheet-of-paper' meeting, and all these citizens suggested the very things that would create a heart for the community. It was inspiring."[175]

The Brentwood City Commission, however, was not inspired. After months of back-and-forth between the public and the consultants, after the Turners spent more than a million dollars putting a master plan together, the commission decided to stick by its 1940s-vintage zoning laws. Cal Turner was visibly disappointed. "I threw in the towel," he said, admitting to reporters that he was "a little frustrated...We had an opportunity to do some out-of-the-box planning. I am disappointed that Brentwood is going to stick with the same old box."

Brentwood Mayor Joe Reagan countered with a few metaphors of his own. "Putting in office buildings and retail and overloading on residential [development] is not thinking outside the box – it's the other side of the coin: overloading the system."[176]

After feeling the heat of disbelieving media and disappointed reformers, Brentwood eventually reduced its lot size requirements, making it possible for builders to sell homes there for less than a half-million dollars. However its citizens may never get their town center, park and streamside stroll. Their traffic problems will likely continue to mount, as three- and four-car families move in and commute to one or two jobs, and as more people drive more miles in search of groceries, restaurants, doctors, clothing and entertainment.

"It was a well-thought-out plan," laments city planner Rick Bernhardt. "We would love to have had that development in Nashville. It provided just the type of environment we want, with different housing types for different income levels, with a well-thought-out design. Unfortunately it did not meet Brentwood's vision for itself."[177]

And who was it that defined Brentwood's vision? It was not the people who spoke in Brentwood, it was the representatives of government. When we approached Brentwood's Planning & Codes Director Joe Lassus for an explanation of the town's rejection, his answer was terse: "The problem that stalled the proposal in question related to the city's infrastructure which could not handle the tremendous loads that would have resulted from this development. Our infrastructure was financed and sized based on a much lower residential density that was proposed on the Turner tract."

Infrastructure – primarily streets, water lines and sewer lines – must be modified to accommodate any sort of development anywhere. In the case of successful New Villages, developers usually work with local governments to make improvements and extensions that generally benefit residents of other neighborhoods as well as those who will live in the new neighborhoods. The conversation in Brentwood never actually got that far, because someone in government said the D word, *density*. Brentwood's commissioners in the 1970s had passed a law that

Another McMansion goes up in Plano, Texas, at the northern edge of Dallas's suburban sprawl.

Photo by Dean Terry from the film Subdivided (www.subdivided.net)

no residential lot could be smaller than one acre, and, by damn, no commissioner in 2003 was going to change that.

THE D-WORD IN DEVELOPMENT.

"Density" has come to strike fear in the hearts of politicians, just as "developer" panics the populace. The word suggests sardine packing, crowded tenements, thick-headedness. When people don't get it, we say they are *dense*. But if you want nice places to shop, restaurants, movie theaters and the like, a little density can be a good thing. Commercial establishments use density as one of the factors in determining where to build their places of business. Businesses need a certain amount of residential density to ensure traffic. If a shop is going to be in a strip shopping center or an enclosed mall, the neighborhood density need not be as great, because such venues are meant to be accessible primarily by automobile. And because we have accepted our fate as shoppers-by-auto, we are blessed with millions of strip malls.

Density has political ramifications. Altering the population density means changing the status quo. It usually means adding a lot of new names to the voter rolls, and who knows how that might influence the outcome of an election. Such potential changes represent threats to the insecure.

"In my opinion," says a real estate developer who makes his home in Middle Tennessee, "the Brentwood issue had far less to do with infrastructure and more with a cultural mindset that many at Brentwood's city government and some residents hold about density. Remember, this is a city that has no zoning for development above one unit to the acre."

The above-cited developer, whose livelihood depends to some degree on the politicians he accuses of thick-headedness, has requested anonymity. While some in Brentwood felt Turner botched the deal himself by coming across as an arrogant, tantrum-prone billionaire, this developer feels government should have taken a longer view of its own self-interest. He points out that the Turner Farm's failure, at least to a degree, has prompted Brentwood's office holders to reexamine their intransigence on density, with the result that Cal Turner has been allowed to sell off significant pieces of his farm to developers and builders who will create somewhat denser pockets of housing, but who will not create the sort of village community that Turner envisioned.

"Their version of density is to allow smaller lots (and now a limited number of townhomes) as part of a master plan," says the incognito developer, "as long as the overall gross density is still at or below 1.0 dwelling units per acre. Many Brentwood residents are proud of this, but others see it as the poster child for sprawl."

And herein lies the sad and ironic truth for the people who live in places like Brentwood. If their government officials fail or refuse to seize the opportunity of New Village development, they are likely condemned to a future of relatively unplanned and uncontained sprawl. Well-planned developments filled with parks and other amenities they might enjoy are forsaken for smaller neighborhoods that actually wind up taking away more of the open space they cherish. Their enclaves will by necessity become more densely occupied, because there will be always be more people. Their roads and streets will become more densely traveled, their water and sewer lines stretched thinner and their taxes raised to make the inevitable repairs and improvements.

That's what's happening now on Bainbridge Island, across wide Elliott Bay and Puget Sound from Seattle. Twenty years ago Bainbridge politicians rejected a master-planned development on a thousand acres of the island. The company that wanted to build it, Port Blakely, is the same company that created Issaquah Highlands. The company had forested the land for nearly a century and had once operated the world's largest lumber mill there, as well as the company town of Port Blakely and the island's only ferry service. It is no exaggeration to say that the company built the island of Bainbridge. But when it proposed a master-planned development, the islanders rose up in protest.

"We were simple, we didn't want it to be anything fancy. We heard them talk and it was too much to swallow. We couldn't deal with a new restaurant, let alone the whole island. Bainbridge wasn't going to let it happen." Sandy Sinton, who lived through the Bainbridge brouhaha, remembers it as an unpleasant time.

The developers may have been ahead of their time, or perhaps heavy-handed in their approach, choosing to partner with a California real estate group with experience in master planning. "There's a lot of people on Bainbridge who could absolutely not stand the folks coming up from California trying to take over their island. They had these hotshots from California, overextending their hotshot-i-ness. People were very angry."

Sinton is in her seventies now, and she and her husband have retired near Bend, Oregon. When she lived on Bainbridge, she rode the ferry home every day from Seattle, where she was executive assistant for the CEO of Port Blakely Tree Farms, the company that was trying to create a New Village on her island. She considers herself friendly and popular, so "the people liked me, but not what my company was doing."

In the midst of their fight to keep the developers away, Bainbridge citizens incorporated the town of Winslow, which subsequently created a Local Improvement District. The District is extending water and sewer lines to areas that have been sold off by Port Blakely, in small chunks, to various builders. Under the company's original plan, Port Blakely would have picked up a significant portion of that cost.

Recently the town has initiated "Winslow Tomorrow" – a plan to create a new Urban Village on the island – spending millions of dollars to get essentially what the developer would have paid for permission to create. The former anti-growth activists on Bainbridge are realizing that a master plan will save them more green space and "small town" amenities than the alternative.

"I would say now that the company vision was the right thing," Sandy Sinton told us in 2006. "I would say that it will probably take twenty years for the people to figure that out. That island belongs to the people. It's humorous and it's sad… And it didn't matter a whit that the company had historically developed Bainbridge." Now Port Blakely is getting out of Bainbridge Island, one typical suburban neighborhood at a time. Denied the opportunity to think big, developers go back to thinking small. Defeated land owners scale down their dreams.

CHANGING THE RULES IN THE MIDDLE OF THE GAME.

On the other side of the country, in Davidson, North Carolina, the exact opposite has occurred. Davidson is home to Davidson College, where Woodrow Wilson went to school, and is pretty much a village in its own right, with quaint shops, variable-sized housing, walkways, restaurants clustered around the tree-walled campus. When they saw what architect Tom Low, a New Village pioneer, was doing in nearby Vermillion, city officials decided to make New Urbanism the law in Davidson, and officials in other small cities on the outskirts of ever-expanding Charlotte followed suit. After a period of celebratory exuberance, Low realized he might have oversold the concept.

"The really big obstacle in Charlotte – which I didn't anticipate – was that when the small towns became so enthusiastic about traditional neighborhood development versus suburban development and rewrote their ordinances, what they did is they basically forced these changes upon the development community, as opposed to giving it to them as an option. What that created was huge – it just polarized the entire development community against the municipalities and against professionals like myself, who were just basically trying to provide the tools to do this. So we were viciously attacked by the local building industry."

Low, who had set up the Charlotte office of Duany Plater-Zyberk and Company (DPZ) in 1995, found himself up against the local real estate and building industry, which in Charlotte, as in many cities, is a major element of the regional establishment. "The development industry doesn't want to be told what to do. They said, 'We know what the market is, leave us alone and let us deliver.' There was a huge backlash and I got the butt of that. So I spent my first five years back in Charlotte basically writing counter-articles and counter-responses and so forth to the people who were attacking us. Basically I was put on the defensive."

No longer defensive, Tom Low has seen New Villages circle Charlotte like fortresses ringed against sprawl. Birkdale Village in Huntersville, Afton Village in Concord, Prosperity Ridge and Ayrsley on Charlotte's outerbelt, Baxter to the south. And in the city's urban core, Gateway Village, First Ward, Latta Pavilion and Ratcliffe on the Green are providing living-working-shopping-entertainment opportunities for citizens of the city that just a few years ago yearned to become a second Atlanta, North America's prime showcase of urban growth run amok.

Ironically, developers who take on projects like these find often themselves doing battle with a city government which by now really ought to know better. As Robert McMillan, of Ayrsley developer Cambridge Properties, puts it, "[Charlotte's] current zoning laws and traffic policies actually serve to promote sprawl and retard smart growth plans like Ayrsley. It would have been much easier to do another big-box suburban project."[178]

URBAN GROWTH BOUNDARIES: LINES IN THE SAND.

Battles between developers and government are being waged from East Coast to West. In the Northwest, the Portland region became the environmentalists' darling for establishing an Urban Growth Boundary back in 1979. But not until the late 90s did growth pressures begin to demonstrate the Boundary's drawbacks: it reduced the acreage of available land for people to live on, and consequently reduced the availability of affordable housing. By 1998 only 35 percent of houses sold in Portland were affordable for families earning the city's median income.

The same effects became more immediately apparent in Seattle when Washington State followed Portland's lead. Despite the sound defeat of a growth management initiative by 75 percent of Washington voters, the state Legislature drew up development boundaries around

Despite homebuilders' concerns, residents enjoy proximity and friendship with neighbors seperated by only a few feet.

Used by permission of Port Blakely Communities (Issaquah Highlands, Washington)

Seattle and other Puget Sound cities as part of its Growth Management Act of 1990. The legislators were assured that there was enough vacant or underutilized land within those boundaries to accommodate twenty years of population growth; however, they missed the fact that building on a lot of that land – wetlands, steep slopes, industrially polluted "brownfields" – would be either prohibitively expensive or actually in violation of other existing laws.

Within just two years of the state drawing up the Urban Growth Boundary, Seattle saw its percentage of owners-vs.-renters dropping dramatically. As many as 70 percent of single family homes for sale could not be afforded by any family at or below the median income level. Significantly, families with children were moving out and not being replaced. "The trend may have more to do with Seattle housing prices and the kinds of people who are able to pay $350,000 for a bungalow," the Seattle Times reported. Since most of the homes were being bought by two-income, childless couples, the city looked "more and more like a theme park for adults."[179] Traffic congestion was getting worse, not better, as working people moved further out and commuted to jobs inside the city.

The business-sponsored Washington Research Council concluded in 2001: "Governments impose regulations on development for reasons they consider sound, but such regulations result in higher prices for homebuyers. Urban growth boundaries, impact fees, sensitive area and wetland ordinances, and complicated, prolonged permitting processes are not only contributing to the costs of developing new housing, but inflating the prices of existing housing throughout Washington and the country."[180] In fact, when developers anywhere today face a threat of government interference in their business, Seattle is held up as the example of all the bad things that can happen when government attempts to tell people where they can live and tell builders where they cannot build – not that government hasn't been doing just that for the past hundred years or more.

When the urban growth boundary was drawn, Port Blakely Communities' Judd Kirk was somewhat disconcerted to find it ran right down the middle of the land his company wanted to develop as Issaquah Highlands. Now Kirk had government agencies from Washington State, King County and the City of Issaquah to deal with.

"People were talking more in symbols and emotional terms," Kirk recalls. "We became kind of the poster child for growth management. Basically, the state and the county said, 'We can't move the line. We just passed this [law] and this is the first test; we can't roll over for this huge massive project, otherwise it doesn't mean anything.'

"The biggest frustration was getting people to consider what the realistic choices were. So we went around for several years and said: Here are your choices. You either have about 400 five-acre estates, which was the zoning at the time – very expensive housing, no public open space, everyone using their single vehicles, all on wells, all with their own septic tank, and no new interchange for I-90 to relieve the congestion, no right-of-way – versus the other way, which would meet the goal of the Growth Management Act, and have affordable housing, public open space, a new interchange. And we just had to convince people about the environmental issues, which we did; convinced them that we could do a better job with some planning, and by giving them about 1,500 acres of permanent open space."

When it looked as though the town of Issaquah might be siding with the naysayers, Kirk took off the gloves. He announced that Port Blakely would be selling off its land in five-acre plots. He even had the For Sale signs printed up and posted. That turned the town politicians around, so that by the time King County officially announced its opposition to Issaquah Highlands, the Issaquah government was in Port Blakely's corner. The town took the county to court and won, thus turning Issaquah Highlands into a true public-private partnership.

This never happened with the New Village of Redmond Ridge, built by another timber-and-land company just to the north of Lake Sammamish and Issaquah Highlands. In this case, the developer is Quadrant Homes, whose parent corporation is Weyerhaeuser, one of the world's largest timber companies, used to getting its way in the Pacific Northwest. Further south in Washington, Quadrant has successfully managed public and governmental opinions to construct the New Village of Northwest Landing near Olympia, and it has had success converting several of its timber tracts to community-fostering neighborhoods in Oregon and California as well. But Redmond Ridge has butted its head for years against a wall of government delays. As Quadrant executive Susan Heikkala sums it up, "People in our communities are blissfully unaware of the struggle we go through to build them."

Peter Orser has been with Quadrant for eighteen years and has been trying to complete Redmond Ridge for sixteen of them. "The issue is that when a Fortune 500 company walks to the plate and says that they would like to build one of those New Villages, it becomes a sinkhole of opportunity for the surrounding cities, for fire districts, water districts, whatever, to correct many of their past lack of investments. So we end up not only mitigating *our* impacts, but also impacts that go well beyond what would have been caused by us."

Orser is bitter about the experience. "People think because we're a Weyerhaeuser company, we get all that land and all those 2x4s free," he told us in an interview squeezed between meetings with county and city officials. "I have been to so many council meetings, sitting there, trying to explain in a very personal sort of way that we are on the same side."

Orser is not at all displeased that Quadrant has decided not to begin any more New Villages in Washington. "They're the best approach, of course, but it becomes financially unfeasible, driving the land developer to go back to the 100-lot subdivisions, without the planning... The master-planned communities that we've done, we've been asked to make *huge* financial commitments up front, and then wait a long time to recoup them. So the time involved is any investors' bane, and the more you put in up-front, and the longer you have to wait, the worse return on your investment there is."

In contrast to Peter Orser, Port Blakely's Judd Kirk has nothing but good to say about the government officials he's encountered in Issaquah. Working closely with town officials, he and his team assembled a number of focus groups to get a feel for what local people wanted when it came to neighborhoods. In addition to the anticipated responses – minimal traffic impact, affordable housing, preservation of open spaces and the like – Issaquah officials were impressed by the number of times they heard the word "community." From one focus group, gathered from an earlier master-planned development called Klahanie, community was the top item.

"We found that all the people who didn't live in Klahanie hated it – it's ugly; it was built on the concept of the automobile, not for walking; it's bad design – but the people who lived there loved it. The residents stayed there, even though they had grown out of their houses, or were ready to downsize, because they loved the community, loved knowing their neighbors. They can get a ride to the airport, or if they're sick, they have friends to call on them. The overwhelming message was that in a real neighborhood you have a sense of community."

Once Port Blakely had its plans in place for Issaquah Highlands, "we wanted to have this central place, where we would have our map, our displays, where people could drop by anytime to understand what the plans were." The town made room for Kirk's display on the second floor of City Hall. As the public-private relationship matured, Port Blakely Communities and Issaquah's Planning Department wound up across the hall from one another. In contrast to Peter Orser's experience, developer and government agencies realized they were on the same side.

"Again, this was this atmosphere of trying to do things differently. How can we break the mold, how can we work together, and not waste money? So it made sense, since we would be working with their planners on a daily basis." Kirk admits the arrangement raised a few eyebrows. "They have taken a lot of heat for it, from some of the usual folks who would be opposing things – 'Oh, you're in bed with the developer' – but that's kind of died down a bit. If I was the city, I would want the developer right there, so I'd know what they were doing. If they need anything, we're right there. They just come over and walk in. Earlier today, I ran into the planning director in the men's room. We were able to talk and get some issues resolved. I know it would have taken two weeks to set up a meeting with him."

INNER-CITY VILLAGES.

While such proximity is unusual, it suggests that when developers and government agencies work in concert, we are more likely to get new neighborhoods that will promote community, rather than more of the same old isolation. Once again, we emphasize that these New Villages need not be located at great distances from central cities. In Florida, Senator Constantine believes that the greatest thrust for community actually will be made within the cities rather than in the exurbs. As the perfect example, he points to Baldwin Park, Orlando's former naval base, now converted to a New Village. With its parks and walkways, shops and markets, its single-family homes, condos and apartments,

Baldwin Park qualifies in every way as a New Village. The principal difference between it and Celebration is that while the Disney village is built out in Osceola County in the Orlando exurbs, Baldwin Park butts up right against downtown Orlando, in fact is *in* downtown Orlando.

"We have good news like this all over Central Florida," Lee Constantine proclaims from his office in Tallahassee. "We suddenly have villages being built right in the midst of cities, and these are living, breathing, shopping, working, playing environments. There's an explosion of condominiums and downtown living in Central Florida." People, he says, want to be near each other again.

In the mid-1980s, as Disney was pondering what to do with the land that would become Celebration, Orlando was "really finding out what it takes to recapture a sense of community," says former Orlando Planning Director Rick Bernhardt. "The city council changed some of our old zoning laws, and people showed a willingness to reinvest in downtown. We realized that people were looking for it, for a sense of community. And the demand of the public generated a response by the private sector." Bernhardt oversaw the initial phase of the base transfer from the U.S. Navy to the city of Orlando. "There were a lot of people who wanted to fight the Navy's leaving, and others who just wanted to turn the whole thing into a park, but the mayor believed we could do better than that for the city."

As soon as Celebration became a success, Bernhardt says, Orlando realized it could duplicate that success within the city limits. "When you see the effort people go through to get into that kind of environment, people who could well afford their own McMansions, you know it will work. At Baldwin Park we skipped several steps of the approval process because we could build on people's acceptance of Celebration. We didn't have the usual objections to mixed use and high density, because people could go out to Celebration and sort of kick the tires, see that it works."

When they can build community at a city's heart, developers generally encounter less resistance of the build-nothing-nowhere sort than they must battle on the city's fringes. While there may be more home- and business-owners in place ready to picket change of any kind, in most cases, city government has first and last say on what happens inside city limits. That generally allows the developer to concentrate his or her energies. But for another closed-down inner-city naval base on the other side of the country, layers of governmental red tape started at the federal level and ended with city government, with county and state agencies thrown in to complicate the mix. For complexity of developer-government relationships, Liberty Station may be the record-holder.

When the U.S. Navy announced the closing of its seventy-year-old Naval Training Center in 1993, it handed over more than 550 acres to the city of San Diego, California. A few strings, however, were attached. The Defense Department said the city had to use the property to create jobs and to stimulate the economy in ways that would soften the impact of the military cutback. Shades of the New Deal and the Federal Housing Authority. Moreover, because of the roles certain buildings had played during wartime, the Navy sentimentally insisted they be left intact.

However, some in city government saw the NTC acreage as an instant cure for San Diego's critical shortage of affordable housing. The city ranks second lowest in the nation for housing affordability at this writing and San Diego County has declared a "housing state of emergency." In the first quarter of 2005, the average new home price in San Diego was $422,220 for an attached unit – townhouse or condo – and $797,041 for a stand-alone home.[181] Those price tags, as it happens, are just about average for housing in what has become of the city's Naval Training Center, a New Village called Liberty Station.

Federal and local agendas clashed from the start at Liberty Station. The Navy's stipulation of economic stimulation, and especially its insistence on leaving certain structures intact left room for building only 349 homes. Buyers for those homes literally lined up for a chance to get into Liberty Station, never mind the county's imposition of a "Community Facilities District" levy of between $178 and $358 per month on prospective residents.

The state of California threw a few regulations of its own at the project, including one that made it illegal to build anything west of Interstate 5 exceeding thirty feet in height; this meant that anything above two stories would need low ceilings and a flat roof to qualify.

It goes on. San Diego's Airport Authority, desperate for a way to expand beyond its city-cramped boundaries, demanded the base property all to itself. In nearby Point Loma, one of Southern California's most desired pieces of real estate, high-powered residents demanded that the city replace their former military neighbors with exclusive single-family homes, so as to further entrench their Point Loma exclusivity. Equally insistent Native Americans felt this was a good opportunity to reclaim lost tribal lands. Advocates of the homeless wanted to occupy the old existing barracks, gyms and educational facilities to meet one of the area's most dire needs.

Into this riptide waded local developer Corky McMillin. In 1998, McMillin beat out a national company, Lennar Homes, for the "adaptive re-use" development of Liberty Station. In the years that followed, McMillin and the city's Redevelopment Agency endured and won no fewer than seven lawsuits. They survived the replacement of several city council members who had voted for the original plan. They watched the Naval Department renege on part of the deal, retaining the southern tip of the base property for enlisted housing. They shook their heads in disbelief as a number of the original base structures – few of them visually entrancing – were entered on the Registry of Historic Places, thus eliminating the possibility of extensive alterations on those buildings.

Through it all they kept going.

"We looked at it as combination of opportunities and restraints," muses McMillin Development's Walter Heiberg. "I give the city and the Navy all the credit for doing the best they could, considering all the conditions."

Heiberg, a slim blond with a pencil moustache over a stiff upper lip, is project manager for Liberty Station. He loves to quote former City Council member Judy McCarty's answer to concerns that his company was less well-heeled than the national developer that wound up second in the bid to design Liberty Station. "If it's the difference between having the money and having the passion," McCarty said, "I'll take the passion. You can always find the money." That is certainly true of homebuyers at Liberty Station, where condos start in the low $400,000s, while townhouses and single-family homes go from the $600,000s to well over $1 million. The Liberty Station residents we met were mostly two-income working families with children. Well-paid but not wealthy, somehow they find the money to buy into this urban New Village.

Liberty Station "is not so much mixed-use as a mixture of uses," Heiberg quips. A past master at interviews, he drives the overly wide streets of Liberty Station (suitable for armored-vehicle parades), pointing out proudly its design features, marching condos, townhouses and single-family homes in close order, up from the new military housing along a wide central walkway spine. While New Urbanists will claim it breaks all the rules, Liberty Station works as a New Village.

At the northern end of the base are seven new office buildings, each more than thirty feet high. The city and the developer took the state to court over that height restriction law and won. Turns out that the law exempted military bases, and McMillin's lawyers got the former base grandfathered in. McMillin has moved its corporate headquarters into one of these spacious high-tech buildings. The central "historic district," which includes the old barracks, is being converted into shops and arts-and-crafts studios, with much of the space having been turned over to local arts organizations – a surefire vote-winning tactic. There are charter high and elementary schools, one small church and one mega-church. One grocery store has signed on at this writing and another is being courted. Along the shoreline, McMillin is constructing a public park, which, along with the arts-and-crafts studios, the developer hopes will make Liberty Station a future must-see destination for locals and tourists. "Five years from now," predicted Walter Heiberg in 2005, "we will be a major attraction."

Libby Day is assistant project manager for San Diego's Community and Economic Development Department, Redevelopment Division, the city's head honcha at Liberty Station. "The San Diego City Council oversees all redevelopment activities and the politicians keep changing," she says. "We have to keep re-educating the council. We have a pretty conservative political climate here. San Diego is really very much like a small town in many respects."

Touring visitors around the work-in-progress, Walter Heiberg says the developer and the city agreed early on that Liberty Station would be completely open and accessible by the public. "Some of the commercial builders said, 'We have to put a fence around our building,' but we told them that was not going to happen." The single exception to open access is the high, black, obviously expensive spiked steel fence the Navy erected post-9/11 around its medical clinic. "Homeland security at its worst," Heiberg complains.

The absence of walls and gates is one of several New Urbanism tenets adopted by McMillin in its design of Liberty Station. Others include walking trails and garages in the rear. Several other rules were consciously violated. The Nuevo-Spanish architecture, for example, provides none of the front porches required in a new urbanist "traditional neighborhood development." In most cases the houses and townhouses are built pretty much right to the sidewalk, while the condos front on common areas studded with fountains and palms that the residents have learned to call front yards.

Perhaps the most conspicuous deviation from the typical Celebration-style New Village model is the grouping of all housing at one end, the southern tip of the old training center, rather than clustering residential neighborhoods around a town center. The reason for this is the proximity of San Diego International Airport. San Diegans call their airport Lindbergh Field because the aviator's "Spirit of St. Louis" was built in San Diego and flew from there on the first leg of what would become the first trans-Atlantic flight. Lindbergh Field is almost in the center of downtown San Diego and its flights take off and land directly over Liberty Station. The nation's busiest single-runway commercial airport, Lindbergh is closed for takeoffs between 11 p.m. and 7 a.m. Nevertheless, the runway's "noise contours" made it illegal to build new housing in any part of Liberty Station other than the southern end, farthest from the direct flight paths. Hotels, office buildings and settings for cultural events are not restricted from the

Community-building events such as Issaquah Highlands' Annual Picnic encourage residents to live not in isolation but together, interacting for their mutual benefit. Notice the display of neighborhood-friendly transportation in the foreground and the trail-filled wilderness area that will remain after the next row of homes goes in.

Used by permission of Port Blakely Communities (Issaquah Highlands, Washington)

more noise-prone areas of Liberty Station, so that is where they are going.

The older Naval buildings retain their military character, with dank arched galleries and curious numerical plaques that have nothing to do with street addresses: Building 201 happens to have been the 201st structure completed on the base. Because of the historic status, the now-meaningless number will stay. An unexpected Naval legacy was a fuel dump that cost McMillin $7 million to clean up. "We were reimbursed by our insurance company," smiles Heiberg, "and then they had to go after the Navy. We've recycled tons of metal, wood and asphalt, and all the old concrete has stayed on-site, as foundation material for the new buildings. We were named recycler of the year in 2002."

Build-out for Liberty Station is expected in 2008, considerably later than originally expected. The 46-acre, $14.7 million regional waterfront park should have been well under way by 2005, but by then the city had fallen two years behind on financing the public part of the project. It was supposed to issue bonds for NTC (Naval Training Center) Park in 2004. Instead, McMillin found a way to place the bonds privately. At first City Attorney Mike Aguirre said that would be illegal, eventually signed off on that approach, then withdrew his approval. Aguirre has been accused by some of political opportunism and headline hogging, but the hostess at our hotel restaurant (who turned out to be the city attorney's niece) assured us that "Uncle Mike is really looking after the people. Everybody says he's doing a terrific job."

Others think the terrific job is the one under way at the old naval base. "They must like what we've done," Libby Day says, pointing to new military housing adjacent to Liberty Station. The neighborhood appears to replicate design elements of the New Village next door. "We've got something worth copying." A sprightly, petite woman who wears wide-brimmed hats to guard her freckled face from the San Diego sun, Day believes Liberty Station will serve as a model for other cities facing military base closures around the country.

That opinion is shared by Harry Kelso, CEO of Base Closure Partners in Richmond, Virginia. Kelso, who says he's "looked at lots and lots of military bases and how they are used," says Liberty Station is a model of how closures and redevelopment can be accomplished "very effectively and done correctly."[182]

Since 1988, when the Department of Defense began its Base Realignment and Closure process (BRAC), ninety major military installations have shut down around the country. Among these was what is now Orlando's Baldwin Park. Far larger than Liberty Station – 1,093 acres compared to 360 – and with nearly ten times the housing units – 3,600 compared to 349 – Baldwin went up faster, mostly because, as we've seen, it had the nearby example of Celebration to still the outrage of political opponents and nervous property owners. Liberty Station, having overcome so much opposition, may well prove to be a more useful model than Baldwin Park for the 33 bases named in 2005 for the next round of closures. Visitors from those other base cities have been impressed by what they see in San Diego, says Marc Kasky.

"There is a model here, with the master developer, the city and nonprofit element, that many cities will be looking at with the next round of base closures," believes Kasky, who is project director for the NTC Foundation, Liberty Station's nonprofit component. "What drew me was the appeal of mixed use - hotels, schools, offices and retail, in combination with a cultural center and open space. It makes for a very compelling project." It was just that combination, the New Village effect, that got official San Diego's attention at the beginning. Former councilman Byron Wear says the plan took into account "the economic considerations of the site, a mix of housing with commercial, having the sense of a village. Liberty Station is a unique village that serves the community and the greater San Diego region."[183]

Echoing the sentiments of Jim Rouse's early homebuyers in Columbia, Maryland, Walter Heiberg says, "Our residents are urban pioneers. They bought into the vision." Indeed, because unlike nearly every New Village we have visited, Liberty Station had homeowners long before it had any of the amenities requisite for the village life. The one thing these pioneers found from the get-go was a spirit of community. So attest the early residents of Liberty Station, who in 2005 were still awaiting the fulfillment of many of the developer's promises.

"MAYBE WE CAN SHARE!"

"People are more hospitable here than in any other place I know of in California," says Guy Hancock, who moved with his wife, Claudia, in the first wave of homebuyers in 2003. "People here just enjoy being together." Hancock is an outgoing business consultant who wears his dark hair slicked back and favors long-sleeved dress shirts even on hot summer days. He's owned homes before, including a couple of two-acre McMansions in Florida and Iowa. "We're a bunch of different types here, from first-time buyers up to and including retirees, all looking for the idea of community," he says. "People have gotten involved. Claudia's on the homeowners' council. The neighbors are driving what's best for the neighborhood, and I want to know who my neighbors are."

Guy was only too pleased to take a couple of hours off from work to meet with a few of those neighbors in Mel and Jim Richardson's condo living room. All of them were looking forward to the 2005 Independence Day picnic, the biggest Liberty Station event yet planned by the residents. Amy Roland, a slim, trim, casual mother of two, couldn't wait to see the neighborhood kid contingent en masse.

"It'll be great to get together with everybody." She goes at a fast clip. "We were renting in La Jolla, and we were able to do a lot of walking there. You just *meet* people when you can walk." Amy and her husband Billy are both video and media producers. He's working at a San Diego television station and she's doing web work from home. "We're first-time buyers, and we were afraid we wouldn't be able to find anything here we could afford. We had to get on this list, and on Saturdays we had to go to the selling office to see whether our name would be drawn for something in our price range. Billy and I thought we were never going to make it. Panic! But at least here the price was fixed; you knew someone wasn't going to come along and out-bid you for the house."

Every few minutes Roland walked across the hardwood floor into the Richardsons' kitchen, where she had a monitor set up from the nursery in her condo unit upstairs. Mel Richardson kept assuring her that she didn't have to worry, because with the windows open they would all know the instant the baby needed attention. "We're the loudest ones around," Amy shrugged, "with our two kids…" The rest of her sentence was drowned out by the noise of a jet climbing into the clear June sky. You could look out the window and see the Alaska Airlines Inuit on its tail. Amy's baby slept through every takeoff and landing that afternoon, and the adults in our conversation seemed unfazed.

Mel – short for Melanie –Richardson would be having her own baby boy in October. She and Jim had been training for a marathon when the pregnancy put those plans on hold. For the moment they were content to take long walks together around the new neighborhood, anxiously awaiting the completion of the waterfront park and the commercial district. "This is going to be an excellent place to run," said Jim, brush-cut and built pretty much like a marathon-running telecommunications designer. "We'll have eight miles of pathways once that park is completed. We'll be able to go across the old bridge, right into the city."

"I've walked to work a number of times already," Guy Hancock chimed in.

"My neighbor, Jeff, walks to work," offered Amy. "Billy and I are thinking we'll rent an office where we can do our video editing, when McMillin opens up more of the commercial space."

"I'm thinking of getting an office too," adds Mel, who has her own real estate agency. "After the baby's born."

A lightbulb flashes over Amy's head: "Maybe we can share!"

Once again, we are reminded of the opportunities that arise only when we get to know our neighbors. As developers and public officials get to know each other, they will discover considerable commonality in the hunger for community.

"We're lucky to live here," reflects Guy Hancock.

Chapter Twelve

A Place to Call Home

In 1993, Robert Kunstler called America a "tragic landscape of highway strips, parking lots, housing tracts, mega-malls, junked cities, and ravaged countryside... a gathering calamity."[184] That seemed hardly an improvement over the "hideous, ghastly mistake," the "colossal world-darkening blunder" of nineteenth-century cities that inspired Ebenezer Howard's Garden City campaign of 1899. But at the end of 2004, Brookings Institution urban expert Arthur C. Nelson rang in with a note of hope, if not outright optimism.

Nelson had considerably more statistics at his fingertips than Ebenezer Howard ever had, and he had powerful computers with which to manipulate those statistics. He noted that because the population of the United States is expected to rise by 60 million in the first quarter of the 21ST century, that the nation will need to replace about 82 billion square feet of "built space" and will need to build another 131 billion square feet of new spaces. That's a total of 213 billion square feet of homes, stores, offices, schools, churches, libraries, movie theaters, symphony halls – you name it.

Granted, those numbers are meaningless to most of us. But to computers and statisticians, they mean that by the year 2030, about half the buildings in which Americans live, work, shop, pray and play will have been constructed post-millennium. Interestingly, nearly half of that new building, more than 100 billion square feet, will be new residences.[185]

All those numbers add up to an almost unprecedented opportunity for those of us living in America today: We have the power to turn Kunstler's "tragic landscape" into something beautiful. We can avert that "gathering calamity" by embracing, by insisting upon *community.* Planners, architects, homebuilders and real estate professionals of every stripe are hard at work deciding where and in what sorts of neighborhoods those homes will be built. The more we raise our voices in support of community, the more community will be forthcoming.

Moreover, the Brookings Institution study goes on to show we are doing just that. Home seekers are demanding, says the Nelson report, "more compact, walkable, and high-quality living, entertainment, and work environments." This is the moment, the report concludes, for consumers to demand change, and to create the right market and regulatory climate in which our cities can grow in more sustainable ways.

This is the moment, in other words, for Americans to demand community, refuse to live in isolation, insist on changing community-unfriendly zoning laws. This is the time for re-villaging America.

THE RECONNECTION REVOLUTION.

The evidence we've gathered suggests that the the movement has begun. "In most metropolitan areas, American households buy into the current settlement patterns because they lack genuine choice," says Laurie Volk and Todd Zimmerman in a report delivered at the 2000 Fannie Mae Foundation's Annual Housing Conference. The change that New Villages represent, according to industry researchers, "is being

By the time these New Village children have children of their own, America can rebuild itself into a nation of community, a land of places in which people are truly able to live their lives.

Photo courtesy DMB Associates, Inc.

embraced by too many builders, developers, financial institutions and government agencies – from local to federal – to remain marginalized as a "niche." With all those disparate factions, along with the isolation-weary public, in agreement, who can long resist such a bandwagon? Yet another report, this one by the Urban Land Institute, puts it in no uncertain terms: "A search for 'community' and 'place' is underway."[186] As of now, the revolution to reconnect is in progress.

Despite all those recent predictions and unhesitant reports of community's demise, the fact is that we never have lost, and surely never will lose our drive and passion and need for one another. The esteemed European philosopher Leszek Kolakowski explains our community-dependence this way: "My way of life, my acts and my emotions depend both on what others expect of me and on the support they offer me... My awareness of the good and evil in me is therefore a condition that makes my being part of the community possible."[187]

That basic human need to connect has not gone anywhere. Nor is it measurable in bowling league shirts or Rotary memberships. As the villagers of ancient Çatalhöyük knew instinctively, as Abraham Maslow codified, as noted psychologists keep telling us, we are social beings. We require interaction. We need one another. We yearn to share our gifts with others and to accept the gifts they would share with us. The yearning for community is real, permanent, non-generational.

Certainly the generations rising at this writing attest to that. We read newspaper accounts of Alaska high-school students creating a system of bike paths with free rental bicycles; of a children's movement started by a Baltimore ten-year-old that now prepares lunches for homeless in 43 states; of elementary kids in Michigan recording music for hospitalized children; of Washington third graders launching a fund drive for hurricane victims.

Authors Neill Howe and William Strauss, who dub this post-Gen-X generation "millennials," have studied the phenomenon. "Millennials aren't doing this as entrepreneurial loners," the authors tell us. "Instead—in keeping with their generation's team orientation—they're banding together" to make a difference. They are building community.[188] And in New Villages across the land – more than 500 of them as of 2006, according to *The Wall Street Journal* – people of all ages are placing community at the top of their priority list for homes. And once they find it, they quickly become evangelists for the movement.

Witness John and Mary Pfeiffer, who bought a home with an apartment above their garage so they could introduce family members to the concept of New Village living in Celebration. Mary's uncle rented the apartment until he moved to the nearby rentals compound, leaving the garage room for Mary's mother. John and Mary's son Tom and his wife bought a home in Celebration, too. Drive way out west on Interstate 10 and you'll find Kyle Campos, who brought his brother and family from California to the Arizona New Village of Verrado, just as Bill Retsinas convinced his parents to join him there. Rick Bernhardt watched Celebration happen while he was Orlando's city planner and that made him prime proselytizer for Orlando's inner-city New Village, Baldwin Park. Back home in Tennessee, Bernhardt now preaches the New Village gospel in Nashville.

Other savvy regional planners and political leaders see New Villages as our best hope of reducing the impact of suburban homebuilding on the environment while providing profitable opportunities for builders and developers. But it is the people who want to live in them who will force the issue. And more than any other amenity in these New Villages – more than convenience or safety or environment or educational opportunity – "community" is the word residents and developers alike cite as the reason for their success.

ULTIMATELY, COMMUNITY IS UP TO US.

Lee Moore, an activist who's developed an almost curmudgeonly reputation around Celebration, concurs. "Disney gave us the tools, but it's the people who come here – they give us our sense of belonging," he says. "This is a place where the family belongs. My mother-in-law lives in town; she moved here after we did. There are a lot of families with one or two or three relatives living in Celebration. My kids feel very comfortable here, I feel very comfortable about my kids' friends. It's a small community – our friends and family around us. I travel around the world, and this is home. You can build lots of buildings, but it's the people who come here – they are the ones who make it home."

Yet those "tools" of community, as Moore describes the design elements of his New Village, provide instant recognition and gratification for the community-deprived. Chris Urwiller, who moved to Verrado from the nearby Arizona city of Buckeye, says, "I would like to see the tools of Verrado brought to Buckeye." Urwiller is on the Buckeye City Council, so he may have something to do with exporting those tools. To plan for community, he believes, is to enable a better life. "A family without a community is starved. An area without community is like a body without food, it's unsustainable," he says. "People are hungry for that connection – I think that's what I've learned here in Verrado. Building community is about working together, not about argument. You've got to find a way to make things work."

Brent Herrington, who satisfied his own thirst for community in Celebration before spreading the word in Arizona, believes he and his company can make money by building opportunities for community, but only people who recognize their need can truly satisfy the craving.

"After you build the development, there is this terrible sense of helplessness," Herrington says. "It's up to the people who live there to make the community work. The highest lesson I've learned in all this is that the biggest mistake you can make is to think that you can design it and cause it to be so. The biggest thing that we can hope is that the people we design for will self-select and self-actualize. All we can do is be a catalyst, set a stage, create the physical possibility."

At least since 1945 and until quite recently, most governments and real estate developers in North America simply failed to create that physical possibility. Most of the "places" they've made for us have stifled our longing for community, bottled it up in ever larger houses on ever larger lots and in ever more self-contained auto-dependent environments. Our governmental agencies have redlined city neighborhoods only to bulldoze them. City fathers have chased us out of cities in fear for our lives and later admonished us for abandoning them. And all the while, when we could scarcely manage to be among ourselves, people of other nations continued arriving here in increasing numbers, longing to be among us.

"This generation of place-making has been a generation of horrors," Brent Herrington says, acutely aware that his industry is only just beginning to understand what people want and need from their neighborhoods. "Ten years ago, it was only a handful of people in the country. We were the canaries in the coal mine. Most laypeople hadn't gotten fed up enough with sprawl. Me, Todd [Mansfield], [Andrés] Duany, [Peter] Calthorpe – five or ten years ago, we'd talk at Urban Land Institute meetings, and we might as well have been from Mars."

No longer. From one corner of the country to the other, enlightened planners and developers and governments are coming to recognize their responsibility to create not simply more tracts of housing but semi-self-contained villages. Their cause is "to shape a place that is better executed," as Herrington phrases it. By enabling community in the places they build, they are building a better America. "We may not see the effects of the community building in our lifetime, but these places will be around for a long, long time, affecting generations, and that's a profound thing. We're living through the moment of realization that community is a necessity."

Seattle's High Point, a public-private partnership, is among the best examples of the New Village's suitability for urban infill. The city's main attractions are just a short bus or water-taxi ride away.

Photo by Fusionpartners LLC for Seattle Housing Authority

Like developer Brent Herrington, Urban Futures research fellow Chris Fiscelli believes that ultimately New Village-type neighborhoods will become the norm for American living. One reason is that they have emerged out of a genuine public need. "[T]hey are not some government version of utopia, but rather a private sector innovation," Fiscelli writes in an op-ed piece for Reason Public Policy Institute. "While planners and environmentalists have wrung their hands, while new age architects have busied themselves with rewriting bylaws, a small number of real estate developers have recognized a need for community in North America. A need is another name for a market... Maybe we've understood a sense of community is a good thing, as long as it's common sense."[189]

Not only common sense, but often enormously profitable for the companies that have the foresight and patience to build New Villages. As James Rouse told *Life* magazine in 1967, "Profit is the thing that hauls dreams into focus."

The focus became sharper in 2006, as *The Wall Street Journal* took note of the New Village wave sweeping America, rather astonished to discover that "roughly 500 of the communities comprising tens of thousands of homes have now sprouted up across the U.S."[190] Using the New Urbanist Traditional Neighborhood Development nomenclature, the *Journal* observes that cities throughout the land are using village-type design elements as part of their effort to corral sprawl.

"TND started out experimental, but it's now becoming mainstream," the *Journal* quoted Jim Constantine, director of community planning for Looney Ricks Kiss Architects in Princeton, New Jersey. Within a decade, Constantine projects, 20 to 30 percent of all new subdivisions will be New Villages. "And unlike the first wave of these developments – such as Celebration near [Orlando] and Seaside in the Florida Panhandle, which tended to be built in the suburbs or beyond – the new communities are being heavily concentrated in cities and on former industrial sites."[191]

Thus Seattle in 2006 has begun a move to bring more residents of diverse income levels back to the inner city. By repealing a seventeen-year cap on building heights, the mayor and city council aim to concentrate in the heart of downtown both jobs and the people to fill them, in multi-use developments that would include village-style arrays of housing, offices, shops, restaurants and open spaces. And to ensure diversity, the council requires developers to pay between $17 and $19 for each square foot they build into a fund for low-income housing. At least ten developers were in line to file permits even before the new law went on the books.[192]

Even Atlanta, one of the East Coast's most sprawl-defined cities, is embracing the concept of New Villages. When internet entrepreneur Charles Brewer looked for a way to invest some of the millions he made from his company Mindspring, he became convinced he could improve people's lives by using New Urbanist principles to build community. He bought an abandoned concrete recycling plant near downtown Atlanta and created the 28-acre New Village of Glenwood Park. Like most New Villages, this one promotes walking, provides destinations and meeting places for walkers, and includes office spaces for those who can take advantage of them.

In the spring of 2006, Brewer stood in front of the coffee shop in his Brasfield Square and showed National Public Radio's Jim Zarroli where the big fountain would go once it was delivered from France. "It's gonna be a great place to hang out," Brewer said.

Zarroli spoke in almost reverential terms of this New Village in the heartland of sprawl: "A kind of easy sociability defines the place." Confirming that was John Shaw, a recent purchaser of a townhouse in Glenwood Park. Shaw enjoys getting together with neighbors in the evenings, when "nobody is particularly a stranger."

Because nearby residents were happy to see the piles of concrete rubble replaced by nice homes, restaurants and shops, Glenwood Park endured none of the zoning battles that can bring down a New Village dream. And because Brewer, though his resources might not equal those of The Disney Company, poured $8 million of his own money into Glenwood Park, banks stepped up in advance of the buyers.

Charles Brewer is convinced that the New Village is emerging as the lifestyle model for 21st century America. "Even out in the new suburban developments," he told NPR, "I think mixing the housing types together, mixing the uses together and making walkable streets again really is going to happen, because I think most people, in fact, if given the choice, end up liking it better."[193]

Liking it better because it is where we were meant to live. Syndicated columnist Neil Peirce admitted as much in a column published the day after Christmas, 2006. "If Christmas is about believing," the *Washington Post* columnist begins, "so are two fascinating new towns I've seen this year." The New Villages that made a believer out of Peirce are Prairie Crossing, near Chicago, and Habersham, in South Carolina's coastal Low Country near the old colonial town of Beaufort.

"Both communities have roots in the New Urbanist movement of focused development," Peirce notes. In fact, they were both designed in part by two of the movement's chief evangelists: Peter Calthorpe was a consultant for Prairie Crossing, Tom Low, the head of Andrés Duany's Charlotte office, planned Habersham. Peirce waxes ecstatic over these two New Villages, with their rail connections and bike paths, their environment-friendliness and energy efficiencies, their gathering places, even – in the case of Habersham – racial and economic diversity.

"By belief and action," writes the columnist, the developers of these New Villages "provide a gift for us all – evidence that America's communities *can* be more social, more beautiful, more environmentally friendly than standard development yet still work economically."

SAVE THE SUBURBS.

Recently, advocates of Smart Growth and New Urbanism have been lumped together in a group labeled "anti-suburbanites," seen as enemies of the "American dream" of home ownership. In a recent book, St. Louis urban policy consultant Wendell Cox argues, "Anti-suburban policies must be rejected and repealed."[194] In a glowing review of Cox's book, *Orange County Register* columnist Steven Greenhut writes, "Unfortunately, Smart Growth and New Urbanism are based on faulty foundations. Those of us who grew up crammed into row houses in dirty East Coast cities… scratch our heads at the otherworldly arguments and analyses these ideologues make." Greenhut hints at the reason for his invective: "Those of us who own homes have enjoyed watching prices, and our equity, soar in California."[195] This is in California's exemplar of suburban sprawl, Orange County, where officials are desperate to create affordable housing, even for renters, and where $500 a month will get you a garage "apartment," *sans* heat, toilet or kitchen.[196]

In fact, the authors of this book in no way recommend an abandonment of suburbia. Rather, we suggest that the suburbia of the future is going to be radically different from the suburbia many others of us grew up with.

Since the end of World War II, land development in the United States has been predominantly on the fringe of our cities. The overwhelming majority of this growth has been low-density and automobile-dependent. The result of this development, in addition to lack of community, is environmental degradation, congestion, and a diminishment in the ability of many of our citizens to pursue the long-standing "American dream" of home ownership. Notwithstanding the increasing desire for city life and the return to an urban lifestyle for some, the overwhelming amount – in excess of 85 percent – of future development will remain at the edge. This will be our only reasonable means of housing our growing population. No amount of densification of existing development or urban infill will accomodate the magnitude of this population growth. Furthermore, a large percentage of this growth will occur in a few states, many of which are in the Southeast.

In cities and in their suburbs across the nation, the rebuilding of our "tragic landscape" has begun. We Americans owe it to ourselves and to our future generations to recognize the movement and to embrace its new set of standards for builders, buyers and renters. Here are those standards, in clear and simple language:

1. Make it foot-friendly. The less auto-dependent we can be, now and in the future, the greater our chance to get to know neighbors. Sidewalks, walking paths, biking paths and trails are essential to our well being and to our sense of place.

2. Design around people, not cars. Ideally, neighborhoods should be accessible by public transportation as well as by automobile. Garages in the rear make houses more pleasing to the eye and less isolated from neighbors.

3. Put shops and homes in close proximity. Mixing uses can draw people to village-centers where there are destinations for walking. Strolling to a coffee shop, a market, a laundry, a movie or a library can make daily exercise an easy habit and break down our dependence on the isolating automobile. A sensible mix of commercial and residential uses will have less impact on the environment than zoned sprawl.

4.   Go for the green. Front yards are more important than back yards, and park areas are more important than either. Living in a place where people demonstrate their care for the environment helps us take pride in our neighborhood and appreciate our neighbors.

5.   Create opportunities to work near or out of our homes. Career demands are among the greatest detriments to community-building. The more we reduce potential conflict between the two, the more complete and fulfilled our lives become. Look for neighborhoods with office buildings and other work spaces built-in or at least close by.

6.   Provide homes of widely varying value. When different types of housing – single-family, townhomes, condos, apartments – are allowed to co-exist, a degree of economic and age diversity is almost guaranteed.

7.   Consider the children. Small children are instant ice-breakers: we benefit from engaging them and they grow through interacting with us. But they do grow, and the needs of pre-teens and teens must be taken into consideration when designing and selecting for community. If a place is not child-friendly, it may not be truly community-friendly.

8.   Encourage engagement. Essential to being part of a place is that we feel ownership and inclusion. We need to be able to get involved and we need to get involved. We don't mind following the rules, but the people who make the rules must be reasonably accessible and open to new ideas.

9.   Deliver diversity. While living among all-retirees or all-golfers or all-singles may at first seem appealing, it is ultimately boring. Our differences stimulate discovery and interest among neighbors, making chance encounters more appealing and more fruitful.

10. Hold government accountable. Whether you're looking for a location to build in or to live in, ask whether its leadership and populace appreciate the value of community. If they are still bound by archaic zoning

laws and unwilling to embrace the village concept, they may not be ready for community.

Already hundreds of such places exist, and others are on the drawing boards. Laurence Aurbach of the bimonthly publication *New Towns* maintains a list of New Village-type developments in "The Town Paper" on the internet. As of the start of 2007, Aurbach listed more than 400 places that met his "traditional neighborhood development design rating standards." These New Villages, both urban and suburban, are drawing homebuyers, renters and shopkeepers in forty states, the District of Columbia and twelve foreign countries. He regularly updates his list, which can be found online at www.tndtownpaper.com/neighborhoods.htm. While the Town Paper's list covers only larger projects that already have their own web sites, New Urban Publications' *Directory of the New Urbanism*, scheduled for publication in early 2007, promises a more extensive list. That directory may be found at www.newurbannews.com/DirectoryPage.html.

In the suburbs and in the cities, village-like developments are changing the way we relate to our neighbors. People get to know each other in neighborhoods with sidewalks, where homes with front porches sit on smaller lots, where folks we walk with and speak to are more real than strangers in passing cars.

Used by permission of Port Blakely Communities (Issaquah Highlands, Washington)

There will be those who suggest that everything we've written here is so much wishful thinking. It must be admitted that this is a possibility. Signs of hope do not necessarily reward the hopeful. For example, despite architect Peter Calthorpe's assertion that the primary community-building feature of Ladera Ranch is its walkability, more than a few residents of the Southern California New Village fail to get the point. "New SUVs dominate the streets," writes Sarah Richards in *Psychology Today*, "and residents often drive instead of walk the few blocks to the Ladera Flower Shoppe or Maggie Moo's Ice Cream."[197]

The truths are that the most ingrained habits are the hardest to change, and that a significant portion of society simply may never get the point. These are the people whose very natures seem to require that they hold themselves apart. It is important to their self-esteem that they seem, especially to themselves, better than the rest of us. They may be happy to have the kids walk to school, because that relieves them of a daily inconvenience. They may visit the local gym for a bi-weekly workout, but they won't be seen walking to the grocery store. They may spout the tenets of New Urbanism and Smart Growth, but the last thing they want is actual community. These are frequently people who consider themselves "players," individuals who, as former teacher and author Garrett Keizer has written, believe they move at a faster pace, possess more power and are governed by a different set of rules than the rest of us.

In a thought-provoking *Harper's* essay, Keizer speculates that the first "player" may have been the first man or woman to mount a horse, this becoming at once taller, faster, stronger and better equipped than those down below. The plutocrats of Rome, he reminds us, called themselves "the equestrian order." Today's thoroughbred may be an SUV or a Hummer – the low-mileage beast formerly known as the army's High Mobility Multipurpose Wheeled Vehicle – suggests Keizer. But: "A player is not ever, if he can help it, a pedestrian."[198] Indeed, one of the meanings of "pedestrian" is "ordinary," and that meaning is not likely to disappear any time soon.

Nor are those "players" who have divided us into pockets of solitude likely to voluntarily dismount their high horses. Gaining back our neighborhood walkability, our sense of place, our community will require the outspoken voices of the rest of us, the ordinary people, to make it clear that we *want* to walk, that "pedestrian" is *not* a pejorative term, that "community" is something we highly value. It is up to us to declare that we are part of what *Tipping Point* author Malcolm Gladwell calls a successful "social epidemic," one founded on "a bedrock belief that change is possible, that people can radically transform their behavior or beliefs in the face of the right kind of impetus."[199]

The real estate industry has begun to feel that impetus. Some believe the tipping point is at hand, that the people who design and build and market our places can no longer avoid heeding our cry for community. One indication is that developers from China – the most rapidly changing nation on the planet – are looking to America's New Villages as models for China's future.

In March 2006 representatives of Chinese development companies toured Verrado, the 8,800-acre live-work-play development in Buckeye, near Phoenix. Pinnacle Consulting Group's John Gallagher, who sponsored the tour, said the Chinese wanted to see Verrado partly because its bleak landscape resembles the terrain outside Beijing where they will be developing China's New Villages. But, he said, the builders also wanted to see Verrado's "town-square sense of community."[200]

The same month that the Chinese developers toured Verrado, about 200 prominent building, development and real estate professionals from the United States met in Santa Barbara, California, to launch an annual conference they call The Vine. The purpose of The Vine, they say, is to "rethink some of the underlying principles about the nature of community, to get to the heart of the matter as it applies to people in today's world."

One of the organizers of The Vine is Sandra Kulli, a high-profile marketer who is former president of the California Building Industry Association's PCBC, formerly known as the Pacific Coast Builders' Conference. In an interview with the Urban Land Institute, Kulli said attendees at the Santa Barbara event asked, "What does it really mean when we create these places for people to live their lives?" The reason such a question is even being asked, Kulli suggests, is that the trendsetters in her industry now are "aging boomers, thinking about the meaning of what we do and how we can have a wonderful impact on community."

Indeed, for decades the search for new homes in retirement has been largely a retreat to sunshine, golf and water sports. No longer is it that simple. 21ST century retirees, reports the *Wall Street Journal*, are looking for "a community where they can make friends and connections quickly, whether it's a small town or a walkable neighborhood in a big city."

By the time sixty-two-year-old John McIlwain became the senior resident fellow at the Urban Land Institute in Washington, D.C., he'd had enough suburban isolation. "Moving to a mixed-use development, a small town, or seeking an urban experience are all elements of the same thing," he told the *Journal*. "It's a community where you get to know each other...You're walking around, and you get to know your neighbors, you get to know the shopkeepers, because you meet them on the street."[201]

Creating community, not just more buildings, concludes The Vine's Sandra Kulli, is in the self-interest of developers and builders, not to mention those of their children and grandchildren. "There are many issues of community we need to remember beyond selling the next million-dollar house," she proclaims, "and I think many people in our industry are vitally interested in that."

It is up to us to keep them vitally interested. It is up to us to let real estate and rental agents know that we want neighbors, not merely a collective hermitage of individuals who nod across expansive lawns or hide behind locked apartment doors. It is up to us to decide what a rebuilt America is going to look like in the year 2030.

It is up to us, simply, to get back together, to re-village America with places in a place we all can call home.

ABOUT THE AUTHORS

As President of The Walt Disney Company's Celebration Company, Todd Mansfield led the planning and development of Celebration, Florida, a leading example of the living-working New Village environments rapidly emerging as the preferred lifestyle of the 21ST century. Now CEO of Crosland, LLC, Todd heads a seventy-year-old, $1.5 billion real estate development and investment firm that is a leader in mixed- and multi-use development in the Southeastern U.S. Praised as a "wunderkind" by *Urban Land* magazine for his achievements in conservation, health-care delivery and conversion of blighted slums, Todd is Chairman of the Urban Land Institute, and past-Chairman of the N.C. Chapter of The Nature Conservancy. He is widely recognized for his expertise in place-making.

L. Beth Yockey is an avid researcher, writer and visual artist in Seattle. Passionate about community and environmental issues, she has participated in a number of social research projects, worked in television and produced multimedia presentations. An editor and designer of several previous books, this her fourth book as author. With her father, Ross, she manages the business book production firm of Yockey Communication.

Ross Paul Yockey is an award-winning author, television producer and filmmaker who has published eighteen previous books, including the business bestseller, *McColl: The Man with America's Money.* Ross has a B.A. in English from Loyola of New Orleans and a M.F.A in Creative Writing from Queens University of Charlotte. He has taught writing on the elementary, high school, college and graduate levels.

ENDNOTES

NOTES FOR CHAPTER ONE, "THE QUEST FOR COMMUNITY"

[1] Gregg Easterbrook. *The Progress Paradox: How Life Gets Better While People Feel Worse.* New York: Random House, 2003.

[2] Kenneth T. Jackson. *Crabgrass Frontier: The Suburbanization of the United States.* New York: Oxford University Press, 1985.

[3] For more on "The Roseto Effect" see the University of Illinois at Chicago's web page
http://www.uic.edu/classes/osci/osci590/14_2%20The%20Roseto%20Effect.htm

[4] Robert Ezra Park. *Human Communities: The City and Human Ecology.* Chicago: Free Press, 1952.

[5] John Bowlby. *Separation: Attachment and Loss.* New York: Basic Books, 1973. Reprinted as *Loss: Sadness and Depression*, 1982.

[6] Thomas Lewis, Fari Amini and Richard Lannon. *A General Theory of Love.* New York: Vintage Books, 2001.

[7] S. Taylor, S.S. Dickerson and L.C. Klein. "Toward a Biology of Social Support." In *Handbook of Positive Psychology*. C.R. Snyder and S. J. Lopez, eds. New York: Oxford University Press, 2002.

[8] T. Berry Brazelton et al. *Hard-wired to Connect: The New Scientific Case for Authoritative Communities.* New York: Institute for American Values, 2003. The executive summary of this report is available on the internet at http://www.americanvalues.org/ExSumm-print.pdf.

[9] Felix Warneken and Michael Tomasello. "Altruistic Helping in Human Infants and Young Chimpanzees." *Science Magazine*, March 3, 2006.

[10] Shirley Russak Wachtel. "Won't You Be My Neighbor?" *New York Times*, June 27, 2004.

[11] Kathleen A. Brehony. *Living a Connected Life: Creating and Maintaining Relationships That Last.* New York: Henry Holt & Company, 2003.

[12] Jane Jacobs. *Dark Age Ahead.* New York: Random House, 2004.

[13] Brehony, p. 54.

[14] Robert Putnam. *Better Together.* New York: Simon & Schuster, 2003.

[15] Lawrence Cheek. "On Architecture: Starbucks puts a double shot of hometown flavor into every store." Seattle *Post-Intelligencer*, April 26, 2005.

[16] Phil Primack. "Taster's Choice." *The Boston Globe Magazine*, May 2, 2004.

[17] Morning Edition, National Public Radio, December 8, 2004.

[18] Heather Havrilesky, "On Bended Knee." Salon.com, June 24, 2002.

[19] Richard A. Posner. "Strong Fiber After All." The *Atlantic Monthly*, January 1, 2002.

[20] Samuel Barber. *Hermit Songs.* Published by G. Schirmer, Inc.

NOTES FOR CHAPTER TWO, "DEFINING COMMUNITY"

[21] Edward T. O'Donnell. "109 Years Ago: Annie Moore is First." *The Irish Echo*, December 27, 2000.

[22] Sue Kirchhoff. "Immigrants chase American dream. "*USA Today,* August 5, 2004.

[23] Dan Rafter. "Won't You Be My Neighbor? Washington Residents Get Invloved for a Sense of Community." *Washington Post*, Oct. 11, 2003.

[24] Urban Land Institute. "From Melting Pot to Stew Pot: ULI Examines Implications of America's Diverse Ethnic Makeup for Real Estate Industry." News release, November 6, 2003.

[25] Ross Yockey. *The Builder: The Croslands and How They Shaped a Region.* Seattle: Abecedary Press, 2004.

[26] Harvey Levenstein. *Paradox of Plenty*. Berkeley: University of California Press, 2003.

[27] David Carr. "Car in Every Garage, Sitcom in Every Cul-de-Sac." *New York Times*, April 2, 2006.

[28] Trend forecaster Faith Popcorn in her 1990s Popcorn Report coined the term "cocooning."

[29] www.welcomewagon.com

[30] Phil Rees. "The Missing Million," BBC News World Edition, October 20, 2002.

[31] Jacobs, *Dark Age Ahead*, op. cit.

[32] Nadine Brozan. "Big-City Buildings Seek A Small-Town Feeling." *New York Times*, Apr. 27, 2003.

[33] Carin Rubenstein. "For Neighbors, Being Close Really Counts." *New York Times,* Sept. 29, 2002.

[34] William Drayton. "Secret Gardens." *The Atlantic Monthly*, June 1, 2000.

[35] L. Beth Yockey and Ross Yockey. *Olympia Federal Savings & Loan: the First Hundred Years.* Seattle: Abecedary Press, 2006.

[36] http://www.communitygarden.org/mission.php

[37] Lisa W. Foderaro. "Under One Roof." *New York Times*, Apr. 24, 2005.

[38] "Evergreen gets an A for academia." *The Olympian*, Olympia, WA, Nov. 9, 2005.

[39] Ethan Watters. *Urban Tribes: a generation redefines friendship, family and commitment.* New York: Bloomsbury, 2003.

[40] Matthew Continetti. "That's what Friendster's for." *Weekly Standard,* Sep. 15, 2003.

[41] Dan Rosenheck. "Will you be my Friendster?" *New Statesman*, Aug. 4, 2003.

[42] Deirdre van Dyk. "Crossing the Virtual Street." *Time*, Jan. 10, 2005.

[43] South Park also happens to be Beth Yockey's neighborhood.

[44] Joel Clement. "South Park, a multi-ethnic jewel just discovered." *West Seattle Herald*, Sept. 3, 2005.

[45] Celeste Smith. "Turning strangers into good neighbors." *Charlotte Observer*, Apr. 16, 2005.

[46] Bradford McKee. "A New-Style Indian Village Rises From the Dust." *New York Times*, Sept. 30, 2004.

[47] Thomas Fields-Meyer and Trine Tsouderos. "Native Son." *People Magazine*, April 8, 2002.

[48] David Melmer. "A Conversation with Lance Morgan." *Indian Country Today*, February 13, 2006.

[49] Rafter, op. cit.

[50] Chris Fiscelli. "A New Sense of Community – Master-planned." Reason Public Policy Institute, June 5, 2003."
http://www.rppi.org/masterplannedcommunities.html

Notes for Chapter Three, "Birth of the New Village"

[51] See: http://www.cotswolds.info/places/cotswold-villages3.htm

[52] For more on Chatal Huyuk, see: C. Eden. "Çatal Hüyük," in P. G. Bahn, ed. *100 Great Archaeological Discoveries*. New York: Barnes & Noble Books, 1995.

[53] Off the western coast of India, scientists in 2002 discovered a sunken city that is believed to date from 7500 B.C., about the same time as the founding of Chatal Huyuk.

[54] Forrest Selvig, Interview with Ben Shahn. Smithsonian Archives of American Art. Transcript available at http://www.aaa.si.edu/oralhist/shahn68.htm.

[55] Alexander Garvin. "Are Garden Cities Still Relevant?" address to the National Planning Conference, 1998
http://www.asu.edu/caed/proceedings98/Garvin/garvin.html

[56] Joshua Olsen. *Better Places Better Lives: a Biography of James Rouse*. Washington, D.C.: Urban Land Institute, 2003.

[57] "On the Rocks," *Time*, November 24, 1961.

[58] Olsen, op. cit.

[59] Michael Chabon. "Maps and Legends," *Architectural Digest,* April, 2001.

[60] "Hope for the Heart," *Time*, March 4, 1966.

[61] Roger Galatas with Jim Barlow. *The Woodlands: The Inside Story of Creating a Better Hometown*. Washington, D.C.: Urban Land Institute, 2004.

[62] Vincent Scully. *The Architecture of Community*/The 1996 Raoul Wallenberg Lecture. University of Michigan, 1996.

[63] Todd Bressi. "Planning the American Dream." Introduction to *The New Urbanism: Toward an Architecture of Community*. Peter Katz. New York: McGraw-Hill, 1994.

[64] Andrés Duany and Elizabeth Plater-Zyberk with Jeff Speck. *Suburban Nation: The rise of Sprawl and the Decline of the American Dream*. New York: North Point Press, 2000.

[65] National Audubon Society. "Smart Growth: History, Tools and Challenges." http://www.audubon.org/campaign/er/library/smart-growth.html#1.1.1

[66] Jo Allen Gause. *Great Planned Communities*. Washington, D.C.: Urban Land Institute, 2002.

[67] Jeffrey Hart. *From This Moment On: America in 1940*. New York: Crown, 1987.

[68] Andrew Ross. *The Celebration Chronicles: Life, Liberty & the Pursuit of Property Value in Disney's New Town*. New York: Ballantine Books, 1999.

NOTES FOR CHAPTER FOUR, MIXING BUSINESS WITH PLEASURE...

[69] Will and Ariel Durant. *The Age of Louis XIV*. New York: Simon and Schuster, 1963.

[70] Edward M. Bassett, Autobiography. Unpublished, in the Division of Rare and Manuscript Collections of the Cornell University Library, Ithaca, New York. Quoted in Knack, Meck and Stollman.

[71] Ruth Knack, Stuart Meck and Israel Stollman. "The Real Story Behind the Standard Planning and Zoning Acts of the 1920s." *Land Use Law,* February, 1996. Available online at http://www.planning.org/growingsmart/pdf/LULZDFeb96.pdf.

[72] Robert K. Murray. "Herbert Hoover and the Harding Cabinet" in E. Hawley ed. *Herbert Hoover as Secretary of Commerce Studies in New Era Thought and Practice*. Herbert Hoover Presidential Library, 1974. Quoted in Knack, Merk and Stollman.

[73] The decision, Village of Euclid v. Ambler Realty Co., 272 U.S. 365, may be read in its entirety at http://www.communityrights.org/legalresources/otherkeysupremecourtopinions/Euclid.asp.

[74] City of Euclid, History. http://www.cityofeuclid.com/about/history.cfm

[75] David Sucher. *City Comforts: How to Build an Urban Village*. Seattle: City Comforts Press, 1995.

[76] James Howard Kunstler. *The Geography of Nowhere: The Rise of Sprawl and decline of America's man-made landscape*. New York: Simon & Schuster, 1993.

[77] Robert D. Putnam and Lewis M. Feldsten, with Don Cohen. *Better Together: Restoring the American Community*. New York: Simon & Schuster, 2003.

[78] Sucher, op. cit.

[79] Andrés Duany with Elizabeth Plater-Zyberk and Jeff Speck. op. cit.

[80] Kevin Nevers. "New Urbanism arrives at LEL in latest Coffee Creek addition." *Chesterton Tribune*, Nov. 18, 2003.

[81] Elyse Umlauf-Garneau, "Sustainable Sites." *Professional Builder*, Sep. 1, 2000.

[82] Janny Scott and David Leonhardt, "Class in America: Shadowy Lines That Still Divide." *New York Times,* May 15, 2000.

[83] Generational Income Mobility in North America and Europe. Statistics Canada's Family and Labor Studies Division, Cambridge University Press, 2005.

[84] Stephen Dunphy. "The Newsletter." *Seattle Times,* Nov. 14, 2002.

[85] Source: California Association of Realtors. From
http://www.downtownsandiegoproperties.com/housing_info.htm.

[86] Hugh L. McColl Jr. "Developing Common Ground." March 30, 1999.
http://www.bankofamerica.com/newsroom/press/press.cfm?PressID=press.20000601.01.
htm&LOBID=2

NOTES FROM CHAPTER FIVE, WALK, DON'T DRIVE

[87] Johnnie L. Cochran and David Fisher. *A Lawyer's Life*. New York: Dunne
Books, 2002.

[88] Max Herman. "The Newark and Detroit Riots of 1967." Rutgers University.
Online at http://www.67riots.rutgers.edu/introduction.html.

[89] Micheline Maynard. "Foreign Makers, Settled in South, Pace Car
Industry." *New York Times*, June 22, 2005.

[90] Prevention Makes Common Cents: Estimated Economic Costs of Obesity
to U.S. Business. *American Journal of Health Promotion*, 1998. cited in
obesity.org.

[91] Todd Zwillich. "CDC: Obesity Is Still An Epidemic." WebMD Medical News,
June 2, 2005. See: http://www.webmd.com/content/Article/106/108330.htm

[92] Howard Frumkin, Lawrence Frank and Richard Jackson. *Planning and
Public Health: Designing, Planning, Building for Healthy Communities*.
Washington, D.C.: Island Press, 2004.

[93] http://www.obesity.org/subs/fastfacts/cities.shtml

[94] *American Journal of Preventive Medicine*. August, 2004.

[95] Joel S. Hirschhorn. *Sprawl Kills: How Blandburbs Steal Your Time, Health
and Money*. New York: Sterling & Ross Publishers, 2005.

[96] Dan Ackman. "Sprawling Cities, Higher Scales." *Forbes*. August 29, 2003.

[97] Howard Frumkin. "Urban Sprawl and Public Health." *Public Health
Reports*, December, 2001.

[98] "Highway Health Hazards: A Sierra Club Report." 2004.
http://www.sierraclub.org/sprawl/report04_highwayhealth/report.pdf

[99] World Health Organization, Global Strategy on Diet, Physical Activity and
Health.
http://www.who.int/dietphysicalactivity/publications/facts/obesity/en/

[100] Jonathan Watts. "China faces up to obesity epidemic." *The Guardian*,
June 20, 2005.

[101] Megan Rauscher. "Daily dog walk works off pounds." MSNBC, October
21, 2005.

[102] Stacy Goodman. "Parks debate stops platting at Highlands." *Issaquah
Press*, January 31, 2001.

[103] See Dr. John Medina, http://www.ethix.org/body.php3?id=234

[104] Frumkin et al. *Urban Sprawl and Public Health*. op. cit.

[105] Charles W. Schmidt. "Sprawl: The New Manifest Destiny." *Environmental
Health Perspectives*, National Institutes of Health, August, 2004.

[106] Ibid.

[107] Peter Calthorpe, Mark Mack and Eric Carlson. "Pedestrian Pockets: new strategies for suburban growth." *Whole Earth Review*, Spring, 1988.

[108] Carole Rifkind. "America's Fantasy Urbanism: The Waxing of the Mall and the Waning of Civility." In Katherine Washburn and John Thornton eds. *Dumbing Down: Essays on the Strip-Mining of American Culture.* New York: W. W. Norton, 1996.

NOTES FROM CHAPTER SIX, PARKS, LAKES AND GREENSPACES

[109] Jo Allen Gause. *Great Planned Communities*, Washington, D.C.: Urban Land Institute, 2002

[110] Michael Chabon. *Architectural Digest*. April 2001, Vol. 58 Issue 4.

[111] Michael Kolber. "Laguna West a decade later." *The Bee [Sacramento]*, October 5, 2003.

[112] Jason Miller. "Walking in Kentlands." http://www.tndhomes.com/tour03.html

[113] Joe Kullman. "Phoenix Eyesore Blossoms as Park." *East Valley Tribune*, November 3, 2005.

[114] Joseph MacDonald and Michael Holmes. "Case Study of Riverside, GA: Comprehensive Report of the Impact of Urban Design on Water Resources." University of North Carolina at Chapel Hill and NC State University, December 2003.

[115] Mike Hassinger. "Williams calls Riverside 'A Living Laboratory.'" *Atlanta Business Chronicle*, March 5, 1999.

[116] Warren Cornwall. "Neighborhood tries to honor Mother Nature's runoff rules." *Seattle Times*, June 10, 2005.

[117] R.L. Thayer Jr. and T. Westbrook. "Open Drainage Systems for Residential Communities: Case Studies from California's Central Valley." Council of Educators in Landscape Architecture, 1989.

[118] Steven Kellenberg. "Where is the Green in Green Communities?" *Making Green Make Sense: Market-Driven Approaches to Sustainable Development*. Washington, D.C.: Urban Land Institute, June 2004

[119] Proceedings, Council of Educators in Landscape Architecture Annual Conference, September 1989, Amelia Island, Florida.

[120] Sharon Apfelbaum. "California Intelligent Communities Announces Development Plans for 9,000-Acre Joshua Hills Community." Desert Publication, Inc. News Release, February 27, 2002.

[121] Benjamin Spillman. "Developer says he's scrapping Joshua Hills plan." *Desert Sun*, July 23, 2003.

[122] News release from the Nature Conservancy, Sept. 22, 2004.

[123] Kellenberg, ULI. Op. cit.

Notes from Chapter Seven, Children in Paradise

[124] Brazelton et al. *Hard-wired to Connect*. Op. cit.

[125] Hara Estroff Marano. "A Nation of Wimps." *Psychology Today*, Nov./Dec. 2004.

[126] Brazelton et al. *Hard-wired to Connect*. Op. cit.

[127] Lisa Foderaro. "Under One Roof." *New York Times*, Apr. 24, 2005.

[128] Marano, op. cit..

[129] http://cuttothechase.typepad.com/chaserpaul/pop_culture/

[130] http://www.34747.org

[131] Mike Schneider, Associated Press. "Disney sells town center of Celebration, city it created." In the *Miami Herald*, Jan. 21, 2004.

[132] www.schoolsecurity.org/trends/school_violence04-05.html+%22celebration,+FL%22+drugs+crime&hl=en

[133] Deanna Sheffield. "Osceola leads in grads continuing education." *Osceola News-Gazette*, December 16, 2005.

[134] Katherine S. Newman. "Too Close for Comfort." *New York Times*, April 17, 2004.

Notes from Chapter Eight, Civic Involvement and Following the Rules

[135] Pearl Seligman. "Roosevelt, New Jersey – A Successful Experiment in Democracy and Creation of Community." Roosevelt Web Site: http://pluto.njcc.com/~ret/Roosevelt/pearl.html

[136] http://www.eastvalleytribune.com/?sty=19287

[137] FBI crime statistics reported at CityRating.com.

[138] http://www.socchambers.com/custom.cfm?name=articlePrint.cfm&id=292

[139] Ron Fournier. "People-Driven Politics." *Seattle Post-Intelligencer*, Dec. 24, 2005.

Notes from Chapter Nine, Company Towns & Hard-wired Community

[140] "Sixteen Tons: The Story Behind the Legend." www.ernieford.com.

[141] http://en.wikipedia.org/wiki/Company_towns.

[142] http://www.ci.seattle.wa.us/ligh.

[143] Jonathan Barnett. *The Elusive City: Five Centuries of Design, Ambition & Miscalculation*. New York: Harper and Row, 1986.

[144] Quoted in "Commuting's Toll on the Workforce." Sierra Club, 2004.
http://www.sierraclub.org/sprawl/report04/commuting.asp

[145] Sonia Krishnan. "'Village' ideal eludes Issaquah Highlands." *Seattle Times*, February 1, 2005.

[146] http://www.issaquahhighlands.com/movies/14_high.mov

[147] Doubleday Anchor, 1996. Today Stoll's statement is easily picked apart by those who get their recipes, dance steps and driving directions from the internet. Both prayer and poetry sites are accessible on the net, and as for gossip, some surveys indicate that there are, at this writing, more than 1.25 million internet chat rooms.

[148] Robert Kraut, Vicki Lundmark et al. "Internet Paradox: A Social Technology that Reduces Social Involvement and Psychological Well-Being." *American Psychologist*, Vol. 53, number 9, September 1998.

[149] Norman H. Nie and Lutz Erbring. "Internet and Society: A Preliminary Report." Stanford Institute for the Quantitative Study of Society, February, 2000.
http://www.stanford.edu/group/siqss/Press_Release/Preliminary_Report-4-21.pdf

[150] Christina Maslach. "Emperor Of The Edge." *Psychology Today*, Sept. 2000.

[151] http://www.americancity.org/Archives/Issue5/florida.html

[152] "Why Cities Will Thrive in the Information Age," *ULI on the Future: Cities in the 21st Century.* Washington, D.C.: Urban Land Institute, 2000.

[153] http://web.mit.edu/knh/www/downloads/khampton01.pdf

[154] Netville Resident, Message to NET-L 1998

[155] Netville Resident, Message to NET-L 1998

[156] Putnam. *Better Together,* op. cit.

[157] Randall Stross. "What eBay could learn from Craigslist." *New York Times*, June 5, 2005.

[158] http://www.craigslist.org/about/factsheet.html as of November 9, 2006

[159] Keith N. Hampton. "Place-Based and IT Mediated 'Community.' Planning Theory & Practice," Massachusetts Institute of Technology, Department of Urban Studies and Planning, March 1, 2002.

[160] Michelle Conlin. "The Easiest Commute Of All." *Business Week*, Dec. 12, 2005.

[161] http://www.digitalcenter.org/pages/news_content.asp?intGloballd=125&intTypeId=1

[162] Michel Marriott. "Blacks Turn to Internet Highway, and Digital Divide Starts to Close." *New York Times*, March 31, 2006.

Notes from Chapter Ten, Technicolor Dreaming

[163] City of Rancho Santa Margarita, www.ocalmanac.com/Cities/ci30.htm

[164] Orange County Housing Authority news release, Nov. 5, 2001.

[165] "Paul Johnson, Rancho Mission Viejo, Q&A." *OC Metro*, March 18, 2004.

[166] Rachel Pennant. "Diversity, trust and community participation in England." United Kingdom Home Office, 2005.
http://www.homeoffice.gov.uk/rds/pdfs05/r253.pdf

[167] Katie Jarvis. "What Future For Our Villages?" *Cotswold Life Magazine*, Oct. 2002.

[168] Eve Gerber. "George W.'s Racial Covenant." Slate.com, July 13, 1999. http://slate.msn.com/id/1003204/

[169] Lornet Turnbull. "Homeowners find records still hold blot of racism." *Seattle Times.* June 3, 2005.

[170] Garrett M. Graff. "Join and Divide: Anti Social Societies." *Harvard Magazine,* November-December, 2004.

[171] Claire Enlow. "Design Perspectives: Take a Look at How Southeast Seattle is Changing." *Seattle Daily Journal of Commerce,* Sept. 28, 2005.

[172] Michelle Norris and Robert Siegel. "Interview with Sheryll Cashin." *All Things Considered,* National Public Radio, May 5, 2004.

[173] Jonathan Rauch. "Seeing Around Corners," The *Atlantic Monthly*, April 1, 2002.

[174] Olsen, op. cit.

NOTES FROM CHAPTER ELEVEN, NO DEVELOPERS ALLOWED

[175] Curtis Johnson. Citistates Group Weblog, January 24, 2003

[176] LaTonya Turner. "Owner will sell prime property." WSMV (Nashville) News, January 15, 2003.

[177] Peggy Krebs. "Vote May Have Clarified Turner Property Debate." *Nashville Tennessean,* 24 January, 2003.

[178] David Walters. "Blueprints For A Better City." *Creative Loafing*, Charlotte. Feb. 28, 2002

[179] Mike Lindblom. "Seattle Leads the way with fewer children." *Seattle Times*, April 8, 2001.

[180] Washington Research Council. "Impact of Government Regulations and Fees on Housing Costs." http://www.researchcouncil.org/Briefs/2001/ePB01-18/Growth9.htm

[181] Source: Building Industry Association of San Diego County, *Industry Informer*, Summer 2005.

[182] Pat Broderick. "Revamp of NTC Hailed as Model Base Closure." *San Diego Business Journal*, 7 June, 2005.

[183] ibid.

NOTES FROM CHAPTER TWELVE, A PLACE TO CALL HOME

[184] Kunstler, *The Geography of Nowhere,* op. cit.

[185] Arthur C. Nelson. "Toward a New Metropolis: The Opportunity to Rebuild America." Brookings Institution, December, 2004. Report available at http://www.brookings.edu/metro/pubs/20041213_RebuildAmerica.pdf

[186] Alex Krieger. "An Urban Revival for a Suburban Culture." *ULI on the Future, 2001: Cities in the 21st Century*. op. cit.

[187] Leszek Kolakowski. *Metaphysical Horror*. University of Chicago Press, 1988.

[188] Neill Howe and William Strauss. *Millennials Rising: The Next Great Generation*. New York: Vintage Books, 2000.

[189] Chris Fiscelli. "A Sense of Community – Master Planned." Reason Public Policy Institute, June 5, 2003.

[190] Jim Carlton. "It Takes a Village to Lure Buyers Back to Town," *Wall Street Journal*, March 8, 2006.

[191] Ibid.

[192] Jennifer Langston. "Seattle's skyline headed upward." Seattle *Post-Intelligencer*, March 23, 2006.

[193] Jim Zarroli. "Atlanta Community Offers Amenities of Earlier Age." *All Things Considered*, National Public Radio, April 12, 2006.

[194] Wendell Cox. *War on the Dream: How Anti-Sprawl Policy Threatens the Quality of Life*. iUniverse, 2006

[195] Steven Greenhut. "Are Suburbs Really a Sin?" Charlotte *Observer*, December 23, 2006.

[196] www.housingadvocates.org/default.asp?ID=149.

[197] Sarah Elizabeth Richards. "Backlash in the Burbs." *Psychology Today*, August, 2005.

[198] Garret Keizer. "Crapshoot: Everyone loses when politics is a game." *Harper's*, February, 2006.

[199] Malcolm Gladwell. *The Tipping Point: How Little Things Can Make a Big Difference*. Boston: Little, Brown and Company, 2000.

[200] Bert Cochran. "Chinese developers given a taste of Verrado." *Arizona Republic*, March 31, 2006.

[201] Kelly Greene. "Forget Golf Courses, Beaches and Mountains." *Wall Street Journal*, October 2, 2006.

Index

Printed in the United States
89739LV00009B/1-102/A